Koa Kai

The Story of Zachary Bower and the Conquest of the Hawaiian Islands

D.R. POLLOCK

ISBN 978-1-950818-95-2 (paperback)

Copyright © 2020 by D.R. Pollock

All rights reserved. No part of this publication may be reproduced, distributed, or transmitted in any form or by any means, including photocopying, recording, or other electronic or mechanical methods without the prior written permission of the publisher. For permission requests, solicit the publisher via the address below.

Rushmore Press LLC
1 800 460 9188
www.rushmorepress.com

Printed in the United States of America

CONTENTS

Preface 5
Chapter 1: The Homestead 7
Chapter 2: Back On The Farm 18
Chapter 3: The Wanderlust 25
Chapter 4: Israel Comes Home 41
Chapter 5: First Love 59
Chapter 6: Off To Boston 77
Chapter 7: Off To Sea 81
Chapter 8: Around Cape Horn 106
Chapter 9: Fair American 115
Chapter 10: Hawaii 130
Chapter 11: Captives 135
Chapter 12: On To Maui 158
Chapter 13: Life In London And California 173
Chapter 14: War On The Big Island 185
Chapter 15: War At Sea 208
Chapter 16: The Final Battles 219
Chapter 17: Peace In The Islands 234
Chapter 18: Homeward Bound 252

Epilogue 269
Glossary 271
Bibliography 275

PREFACE

A COUPLE OF decades ago when my wife and I lived in Ka'a'awa, Hawaii. Spending six years with the local people was a complete joy. I love the Hawaiian people they are the kindest and gentlest folks that I have ever met. It does not take long for one to find pretty quickly that *aloha,* is real. It is hard to believe that the great grandfathers of the loving people we know were fierce warriors who partook in ritual cannibalism.

While in Hawaii I studied the history and mythology of the islands, finding the true history to be an intriguing mix of shifting political affiliations, and amorous interludes which made for a story that sounded way more like a novel than actual history.

Among the books I read was *THE WARRIOR KING, Hawaii's Kamehameha the Great* by Richard Tregaskis. I found it to be a very good historical novel documenting Kamehameha's several wars before he conquered most of the Hawaiian Islands. From the history books, it appears that Tregaskis stuck pretty close to the actual events and the legends that go with them.

In the following pages, I have taken a different tack to tell the Hawaiian story. The novel follows the actual history of Kamehameha's campaigns with the addition of a lad from New England who due to a number of misadventures, finds himself in Hawaii and a warrior in Kamehameha's army.

CHAPTER 1

THE HOMESTEAD

A COLD AFTERNOON wind blew autumn leaves across the field of impending battle. The Sun was low and filtered by clouds in the gray November sky. It was cold enough for snow to flurry through the crisp air.

"Company, Left Wheel!" Moments later as the unit broke to the edge of the thicket, "Company, Halt!"

Suddenly, it was mysteriously quiet in the ranks, only the occasional rustle of the men behind him broke the silence. Zachary saw the flags and lines of red clad soldiers at the opposite end of the pasture. He heard the enemy's officers barking orders that were parroted by their sergeants. The roll of their drums began as the long lines of soldiers moved forward onto the field. A few cannon volleys broke and added to the mounting noise at the far end of the pasture.

When the advancing units reached the middle of the field, their first ranks stopped to fire a volley. "Steady, Men!" Zachary commanded.

A second volley ripped through the air around them. One of Zachary's men moaned as a musket ball ripped through his thigh. "Hold Your Fire!"

The lines of British Regulars advanced again. When they were almost two-thirds of the distance across the field, it was time to respond. Drawing his sword from the rope he used as a belt, Zachary ordered the first platoon to fire, and then the second platoon. Through the acrid smoke of the spent black powder he could see a number of enemy soldiers fall before his guns. After another volley the red line halted, then wavered. After the next thunderous volley, the remaining enemy soldiers began to withdraw.

"Fix Bayonets!" Zachary shouted to his imaginary troops, "Charge!" He ran out into the field, waving his wooden sword at the retreating enemy. He personally slew a large number of the foe and declared the day's battle a victory, waving his sword wildly in the air, as the remaining imaginary redcoats beat a retreat.

This was the same way the stories were told by Zachary's big brothers, Matt and Luke. Pa, also named Matthew had also fought in the War for Independence, but like most men who have seen the horrors of war, Pa didn't say much about it. The brothers on the other hand were coaxed by Zachary unmercifully to tell about their adventures fighting against the British. In the evenings after supper Zachary begged for a story, even though he heard most of them, numerous times. As time went on the stories became more grandiose. The brothers left out the fact that being in General Washington's Army meant spending most of their time in retreat. They left out the numerous casualties, the near disaster at Monmouth and the retreat afterwards. They touched on, but didn't go into great detail about the long winter encampments where if a soldier didn't freeze to death, he almost starved.

When it came to telling a story, no one could sling the bull better than Matt. Luke would add the color and fill in the parts that Matt might leave out. The stories they told were of the few good times they had had with their comrades.

Matt, "Well Zach, there was the time in the winter of '79 when we were so hungry, we begged an old farm woman for a chicken. She wouldn't give it to us, but accepted some store-bought buttons and a few coins for a tough old laying hen that was nearing the end of its days. Luke and I befriended a young lad from Philadelphia named Willy, who lead a pampered life as the son of a wealthy merchant, until he ran off and joined the Army. Willy had a kind nature and could withstand a lot of kidding. We spent a lot of time pressing his good humor. He never hunted, fished, or even butchered an animal before he became a soldier." Luke, "Come on Matt, get back to the chicken."

Matt continued, "Well, we convinced Willy that before he was properly fit to kill Redcoats, he had to start small and work his way up. We suggested he kill the hen. Luke here tied the hen's legs together and placed the hen on a stump while I briefed Willy on how to chop its head off with one hit of the axe. Willy addressed the hen offering his condolences, but then closed his eyes when he swung the axe and chopped off the hen's feet instead of its head."

Luke broke into the story, "The hen took off across the barnyard on its stumps, squawking its fool head off. Matt took out after it and dove on it comin' up covered with mud, snow and cow shit."

Matt said, slapping Luke on the knee, "You know Luke, that was the toughest old bird I ever et', but it sure tasted good that day." The boys laughed. Matthew always of a quiet nature, smiled as he emptied his clay pipe into the stone fireplace.

The brothers then solemnly noted the death of their friend Willy, in a cornfield, in an unnamed skirmish, somewhere near the border between Delaware and Maryland. The brothers never went into the details of this event.

The stories of actual engagements with the enemy were few and only those were the brothers believed they had won the day. Feeding on each other's elaborations, the stories of the brother's exploits grew with each telling.

War is not hell for a boy of ten; it is a man's most glorious adventure. Zachary soaked up every word that his brothers spoke and imagined himself in the center of the fray. A boy on a small farm in Connecticut did not have much time to play, what with chores and his mother's insistence that he learn to read and write. When he did play, sometimes he had to fight it out with Indians, but mostly he reenacted the glory of his brother's stories.

When he played, he could not bring himself to pretend that he was the great General Washington. That would have been just too presumptuous. He did not want to pretend that he was one of the lesser generals or colonels in his brother's command. The boys made so many derogatory remarks about the failings of their senior officer's that Zachary could not see himself in such in adept roles. Instead he selected his brother's company commander, Captain Murphy, as his role model. His brothers spoke highly of their captain who led them through many harrowing experiences during the war.

Their Ma, Martha Bower, was a slender built woman, five foot three, with dark but graying hair; green eyes and a sharp nose that betrayed her obvious Anglo-Saxon heritage. She did not approve of all of this talk of fighting and war. She was the daughter of a Tory merchant who supported the British cause during the war, as it would have been bad business to do otherwise. Martha thought Christians should concentrate their thoughts on love and peace, and not dwell on man's propensity for war.

Though she kept her Tory feelings to herself, she could not help but feel that a war against the king whom she had been taught to revere, was not only wrong, but almost sinful. But she married a man who was a staunch patriot and not only her husband, but her two oldest sons had fought and suffered in the war for independence. Her Tory views were not welcome in her home and she honored her sons and husband by not mentioning her feelings to them.

Martha had been raised by parents who believed that women should receive some education, and she saw to it that her boys were given the same opportunity, whether they liked it or not. Her husband had even learned a bit, while listening to her instruct their off spring on proper use of the English language.

The conjoining of Martha Collins and Matthew Bower was an unlikely match. Martha was not only a prosperous merchant's daughter, but she believed in what her father, a deacon in the Church of England preached and tried to live to those standards. Matthew was the son of a frontiersman married to a half-breed, having the lineage of a British trapper and an Iroquois squaw. Matthew was a trapper and hunter, taught by his father. When Matthew came to town and was goaded, by his equally disreputablefriends, into dancing with the freckle faced local beauty; he was smitten by the end of the dance.

Matthew hotly pursued the dark-haired lass, much to the chagrin of her parents. At first Martha was flattered by the attention of this stranger and soon she found him to be the most interesting man she had ever met, much more exciting than the sons of local merchants and farmers. Matthew was tall with brown hair that just touched his broad shoulders; His muscles were pronounced from years of hardwork. His years of living and working in the wilderness had burned his skin to a dark bronze. He and his buckskins did not smell the best, but that was part of his persona. He was a quiet young man with a hard expression until something tickled his funny bone or awakened his mischievous side: then his eyes would smile revealing his true self.

Her father blustered, "How can you be seen with this backwoods boob. He probably only bathes for Christmas and Easter, if he knows when they are."

Martha's mother was also distressed, but in her understated manner, her fear and anger at the thought of her oldest daughter who she brought up to be a lady, the wife of a banker, or lawyer, or maybe even a man of the cloth, caused her voice to come out as a whine. "Now Martha, I just cannot see what attraction you find in this young man. Mr. Biddle's son Nathan has shown great interest in you for years, and you continue to ignore him. The Biddles have the finest carriage in the county and youcould be riding in it, like a proper young lady."

"Mother, Nathan is a pussy wlg. He probably drives the carriage or his pony cart, because riding a horse would chafe his flabby bottom."

"Young lady, you do not have to be crass and crude. The young Mr. Biddle may be a little rotund, but he is well read and an accomplished musician. If your friend Mr. Bower plays an instrument at all it is most likely an Indian drum."

Martha's interest in Matthew increased partially due to a seventeen year old's need to defy her parents. Matthew lingered in town after his companions returned west on another trapping expedition. So, Martha's interest had time to flare into true affection for her untamed suitor.

When Matthew finally proposed, Martha accepted, but did so with the stipulation that they compromise with regard to their lifestyles. Though Martha was fascinated with the exploits of her frontiersman, she could not quite bring herself to trekking through the woods most of the year, sleeping on the ground under a lean-to. Matt on the other hand had figured on spending his life doing just that. That was until he met the woman with whom he wished to spend the rest of his days. When one is in love he will live anywhere and do anything, just to be with his chosen mate. The compromise was that they would farm close enough to what Matt considered wilderness, so he could maintain contact with his current way of life, but also be at home most of the time with his beloved Martha.

Matt bought a mule, a cow and some land which he would make into a farm. The land was mostly wooded, and Matt cut the farm out of the forest. They lived in a rude lean-to for much of the spring and summer. Matt first cut and removed the trees from the fields and planted enough corn, turnips and potatoes to support them through the next winter.

After the planting was done, Matt began to build the log cabin that would be their home. The work was slow, hard labor; cutting the logs to size, notching the points where they intersected with another log and then moving the log into place. Martha helped as much as she could, but Matt had to build a rough crane from a tripod of logs and use a block and tackle to lift the larger logs. Cutting and fitting a single log was sometimes an all-day project.

Though the work was slow, help came early in the project. Matt's brother Josh and his two cohorts arrived in town from an expedition to the western territories. They heard of Matt's marriage and his purchase of land. The three woodsmen sought out Matt's property and arrived when the outline of the cabin was roughly three feet high. Having four strong males speeded the job immensely. Within three weeks the cabin was complete and the four began to build a small barn and other outbuildings.

Martha missed the contact with other people and therefore enjoyed the arrival of the three other men. Though rough and tumble woodsmen, they were almost always in good humor and added much joy and laughter to the quiet of the woods and farm. In the evening the men would tell stories of past adventures and joked and carried on like schoolboys. It was a sad day for Martha when the group finished their job and headed west again. The gregarious Martha was stuck in the wilderness with a less than talkative Matt, who was the only person with whom she could communicate.

This compromise worked for their first few years of married life. Matt sometimes longed for his lost freedom, and hated being a dirt farmer. Their mutual love overcame Matt's wanderlust for the time being. They soon became not only lovers, but also friends. They were a true team.

Matt was born in 1760, twelve months to the day after they arrived on the farm. Luke followed eighteen months later. Both boys took after their father, having dark hair and brown eyes. Matthew now had more than he ever planned on a wife, children, and property. He considered himself respectable.

In their remote location it took time to hear news from the rest of the world. Passers-by were always welcome at the Bower's farm, and Matthew would glean all the news he could from these travelers. Matthew heard tales of the increasingly strained relations between the colonies and Britain.

He learned of the military engagements that had taken place in Lexington, Concord and the valiant stand at Bunker Hill. His adventurous spirit was aroused. His wanderlust was back; he longed to participate in this greatest of adventures: war. He had heard stories around the campfire, of the French and Indian War from the older trappers and hunters. He was assured that the English-speaking successes in that conflict were in large part caused by the aid of frontiersmen, just like him. Matthew believed he and others like himself were the lifeblood of the struggling colonies. It was his duty to aid America. He had to go.

As they lay in their bed one night in early May, he explained himself as best he could to Martha. "Martha, the crops are all in, the farm has never been in as good a shape as it is now, and the boys are old enough to keep after the weeds and do the other chores. Last time the militia came through looking for volunteers, the Captain said that he expected to be home by harvest." Matthew told her he was sure that once the King saw the resolve of the Americans, he would settle the matter peacefully rather than fight with his own people. "I'll be home before you know it."

"Matthew, I have expected this for a while. I could see it in your eyes every time people told us what was going on." Martha rolled on to her back, and took her political stand. "Matthew, I have never expressed my opinions on the treasonous acts of a few revolutionaries, but it is wrong. We are subjects of a King who has protected us from Indians and the French. Our heritage is directly linked by our English roots. I was raised to respect the English system of government and law. The acts of these so-called patriots is like an unruly, unappreciative child striking out at its parents. This is wrong!"

Matthew knew that Martha had Tory leanings, but he had not expected such a vehement stand by his wife. He reached for her hand under the covers, but for the first time in their married life, she pulled it away. He responded slowly, thoughtfully, "Martha, your King has used America not as a beloved child, but as an indentured servant, to use as he sees fit. We are obliged to buy England's goods, to obey English laws and pay English taxes, whether or not they be just. Loving parents do not kill their children, and now the King's armies are doing just that."

Matthew was no match for a debate with Martha; he had learned better on minor issues, during their years together. She switched tactics, "I don't want you to go to war against the world's greatest army." Now she rolled over, curled up against him and hugged Matthew. "A bunch of farmers and clerks cannot stand up against the might of a real army." She squeezed Matthew a little tighter. "I love you. You are the father of my children, the love of my life. I do not want you to be killed. The only possible outcome of this folly is that you will either be killed in the war or hung as a traitor."

Matthew was dismayed. Martha's view imposed on his patriotism and his warrior's pride by adding the word "love" to the issue, in the same breath seemed completely unfair to him. He could not win this debate, so the only option was to take a stubborn masculine stand. "Martha, I have made up my mind. I have to do what I believe I have to do." Martha could feel his back stiffen and knew that even though she had won the debate, she had lost. Matthew went on, "I am not plannin' on gettin' myself killed in battle or hung. Once King George sees that we Americans are serious, he will take his armies back where they belong. I will be home by the harvest."

Martha conceded her loss, "Matthew, I don't want you to go to this sinful war, but I know that you'll just fester here, if you don't do what you think you must." She rolled onto her back. "Go, do what you must and come straight home to the boys and me." Martha then rolled away from Matthew and quietly sobbed until she fell asleep.

Matthew lay awake for a long time, staring into the darkness, trying to decide if the war for independence had just claimed its first casualty, his happy home.

In the morning, Matthew Bower packed his possible bag with personal effects, cleaned his musket, filled his powder horn, sharpened his skinning knife, and set off before noon, heading east. The goodbyes were short. Martha did not want to show her fear and sadness at his leaving, and Matthew wanted to get an early start, before Martha found some valid reason that he should stay a little longer.

Neither Matthew nor Martha had a clue that the week before his leaving, Matthew had planted the seed that would become Zachary Bower. As Matt and Luke grew, they not only looked much like their father, but grew big at early ages and emulated Matthew's woodsman persona. Zachary on the other hand was born very much the image of his mother with blonde hair, blue eyes and a much more delicate nature than his older brothers.

Matthew was not back by the harvest of 1776. It was three years since he had left the farm, when he finally returned to the clearing in the woods where he had carved out his home.

Matthew had seen more of war then he ever cared to again. He had been wounded twice, once from a knick in the arm by a musket ball and once across the cheek by the glancing blow of a British bayonet while Matthew thrust his bayonet into the charging adversary's midsection. Matthew did well at soldiering and rose to the rank of sergeant before he was released to return home.

What the enemy could not do, the cold winter of 1779 did. Matthew got a minor case of frostbite after marching all day in a cold rain which turned to snow as night fell. It continued to get colder as the night went on. He always impressed upon his troops the importance of keeping their feet as warm as possible, but by the time his units pitched camp and built fires, the damage was done. The surgeon ended up removing one toe on his left foot. The surgeon feared that he might have to go back and remove the entire foot, but Matthew's circulation to the discolored members improved dramatically, forced mostly by Matthew's tenacious strength of will.

After three months, Matthew rejoined his men and attempted to resume his duties, but he was not so strong willed that he could keep up with the moving columns. He cursed his bad luck and his inability to perform as he had in the past. As much as his captain wished to retain this excellent soldier, he finally talked Matthew into ending his enlistment and returning home. His boys, Matt and Luke, had been itching to join their father in General Washington's Army.

Martha would not hear of it. "You boys are needed here on the farm. Lord knows I can't keep the place up by myself. Besides, you have not been paying attention to your studies, spendin' too much time messing around in the woods."

"But Ma, Luke and I are men now, and Pa needs our help." The boys found little or no value in studying and had inherited their father's thirst for adventure. They feared they would miss this great opportunity.

The controversy went on particularly hard for the last year that Matthew was gone. When Matthew returned from the war the boys expected to have an ally, but Matthew had lived the horrors of war for three hard years and was not about to subject his sons to the experience, if he could help it.

He tried to explain to them that the glories they imagined were just not so. "Boys, there is no glory in wearing rags and forcing yourself to keep marchin' through the rain or snow, particularly when you can't remember your last good meal."

Matt, always the leader of the two brothers, led the response. "But Pa, you went to do your duty for the good of our country. Now that we are men, Luke and I have the same duty to finish the job you started."

"Start it I did, but no one knew that the King and the Parliament had the gumption to carry on this long. I took my licks for the cause, and I won't hear of my boys doin' the same."

Late one night in September Matt talked Luke into sneaking off to do their duty. They would wait until Ma and Pa were asleep and slip away.

Luke, "Come on Matt, we can't just up and leave Ma and Pa. I have never seen Pa so adamant; we can't just disobey him."

Matt said in his most persuasive tone, "Luke we have done most everything together since you were old enough to stop pissin' in your breeches. I am goin' to join the militia and do what I should. Now you can come along or stay and explain to Pa how you let me go, but I'm a goin', with or without ya."

Luke, rubbing the side of his face with his hand, "Big brother I'm not sure who has looked out for who over the years. It appears that I have had to save you from yourself on many occasions. I guess I couldn't let you go off to war without me there to look after you."

The pact was sealed and that night the boys left a note to their parents and slipped down the same road their father had followed, over three years before.

There are certain things that cannot be adequately explained in words. There was no way that Matthew's attempts to dissuade the boys from war could have prepared them for the rigors of being a soldier, or the mixture of adrenalin and stark fear that came with their first engagement with the enemy. But the boys were young and strong and too proud to turn tail and run from the field.

CHAPTER 2

BACK ON THE FARM

ZACHARY BOWER GREW up a rather pampered child as compared to his brothers. He was born a couple of weeks early and was therefore smaller and weaker than his parent's previous offspring. In many cases children who are born weak do not survive very long, but Martha did all she could to keep Zachary warm and fed and soon he made up for lost time and became a healthy, intelligent child. Once a parent begins to baby a child, it is hard to stop, and the child continues to demand the attention they were used to as infants.

Since his brothers were off at war when he was very young, Martha had only the one child to look after. Not knowing the fate of her other offspring, she wanted to nurture and fiercely protect the remaining child. Also, since the older boys had spurned her attempts to properly educate them and followed their father's image as a man of the frontier, she would make sure that this last child received a proper education.

That is not to say that Zachary was a wimp by today's standards, that would be hard to do on the frontier of early America. He did become a sort of mama's boy as compared to his brothers who tended to follow the untamed nature of their father. Zachary did his studies and found enjoyment in reading and writing. He asked deep questions at an early age. Martha was sure that she had a future scholar on her hands. In spite of an interest in learning and a tendency to stay close to his mother's protective nest, Zachary was the hero of his own dreams. He saw himself one day following his father and brothers before him, to partake in the glories of war.

In 1781 General Cornwallis surrendered at Yorktown and the colonists including Matthew and Martha hoped that the long ordeal was over. This victory for General Washington's army did not end all hostilities, but it was true that the end of the war was near. Five months after Yorktown Matt and Luke were discharged and returned home.

Winter life on the little farm was good. Zachary helped his brothers tend their traps. Whenever he could, Zachary joined his father and brothers on hunting treks into the woods.

March remained cold and rainy. The sun had not been seen for almost two weeks. Martha complained of the chills and coughing for several days before she got a high fever and could not leave her bed. There were few cures in rural America, but Matthew did what he could. He fed Martha soups of his own concoction, trusting that Martha's body would take control and help her recover from her malady.

In the close confinement of the small farmhouse, Matthew and his three sons made as little noise as possible moving about with deliberate silence and speaking to each other just above a whisper. They wanted Martha to sweat out and sleep away her fever.

Matthew and the boys had minor chores around the farm. In the winter there are few pressing chores. They tried to stretch out the chores as the only means to stay out of the house, but the extended period of rain made it miserable to be out of doors for any extended length of time.

In normal times the rain would not have stopped the boys from hunting for some fresh meat, but with Martha this sick they felt obligated to stay close at hand. Matt was working on building a new chair. Luke twiddled to pass the time and helped Matt when needed.

Zachary had his studies to occupy some of his time. Many times, he procrastinated or rebelled when Martha made him spend time reading and writing. In a strange way, he felt that if he did his mother's bidding of his own accord she would somehow get well.

But Martha did not get well. She continued to grow paler, her breathing became shallower, and her fever would not break. She passed away in the middle of the night with no sign other than her coughing ceased.

Matthew awoke at dawn to check on his wife. In the pale light, he saw her lying in her bed. Her expression was more peaceful than it had been through the several days of her illness. He checked and found no pulse; her body temperature was cooling from the fever she had endured. Matthew quietly crossed her arms over her chest and pulled the cover over her face, saying a silent prayer as he did so.

He did not want his sons to see their mother like this. He hoped that they would remember her as the handsome, vibrant woman who had given them life and all her love.

As Matthew finished his solemn task, the boys awoke. Matt, upon seeing the cover over his mother, woke Luke and Zachary. They arose and went to their father who was now sitting in the corner in quiet repose.

Matthew stood and said, "I'm sorry boys."

The four men hugged each other and all quietly wept, each brother blessing their mother in his own personal way.

Matthew asked Matt and Luke to prepare a proper coffin for Martha's remains. With no readily available lumber, the boys pulled off some boards from the lien-to behind the barn and built a long rectangular box.

It had stopped raining during the night, but the sky was still overcast. Without being asked, Matt and Luke dug a grave behind their mother's vegetable garden. The first foot of dirt was heavy with water from the previous day's rain. The boys continued to dig in the dirt removing rocks and roots as they went. At one point Luke slipped in the wet soil and slid into the hole. He began to curse but caught himself. There would be no foul talk or sacrilege on this day.

By early afternoon the grave was dug, and the box was ready. Matthew did not want to drag this ordeal out any longer than necessary. He asked the boys to bring the coffin and then he bid them wait on the porch. He placed the love of his life into the box. She was still dressed in her nightgown. His thoughts were of the many good times they had in their youth and the many joys as a family.

Matthew made Martha as comfortable as possible. He nailed the homemade lid in place and called for his sons to help him carry the coffin to its destination.

It began to rain again as the four carried the barn board coffin across the yard to the waiting gravesite. They lowered the coffin into the waiting hole on two ropes, each having an end to slacken.

Matthew produced the old Prayer Book given them by his father-in-law on their wedding day.

The four stood, the rain soaking their bowed heads. Matthew began to read the rites of burial. "I am the resurrection and the life, saith the Lord: he that believeth in me, though he were dead, yet shall he live: and whosoever liveth and believeth in me, shall not die." He stumbled through the words, not being the best at reading. His emotions caused his voice to break on several occasions. "Zachary, help me," he implored. "You are the best reader in the house."

Zachary stood stoically and read the words of the prayers. It continued to rain as he finished the rites.

"I know that the redeemer liveth, and that he shall stand at the latter day upon the earth...." Zachary finished the section and Matthew helped him select a psalm, which he then read, "The Lord is my light and my salvation; whom then shall I fear?" The Lord is the strength of my life......."

Zachary finished the psalm, wiped the rain from his eyes and went on to the Lord's Prayer. The four prayed in unison. "Our Father, who art in heaven. Hallowed be thy name. Thy kingdom come..."

Zachary continued through the liturgy. At times he could hear his voice waiver with emotion, but he summoned all his courage to finish in a strong voice. "O Lord Jesus Christ, who by thy death didst take away the sting of death; Grant unto us thy servants so to follow in faith where thou hast led the way, that we may at length fall asleep peacefully in thee, and wake up after thy likeness; through thy mercy, who livest with the Father and the Holy Ghost, one God, world without end. Amen."

At the conclusion, Matthew added, "Rest ye well my love." He then hugged his sons. He turned away, taking Zachary with him back to the house. "Thank you, son, I just couldn't do it."

Matt and Luke silently shoveled dirt into the hole, each with thoughts of their mother's kindness and love.

When all were inside before the fire Matthew produced a jug of sour mash whiskey and took a swig to counteract the cold and wet and to deaden the pain of the day's events. He passed the jug to Matt, then to Luke and finally to Zachary.

Zachary winced, his eyes watered as he swallowed the strong liquid. Though it burned going down, the act made him feel more a part of this band of men.

"Thank you, boys, for all your help today." Matthew went to each of them patting them on the shoulder. "I couldn't have made it through the day without you."

Luke warmed leftover soup over the fire. Matt removed two of the rungs from the chair he had almost finished and lashed them into a cross for their mother's grave. There was not much said that afternoon and evening. Each contemplated their mother's fine life and mourned her loss in their own heart and mind.

The rain stopped during the night and the next morning was bright and clear. Matthew wanted to break the pall that was over the house. He did not want his sons to mope around the house any longer.

He announced they had no fresh meat and asked his sons to hunt up something for the night's dinner.

Matthew knew his directions would aid their pain. There is not much chance to think of anything else when hunting. The boys stalked through the woods west of the farm.

The woods were still wet from the previous rains. The smell of the moist leaves and bark filled the boy's nostrils. As beams of sunlight penetrated the forest canopy attempting to dry the foliage, wisps of mist rose above the wild bushes and saplings.

Matt and Luke had taught Zachary to fire their muskets, though they had to help him support the long weapon and hold him from behind to keep the recoil from bowling him over. Zachary had learned to take aim and had successfully hit some targets, but he was a long way from the marksman that he would have to become to match his father and brothers.

The three brothers moved quietly out of the woods to the edge of a clearing. They crouched down. At the opposite side of the clearing three doe were grazing in the field of tall grass. The deer were up wind, so the boys had a chance to maneuver for a clean shot.

The three moved back into the woods and worked their way to the left where they emerged from the woods behind some bushes a mere fifty yards downwind of the does. As Luke raised his musket to take a shot, Matt poked him and pointed to Zachary.

Luke lowered his weapon handing it to Zachary. Matt supported the barrel; Luke took up the station behind Zachary's back. Zachary took aim at the largest of the three does. Matt whispered, "Remember to squeeze the trigger, not pull." The three sensing danger raised their heads, but before they could turn and run Zachary squeezed the trigger. The gun's loud report broke the silence.

The deer was hit in the thickest part of the throat and thrown to the ground. Responding instinctively, she leapt to her feet and ran into the woods, bleeding profusely from the wound. The two other deer also dashed into the woods.

"Come on boys!" hollered Matt, "It's a chase!"

The three dashed across the clearing. Luke let out a war hoop, as was his custom when giving chase to game. Bounding through the woods Matt followed the broken branches and patches of blood that marked the trail of their quarry. Luke and Zachary chased behind their brother.

The deer was faint from loss of blood and fell about a hundred yards into the woods. The doe's sides were still heaving when the panting trio caught up to it. Matt fired a shot into its head to end its life.

Luke quickly found some flexible bark and cut a piece to form a cup. He then slit the deer's throat running some blood into the improvised cup. He handed the cup to Zachary saying, "To be a true Indian hunter and warrior you have to drink the blood of your first kill."

Zachary's eyes widened. He looked quizzically at Matt. Matt responded to the questioning look, "It is a sacred tradition of the Iroquois that has been handed down to us, their white brothers."

Zachary complied, taking a small sip of the warm red liquid. It was not as bad as he had anticipated. Matt and Luke also took a sip to prove to their younger brother that they were not just pulling his leg. Matt dipped two figures in the remaining blood and marked each of Zachary's cheeks as with war paint.

After the ritual was completed, Luke field dressed the deer while Matt cut down a sapling to carry the trophy back home. Within a half hour the three were headed home. Matt and Luke carried the sapling across their shoulders with the deer hanging between them. Zachary carried both muskets over his shoulders.

As they came up the lane and approached home, Matthew came out the door to fetch some firewood. Zachary ran to him with the gun barrels bouncing on his shoulders. "Pa, I shot a deer!" he shouted with unmasked enthusiasm.

Seeing the two remaining brothers with the fresh carcass, Matthew responded, "Well I see you did."

Matthew and Zachary stood waiting for Matt and Luke to make it to the barnyard. When they arrived, Luke declared, "We eat tonight," he raised his end of the sapling. "Zachary bagged his first kill and a good clean shot it was."

Seeing the dried blood on Zachary's cheeks Matthew pointed to it. "I see he got the kill and the ritual."

Matt replied, "Pa, some things are sacred."

It occurred to all three brothers at once that they were being awfully exuberant considering their mother's recent demise. Their heads dropped in silence. Matt as the oldest felt it was his place to apologize. "Sorry Pa, we weren't thinking."

Matthew responded, "That's alright lads, your mother would have wanted us to go on as a family." He patted Matt's arm, "I know that we will all miss her, but we have to carry on." He paused a bit, saying to himself more than to his sons, "There is nothing else we can do."

CHAPTER 3

THE WANDERLUST

Three months after Martha's death, Matt started working on Luke to quit the life of a dirt farmer once and for all. "I have heard that in the Ohio and Illinois territories, there are more game than a man could ever hope for. Luke, Lord knows what wonders lie beyond the Illinois territory, it may go on forever."

Luke was interested, but always the cautious one, "Matt we can't just go gallivanting off into the woods and leave Pa and Zach here to tend the farm."

"Hell no, we'll all go. You know that the only reason Pa ever became a farmer was for Ma's sake. He'd go with us in a minute. Zach is old enough to carry his own weight, so we'll all go."

It was all just talk until the evening Uncle Josh arrived with two of his cronies. They arrived just before sunset, bringing a couple of rabbits to add to the stew pot. "Matthew I'm grieved to hear of Martha's passing. She was a good woman and you know I loved her dearly."

After dinner Josh produced a jug of rum that he had gotten as trade for some pelts. He passed it around for all to sample. "Matthew, I been thinkin', you can't spend the rest of your life moping around, and you sure weren't cut out to be a dirt farmer. You ought to sell this place and join me on my next expedition."

Matt broke in, "Yeah, Pa, Luke and me have been talkin' about doin' just that." Zachary added his enthusiasm, "Come on Pa, we could be the best."

The jug was passed around again, and Matt responded to the growing mandate, "Joshua Bower, it seems to me that you have gotten me liquored up and talked into your questionable schemes, before. I must say the proposition is of interest, but I want to sleep on it before jumpin' into anything."

Zachary pleaded, "Come on Pa, Uncle Josh needs our help."

Matt, "I said I was goin' to think on it and that is that." He got up and retired to his bed. "You lads don't let me hold up the festivities, and Zach, no more pulls on the jug for you, I don't want to be holdin' your head over a bucket all night."

Zachary, "Oh, Pa."

"You heard me." And with this Matt retired for the evening, to contemplate a decision that would be harder to make than the others knew.

Josh, passing the jug to Luke, said, "I hear tell, you boys made it to Yorktown, to whup up on ol' Cornwallis. I didn't know the militia made it down there."

Matt: "Luke and me were regular army soldiers, just like Pa, and yes, we was there." Josh: "Tell me about it lad."

Matt: "It appears that General Washington heard that ol' Cornwallis was hold up on this peninsula down in Virginia, so he ups and moves the whole danged army down to see him. We'd had a bunch of Frenches help us for quite a while and after we had the British stuck in place, the Frenchie brought out the biggest cannons Luke and me had ever see'd and began pounding them Redcoats into the ground with balls that weighed as much as a man."

Luke broke into the story, "Uncle those cannons made more noise than the Lord ought to allow, and the Frenches kept up the shootin' for days."

Matt, "Finally, we made a night raid, led by Colonel Adams. We caught the Redcoats by surprise and captured two of their key redoubts."Luke, "It was tough stumbling around in the dark with craters from the cannon balls, as big as a house."

Matt, "Luke's just sayin' that cause he managed to fall into a hole, face first."

Matt continued, "When ol' Cornwallis woke up in the mornin' and figured out we were close enough to blow them all to hell, he had his boys wave the white flag."

Luke, "You could believe the whoopin' and hollerin' and dancin' around when the British surrendered. That has got to be the best day in our lives."

Josh raised the jug, "Here, here, I'm right proud of you boys, ya serviced your country and did the family proud."

Soon the jug was empty. Josh and his companions spread their bedrolls, and everyone turned in for the night, in high spirits.

Though he had trouble sleeping during the night while thinking about the coming great adventures with his uncle, father and brothers, Zachary dutifully got up before dawn and milked the cow. His mind was still racing with thoughts of seeing places other than the farm, of hunting and trapping and maybe even fighting Indians.

Most of the crew rose slowly, but still carrying the glow of the previous night's good company, and of course the rum. Matt had not slept well, because he knew the decision which he would disclose that day would be one of the hardest things he ever had to do.

Matt and Luke were babbling on with Josh about when and where they would trek. There was no doubt in their minds that their father would accept Josh's offer and return to the life he once loved.

When Zachary came in with the bucket of fresh milk, he joined in the banter, "When will we be goin', Uncle Josh? I got my own possible sack and powder horn, and Matt and Luke have taught me to hunt and fish and all kinds of stuff."

He knew it would be tough and hearing Zachary's enthusiasm made Matt's situation even worse. Patting Zachary on the back of the shoulder he said, "Come out to the shed son, there's something we have to talk about."

Zachary, still caught up in the enthusiasm, was sure that his father wanted to give him assignments in preparation for their departure. "Sure Pa, I want to show you the backpack me and Luke have been workin' on."

Once in the shed, Matt said softly, "Zachary, before your mother died, she voiced her concern for your future. She said, and rightly so that Matt and Luke are a lot like me, bumpkins at heart with no use for book learnin'. But she said how different you were and how you deserved the chance to get a real education, in a school and all. She made me promise that I would see to it that you got that chance."

Zachary was not quite sure where this discussion was going, but he was on his guard, because it sounded as if he were being betrayed. "Pa, I don't want book learnin' I want to be with you and the boys."

"Son, I wrote to your Aunt Jessica about your mother's request and asked for her counsel. I received a letter from her two weeks ago and have been studying on it ever since. Your aunt has offered to take you in, see that you get a real education, and aim you towards a promising future. I hate to break us up and that is why I have been studyin' on the letter for so long. Now with Uncle Josh showin' up and gettin' your brothers in a dither, I figured that I had better do something, before you pack up and head for the woods."

Zachary could not believe what he was hearing, the chance for the greatest adventure of his life and he was being left behind. He felt completely betrayed. As much as he wanted to act like a man and show that he was old enough to join them on the expedition, the tears welled up in his eyes, his voice wavered as he blurted, "You can't, I won't go, you are jus' doin' this cause you don't want a kid along. But I won't be a bother, I can pull my weight."

Matthew said softly but authoritatively, "Son, you know that I'm a man of his word, I made a promise to your mother, and you're going to have to help me keep that promise."

Zachary, "Please Pa let me go with you, we're a family, you can't break us up."

Matthew wrapped his big arms around Zachary, "Son that is why I spent so much time studying on the situation. We will always be a family, whether we are together or apart, makes no difference.

Me and your brothers love you very much, and always will, but now you have to be a man and do the hard thing. I've done decided what you are gonna do and it's done with. Now clean yourself up a bit and I'm goin' to talk with your brothers."

Matthew explained his decision to Matt and Luke; they were more vocal in their protest than Zachary. Luke usually the quieter of the two spoke up, "How can you do this to Zach, first Ma dyin' and now we are goin' to up and leave Zach with strangers."

Matthew retorted, "Aunt Jessica is family just like Josh, she'll take good care of Zach. I made a promise to your Ma that Zach would get a chance to be somethin' and that's final. Who knows Zach may become a teacher or a lawyer or somethin' that we can all be proud of."

The decision having been made, the plan was set to get Zachary to his Aunt in New London, Connecticut. Uncle Josh and his cronies were heading into Hartford to do some trading for supplies and general gallivanting around the city. They would return to the farm in six weeks to begin the expedition. During that time Luke and Matt would take Zachary to his aunt's and return to help Matthew harvest the early crops, which would be sold to help finance the venture. Uncle Josh had suggested selling the farm, which was easier, said that done. Anyway, Matthew hated to sell the place which had become a part of him, and where he and his beloved Martha had spent so many joyful years. The decision was made to sell off the mule, cow and farm implements and then board the place up for future use.

The morning of Zachary's departure came soon. If young boys are anything, they are resilient.

After Zachary accepted his fate, he began to look forward to the upcoming trip. For a boy who had never been anywhere, this too had become a chance for adventure. Zachary was up and about long before sunup. He milked the cow and packed his few belongings into his rawhide possible bag.

Matt and Luke awoke a little before sunup and prepared themselves for the journey. By eight in the morning all was ready and Zachary hugged his father goodbye. "You learn good, boy, and pay heed to what your aunt tells you." As he kissed Zachary on the forehead, he said "The Lord be with you son, we will be thinkin' of you."

As the three brothers headed down the road that had led Matthew and his older sons to war, Matthew lost the tears that he could not show in front of his young sons. He silently prayed that he had done the right thing.

Both Martha and her sister had left their sedate upbringing to marry men who would add some excitement to their lives. Martha of course married a frontiersman and left civilization to live in the wilderness. Two years after her departure, Jessica met a young sailor who was already a first officer on a coastal trading ship. They were married and moved to New London and in a few years, Israel Redden became master of a fine ship.

At first Jessica sailed along with her husband, a privilege given only to the captain. She learned to love the sea and the chance to visit the major seaport cities, such as Boston, New York, Philadelphia and Charleston. When Emily their daughter was born, Jessica was forced to settle down as a mother and oft times be the lonely wife of a sailor   When Emily was three, Israel received an offer to be the master of a brig that traded in France, England and several ports in the Mediterranean. Israel took the offer in spite of the fact that this would mean months away from home and family, instead of the weeks to which they had become accustomed.

When Jessica heard of her sister's passing, and her sister's request of Matthew to get Zachary a good education, she was more than happy to help. "Anyway," she thought "it would be nice to have a permanent man around the house to aid with the heavier chores."

Zachary, in the company of his two brothers, arrived on Jessica's doorstep late one evening.

They had been traveling on foot for two weeks in the August sun. They looked like savages to Jessica and Emily and smelled like goats. Jessica had never seen her nephews and had to overcome her repulsion, in order to hug and kiss them hardily. Emily on the other hand felt no such kinship and had to be prodded by her mother before she would get close enough to shake hands with these obviously downtrodden kin.

Jessica, "Boys, I am sure you're hungry from your journey. Why don't you go out back and wash up, while Emily and I fix you something to eat?"

The boys marched out back, found the pump and set about washing their faces and hands in the cold well water. As soon as they had gone, Emily voiced her disapproval of the invading horde. "Mother, I have never seen such dirty, smelly people in my life. I can't believe that you are going to let them sleep in our house. Perhaps I can find accommodations in the barn that would make them feel more at home."

"Emily that is enough!" chastised Jessica. "Your Aunt Martha was very dear to me and anything that I can do to help her children, I will do, and you will assist me in doing so. Have I made myself clear?"

Emily pouted to show her displeasure. Jessica, "Have I made myself clear?" Emily condescended, "Yes mother."

Jessica was a petite five feet with dark hair, green eyes and the pale and freckled Anglo-Saxon skin that cannot be left in the sun for long without burning. Though girls with this fairest of complexions are among the most beautiful of children, they do not age well, and Jessica already had crow's feet and other wrinkles at an early age.

Emily had a complexion very much like her mother, though her hair was several shades lighter.

From her early height it appeared that Emily would be taller than her mother by the time she was sixteen.

Israel had built Jessica a fine house. The biggest house Zachary had ever seen. The façade was shingled with a balanced number of windows on either side of an impressive mahogany front door.

Upon entering the house there was a parlor on either side of the front hall. Past the staircase was a formal dining room followed by the kitchen. On the second floor, the "T" design of the house was even more evident with two bedrooms, one over each parlor and then a straight corridor past three smaller bedrooms over the dining room and kitchen.

After supper Emily showed the boys to their rooms over the rear of the house. Matt being the oldest got a guest room of his own. Zachary and Luke had to share a high poster, double bed. Emily attempting to comply with her mother's direction and be civil to her cousins, announced, "Zachary, this will be your room for as long as you are with us. I hope that you two sleep well." As she closed the door behind herself, she hoped that the stay would not be too long.

The boys had never slept in so luxurious a bed. Luke, "Dang, boy, you have fallin' into it. This is a fine place to be, the food is good, Aunt Jessica seems to be nice enough and this bed of yours is fit for General Washington himself. You might keep an eye on Cousin Emily though; she seems to be a snippy little thing."

Zachary didn't respond, he had slipped off to sleep with his head resting on the comfort of a real pillow.

Aunt Jessica insisted that Matt and Luke stay around for a couple of days and rest before their return journey. Most of all she wanted to talk with the young men about their mother and how she had fared in the wilderness. They had some pleasurable discussions as they all got acquainted. Even Emily warmed towards her cousins a bit. She was somewhat taken at having a couple of young men around the house, even if in her estimation they were of lesser stature.

On the morning of the third day, the brothers made ready for the long trek back to the farm. The parting was mildly emotional. The boys hugged and kissed their little brother, though Zachary was not sure that this was a manly thing to do.

After the departure Jessica asked Zachary to come with Emily and her to the parlor to discuss his future. Jessica, "I trust you find your room satisfactory?"

He was somewhat intimidated by his aunt, "Yes Um."

Jessica recognized his discomfort and softened her voice, "Please don't be so formal, Aunt Jessica will be fine."

"Yes, Aunt Jessica."

Jessica, "Now for your education, school does not start for a month or so, but Emily and I will be happy to tutor you in the meantime."

Zachary, "My mother learned me how to read and write and cipher."

Jessica, "Your mother 'taught' you how to read and write. We must work on your grammar.

Other than that, I am sure Martha did a splendid job in teaching you. She was always ready to help me in my studies. We will have to see what you have learned and then we will go on from there. But first, we have to do something about those smelly old clothes."

Turning to Emily, "Please take Zachary and introduce him to the bathtub and soap. I took the liberty of buying some breeches and a shirt in hopes that you were actually coming. I think that I got about the right size."

He followed Emily to a room off the kitchen where they kept a large copper tub for bathing purposes. Three buckets of water had been placed next to the tub. Emily felt less need to be civil now that her older cousins had departed, she could not help but attempt to press her dominating air on this youngster. "Fill the tub with those buckets, boy. Take off your clothes and get in the tub."

"I ain't takin' off my clothes in front of some girl," said Zachary.

"I will of course turn my back; I wouldn't want to look anyway." Emily being an only child had little opportunity to see how the other sex was plumbed. She turned around but could not help but try and see what she could see, out of the corner of her eye. Zachary in the meantime was attempting to slip out of his buckskin breeches, while squatting down as far behind the tub as he could in a valiant attempt to protect his privacy.

Five minutes after he got into the tub, Emily reappeared with the new shirt and breeches. "When you are done dry yourself and put these on."

"Where are you goin' with my breeches?" blurted Zachary.

Emily retorted, "As much as I hate to touch them, I'm taking them outside." And she was gone.

Zachary jumped from the tub hurriedly, dried, and put on the new clothes. He did not have many possessions, but his mother made those buckskin breeches from the hide of a deer killed by his big brother. They were his and he was proud of them. He took off in pursuit of Emily.

When he found Emily, she was nonchalantly swinging on a two-seater swing under a large oak tree. "Where are my breeches, Emily?"

"You have no need of them, they were old and dirty, and you are about to learn how to be a clean young gentleman."

"They are mine, where did you put them? You bitch!" The use of this word had no meaning for him. His brother had used it towards a stubborn cow. It had gotten a great rise out of his mother.

"I put it on the burn pile, you little savage." Emily took off to find her mother and report what she had just been called.

Zachary began trucking around the yard in a frenzy looking for his prized pants, before they were burned. Rounding the corner of the barn he spied the breeches on top of a pile of branches, which were stacked for future burning. The buckskins were dirty and odoriferous enough to attract a local dog that beat him to the pile and took off with them, for an afternoon snack. He ran after the dog, tackling it as it made it to the dirt road in front of the house. Grabbing the pants, he pulled them, but the dog would not let go. The dog considered this a great tug-of-war. As Jessica ran towards him with Emily trailing behind, Zachary jumped on the dog again cussing and punching at the dog's midsection. The dog had enough of this sport and fearing that he was about to be ganged up on by the woman who had chased him with a broom in the past, dropped the breeches and took off down the road.

Zachary held the breeches tightly under his arm. "You can't have my breeches." Emily, "I told you that we couldn't civilize this little savage."

Jessica, "We don't want to keep your pants; we were just going to air them and attempt to clean them."

Zachary stood his ground, "Emily was going to burn them!"

Jessica, "Young lady I think that it is time that we have a little talk again. And as for you" pointing at Zachary, "You have undone all of that cleaning in only five minutes. It is back into the tub for you."

This time Jessica supervised the bathing. The good news for Zachary was that she provided a bucket of hot water to be added to the existing water. "Emily, take Zachary's clothes and wash them."

"Mother," Emily protested.

"You heard me. It appears that you had a hand in this mess, and you can help clean it up."

After five minutes in the tub he was ready to get out but was now stuck with no clothes. Jessica seeing him squirming commanded. "You, soak!"

Still firmly in control, Jessica then commanded, "Emily get one of your nightgowns and bring it to me."

After twenty minutes in the tub, Jessica presented him with the nightgown, and ordered, "Put this on until your clothes are cleaned and dry."

Zachary reluctantly complied. It did not look like a good time to challenge this seat of authority. A bit later he sat subdued in the corner of the kitchen. What humiliation, here he was wrinkled from the bath and in a girl's nightgown. The only good thing he could think of was that his brothers were not there to see it. They would never take a boy who wore girl's clothes with them to the wilderness. Oh, the humiliation!

Jessica reappeared with a pair of large scissors and proceeded to cut his shoulder length hair to just below his ears. Would it ever stop? He wanted to protest, but again decided that it was safer to maintain silence.

Later, with fresh cut hair and again dressed in his new outfit, Jessica stood him in front of a mirror. "There," announcing her approval, "That is what a young gentleman should look like. I will help you stay this way."

Looking in the mirror he saw his new image. His blonde hair was shorter than he could ever remember. The short pants and white shirt made him feel all sissified. He squirmed and scratched his itches from the wool pants and stiff collar. He may have looked like a sissy, but he knew who he was underneath this façade and in some ways, he was not entirely displeased with his new image.

At lunch Jessica addressed the young combatants who were still subdued from the morning's chastising. "You two do not have to like each other, but you are both going to live under this roof for a long time, and you will tolerate and show proper respect for each other."

Zachary and Emily chorused a "Yes Um," in unison.

Jessica, "Good, that will be the end of it! Now, Zachary let's go into the parlor and see how well your mother taught you to read."

Jessica was pleased with his basic reading ability. She had been certain that her sister would have done a good job. One of the first apparent problems stemmed from the fact that one of the few books that Martha had used as a reading primer was the family's King James Bible. He stumbled a bit in Jessica's reader because he was not finding the requisite number of "thee's" and "thou's.

After a week of restless peace with Emily and many hours of studying, Zachary was falling into a routine. The only time he had been out of the house and into the adjacent yard was to accompany his aunt and cousin to church on Sunday.

Jessica could see the cabin fever building in her young charge and decided to send Zachary and Emily into town for some groceries. She also thought this would be a good opportunity for the cousins to do something together and possibly build some more tolerance for each other.

Being a proper young lady, Emily put on one of her better dresses for the short walk to town. One never knows whom one might meet. She combed her long blonde hair, forcing as many curls as possible. She placed her brush, the small mother-of-pearl backed mirror that her father had brought her from Europe, and a few other valued possessions into her small drawstring handbag. She then made sure, that Zachary looked as presentable as possible. Again, one never knows whom one might meet, and if she must introduce him as a blood relation, she did not want him to look too disreputable.

Emily took the opportunity to show Zachary around town. There is little more satisfying than showing a stranger the local attractions of your town. Zachary was enjoying all of the new things to see. He had never seen a ship before or all of the seafaring paraphernalia that was spread on the decks of the ships and on the docks.

Emily, as the daughter of a sea captain spoke with great authority while answering his many questions. They both truly enjoyed themselves.

Emily, "Zachary, it is getting late. We had better get the groceries and head home."

They headed up the next street heading away from the docks. As they approached the store, which was on the other side of the street, Emily saw three boys appear from between two buildings and head their way. Emily reached out her hand and stopped Zachary in his tracks. She directed, "Let's cross here." She hastened him across the street.

The first and biggest boy was Toby McPhee, the son of a fisherman who liked to guzzle rum much more than work. No one in town knew where Toby's mother had gone, but she got up and disappeared leaving her only son with his alcoholic father. Toby was mean natured. His father abused him, and Toby spread that abuse onto the rest of the world, whenever he could. Toby was only a year older than Zachary but was half again as big. His two companions were known for being almost as big bullies as their leader.

Emily was known for putting on airs and was therefore not one of the favorites among the local youngsters. Harassing a prissy young lady was a source of great amusement for this disreputable crew. They accosted Emily and Zachary just before they reached the entrance to the Widow Saunders store.

Toby was carrying a homemade fishing pole and held it out to block their route. "Where you goin' in such a hurry, Emily," he said with a mocking whine in his voice.

"Out of our way!" Emily demanded.

To impress his friends, Toby reached out with the butt-end of his fishing pole, lifting the front hem of Emily's ankle length dress about three inches before she stepped back, and it dropped back in place. "You got anything in there for me?" he sneered.

Emily's face turned red more from anger than from embarrassment. Her eyes flashed with rage at this affront by these louts. Before Emily could do anything, Zachary also enraged by this assault on his female cousin, charged forward. He tackled Toby to the ground and fell on top of him in the process. He punched wildly at Toby's bulbous body, while uttering every curse word he had ever heard from his brothers.

"Get this little shit off of me" Toby commanded his cohorts.

They grabbed Zachary, one on each arm, pulling him up to a standing position. Toby immediately stood up, punched Zachary in the stomach and knocked the air out of him. Toby followed that punch with a blow to the face which glanced off Zachary's nose as he turned his head to avoid a direct hit.

Emily had not moved. Now she joined the fray by swinging her handbag against the side of the head of one assailant and then the other. As they let go of Zachary's arms, she brought the bag down on top of Toby's head with her full force Mrs. Saunders, seeing the altercation in front of her store, charged through the doorway wielding her trusty broom. She swung at each of the local bullies which caused them to beat a retreat down the street, uttering a few idle threats at Zachary and Emily as they went.

"Ruffians," barked Mrs. Saunders at the departing trio. "Are you children alright?"

Zachary stood there covered with dirt from his fray on the ground. A trickle of blood dripped from his nose onto his new shirt.

"Put your head back until the bleeding stops, boy." Mrs. Saunders motioned them inside her store. "I'll get some stuff to clean you youngin' up."

Emily was not too much the worse for the engagement. Her dress had become a bit wrinkled and her prized hair was mussed, but other than that she was fine. Having regained her composure, she proceeded to select the items on the grocery list, while Mrs. Saunders wiped Zachary's face with a wet rag and aided him in tidying up.

When Emily reached into her bag, tears welled up in her eyes. She extracted the prized gift mirror, which had been broken during the scuffle.

Mrs. Saunders consoled her, "There, there child, I'm sure that you can have another mirror cut to fit that pretty case."

On the walk home Emily smiled at her cousin, "Thanks for defending me. We may make a gentleman of you yet."

Zachary smiled back, "It was my pleasure."

Emily went on, "You are a pretty tough little kid."

Zachary, "Ah, I used to tussle with my brothers, and they taught me to fight. You swing a pretty mean bag yourself."

Jessica saw the duo coming across the front yard and went to the door to meet them. Seeing the dust and blood, she began a reprimand, "Can't you two stop fighting with each other!"

Emily broke in before she went any further and explained how Toby and his cohorts accosted her and how Zachary had come to her aid.

As she described the fray, Zachary broke in with great excitement and described his assault on Toby.

"Well, fine. I guess fighting with the local toughs is better than fighting with each other," Jessica, quipped. "But just slightly. Both of you better get cleaned up, especially you young man. It's off to the tub with you."

Though Jessica voiced her disapproval, she was secretly pleased. She could see that a bond had been built between her two charges.

While he was in the tub Zachary recounted the engagement in his mind. His first real fight and despite being outnumbered, he figured he had handled himself pretty well.

Jessica entered and took his clothes to clean them. Zachary thought to himself, "Oh no, not the nightgown again. But Jessica reappeared with his buckskin breeches and shirt saying, "I have to soak your shirt in cold water while the blood is still wet. It will stain it for good if it dries. I have cleaned these breeches as best I could. You may as well put them on."

Zachary was out of the tub as soon as she left, drying quickly and donning his own clothes. He was exhilarated, "What a great day. Pa and the boys would have been proud." As he headed out the door he thought, "Maybe I will become an Indian fighter after all."

Jessica and Emily aided Zachary in his studies until school started. He was enrolled to broaden his knowledge. Zachary was fortunate to be educated in Connecticut which was a leader when it came to education. As early as 1650 Connecticut required that all children be taught to read. Zachary attended the local grammar school which used the *New England Primer*, *The Tutor to Writing and Arithmetic*, the *Bible* and other tools to teach reading, writing, and arithmetic.

Only boys attended the grammar school. Emily and the other girls whose parents valued education attended a "Dame School" operated by a local widow. When school was not in session, Jessica added to Emily and Zachary's education by tutoring both of them.

Zachary lived with his aunt for the next four years without major incident. Emily and Zachary continued to have their spats, but the battle with Toby and his friends left them both quietly reassured. They both believed when things got tough, they could count on each other.

CHAPTER 4

ISRAEL COMES HOME

ZACHARY HAD BEEN in residence with his aunt Jessica for almost three months when her husband Israel returned from a trading voyage to the Mediterranean. The day started like any other with morning chores followed by Jessica's tutoring. In the middle of the lesson a fisherman knocked at the door. As Jessica opened the door, he was waving his arms excitedly. He exclaimed, half out of breath, "I bin fishin' out on the point and I seen the *Setauket's* out on the sound! She was showing her colors!"

The normally sedate Jessica responded by mirroring the fisherman's excitement, "Thank you, thank you, for telling me."

"My pleasure Miz Jessica." He tipped his cap and departed.

Jessica's nervous excitement remained. "Emily, your Father's home." She looked in the entry hall mirror and ran her fingers through her hair. "Emily, Zachary, clean yourselves up, we want to look our best."

The excitement carried on for the rest of the day. Jessica gave orders, planned a fine dinner, cleaned the house, and made Zachary and Emily put on their Sunday best clothes. After a thorough inspection, Jessica ushered Zachary and Emily out the door and down to the docks.

When they arrived at the dock, they could see a barque working its way into the harbor on its fore and aft sails alone. The crew was in the rigging furling the square sails. After a month at sea doing quick and dirty sea furls, the crew was, as instructed, to do a tight harbor furl, a roll of the sails, a sign of pride in their vessel. It was indeed *Setauket*, as she was flying her company pennant from the top of the main mast.

Setauket was a barque rig with square sails on her fore and main masts and a fore and aft Spanker on her mizzen. With her inner and outer jibs, fore, main and mizzen staysails, she carried a total of nineteen sails. She was 152 feet on deck and 205 feet overall from the aft most taff rail to the tip of her jibboom. She had a 28-foot beam and drew 10 feet when not carrying cargo. Not a turtle, as she had attained almost 16 knots on occasion.

Setauket was built on Long Island five years earlier. Her fearsome figure head and name come from the Indian tribe that once populated the North shore of Long Island.

For the next two hours *Setauket* worked her way toward the docks. Zachary had watched ships come and go from the harbor since he had lived in town, but this was different, as he felt some family attachment to this ship. He watched intently as the crew descended from the masts and manned the sheets and braces as the ship tacked up the Thames River.

When *Setauket* was within one hundred yards from the dock some crew again ascended the rigging to furl the staysails, while others lowered the boat to tow her the remaining way into the dock. Zachary could hear that commands were being shouted onboard but could not quite make them out until the ship was close.

Israel was not as tall and lanky as Zachary's father and big brothers; he was five foot eight inches tall which was not particularly short for that time. He was of stocky build and maintained bushy lamb chop sideburns and a matching mustache.

Israel was quiet and obviously contemplated his comments before giving a response. Now at home, Israel could be a loving and gentle husband and father, a role that he relished and much the opposite of his role as the captain of a ship.

Zachary was dutifully impressed with his uncle. He had a fine looking uniform and his entire demeanor exhibited a person that was in command. Israel was pleased to have a boy around the house. Israel loved and pampered Emily and was as proud as could be over his lovely young lady, but there are things that a man wishes to do with his children that just do not fit with raising a proper young lady.

Zachary missed the male companionship of his Father and brothers and was ready for a new male role model.

Israel's ship, the *Setauket* needed some serious bottom work and had to be dry-docked for several months to repair the bottom and complete other items of maintenance and overhaul. The ship's owners had contracted with the local yard to do the work. Most of the crew were mustered out and went off to other ships. *Setauket's* officers, remained. Also, four of the best seamen were kept on board to man the watches and perform routine ships chores while she was laid up.

During this period Israel enjoyed the company of a son. He taught Zachary the things that a young lad raised near salt water should know. These things included fishing, crabbing, digging clams and most importantly seamanship.

Israel borrowed a sailing skiff from a boyhood friend who made his living as a waterman. The skiff was twenty feet long, catboat rigged, with a wide beam and short stubby keel to give it stability. A perfect boat to teach the art and science of sailing.

Zachary quickly discovered that there was an entirely new language that went along with boats, ships and the sea. He paid close attention to the terms used by his uncle and strove to understand their meaning. Fore, aft, bow, stern, abaft-the-beam, were fine sounding nautical terms to Zachary's ear, though the differences in meaning took a little time to sink in.

He was excited at the prospect of learning this new skill. He had been on the *Setauket* at dock and since it had been hauled. He had seen sailing vessels of various sizes and shapes going in and out of the harbor. He had yet to be on a sailing vessel that was underway.

Zachary awoke before sunrise. He could not sleep. This was the morning appointed for his first sailing lesson. It was a glorious morning; the sun rose boldly out of the east. The clear blue sky was punctuated with occasional cumulus clouds. The light breeze fluctuated from five to ten knots. It was a perfect day for a sailing lesson.

Zachary dressed quickly, splashed some water on his face so that if quizzed he could assure his aunt that he had washed this morning. He hurried through his morning chores and was at the kitchen table munching on a piece of bread that was left from the previous night's supper, when Israel appeared in the kitchen.

Israel patted Zachary's shoulder as he passed his chair. "Good morning lad, are you ready to go sailin'?" He responded in the affirmative while getting up and heading for the door. Israel stopped his advance, extolling the virtues of a proper breakfast before one goes to sea.

After what he felt to be an eternity, breakfast was completed, Aunt Jessica was duly hugged and kissed and the would-be sailors set off for the short walk to the dock. The little skiff bobbed at the end of a rickety old dock.

"Zach step into the boat and take a seat." Israel then passed the lunch sent by Jessica and stepped aboard. He instructed Zachary to bail out the bit of water that had accumulated in the bottom of the boat. Meanwhile Israel fastened the rudder to the stern, tied the main halyard to the head of the sail and stowed loose items, preparing to make way.

Israel untied the furling lines from around the sail and boom. "Help me pull up the sail Zach." They hauled on the halyard while the little boat dutifully stood with its bow into the morning breeze.

Israel turned the tiller and tightened down the mainsheet. The little boat moved smartly off on a port tack. Israel explained the point of sail and every step of what he was doing to control the boat. "When the breeze is off our side as it is now, it is called a 'Reach'. If the breeze is aft of the beam it is called a 'Broad Reach', if it is on our beam, it is a "Beam Reach' and if it is forward of the beam it is a 'Close Reach'. If we are as close to the wind as we can it is called 'Close Hauled' or 'Beating'. If the breeze is off our stern, it is called 'Running'. The point of sail is also defined by the direction from which the breeze is coming. Therefore, if the breeze is coming from our starboard beam we are on a 'Starboard Beam Reach'. Do you have all that?"

Zachary nodded affirmatively, but Israel could see the bit of bewilderment in his expression.

Israel thought to himself that it will all make sense as we do it.

As the skiff healed from the press of the breeze on its sail, Zachary could feel a glow of exhilaration come over him as the boat began to pick up speed. His mind was racing with numerous thoughts. To think that the weight of two people and the boat could be moving along pushed by this relatively gentle breeze. He had questions fleeting through his mind, but as yet he did not know enough about the subject to ask proper questions.

After two hours of tacking out of the harbor, Israel eased the skiff into a cove on the north side of the harbor's entrance and headed up into the breeze, causing the sail to luff and the boats forward progress to cease. "Zach throw the anchor over the side."

Israel loosened the halyard, letting the mainsail drop on to the boom. He quickly lashed the sail to the boom, pulled up the topping lift raising the boom up and away from their heads. Producing two fishing poles from under the starboard gunwale Israel announced, "It is time to catch our dinner."

Israel and Zachary spent the rest of the morning and early afternoon fishing, talking of sailing and places far away. Zachary finally organized some of his questions regarding his sailing experience. After successfully catching two croakers and three medium sized flounders, with much cheering and carrying on over each landing, Israel announced that it was time to head in.

The mainsail was hoisted, the topping lift eased, the anchor weighed and Israel headed across the mouth of the harbor on a beam reach. Israel said, "Zach, come take the tiller."

Israel continued his instructions "see the yarns on the front edge of the sail, keep them streaming straight and you are in the groove."

At the south entrance of the harbor Israel instructed Zachary to bare off the wind. Israel eased the mainsheet. With the breeze two points abaft the port beam, the skiff flattened out into a broad reach. They headed for home.

After a fine dinner of fresh fish, and equally fine fish stories at the dinner table, Zachary followed his uncle to the back porch. Israel always had to smoke his pipe after supper. On a fine summer night, it was only appropriate to watch the sunset over the woods behind the house. Plus, it was better to be outside than to listen to Jessica's complaints about Israel smelling up her house. They engaged in small talk of the day's events and agreed to do it again in the near future.

Zachary retired to his room, but his mind was not about to go to sleep. He gazed out the window at the night sky. He contemplated the day's great events, and the wonders of going anywhere in the world, pushed by the wind. He pictured those great places, far away, which he had only heard and read about. England, Spain, the Caribbean, how wondrous they must be. He was hooked. As Israel would say, he had gotten saltwater in his veins and would forever after be tied to the sea.

During the following weeks Israel and Zachary did get to sail on several more occasions. He took every opportunity to learn his new skills and soaked up all the knowledge he could. Israel enjoyed Zachary's company and enjoyed being the instructor on a subject that was also one of his true loves.

While *Setauket,* was in dry-dock Zachary spent as much time as he could aboard the ship.

Jessica had daily chores and daily studies for him, but other than that he was down on the dock. Israel had the First Mate; Mr. Bolton give Zachary tasks on the ship to keep him out of the way and to give him the experience. He found chores on the ship much more fun than chores at home.

Jessica ordered up a number of cleaning chores for Emily and Zachary. "Mr. Worthington is coming to visit, and this house is a mess."

Though everything looked fine to Zachary, he knew better than to question the degree of cleaning prescribed by his aunt. He was however interested in the fuss that was being made for the impending visitor. When asking regarding Mr. Worthington he found this was an attorney from Boston and one of the owners of *Setauket.* He also found that the visit was most likely to tell Israel of the next voyage for the ship.

When Mr. Worthington arrived, he was ushered to the guest bedroom that had been occupied by Zachary for the past years. Since it was summer, Zachary was relegated to the back porch and a hammock that had been borrowed from *Setauket*.

Israel treated Mr. Worthington with the greatest of respect, not only as an employer, but because over the years he had learned to trust his business judgment. Israel gave his guest a tour of *Setauket* and the progress that had been made on its repairs. That evening Jessica served the best dinner that Zachary had ever seen. Emily and Zachary were at the dinner table to be seen, but not heard.

Worthington was a rotund and jovial man in his mid-fifties. He made light conversation at the dinner table and was personable enough to include Emily and Zachary in the conversation so that they could feel a part of the group.

After dinner, Israel and Worthington retired to the back porch for cigars and serious discussion.

As Israel had hoped the subject was the next voyage for *Setauket*.

Worthington began, "Captain the other owners and I have been very pleased with the profits made in your past voyages and your command of the ship."

Israel responded, "Thank you sir. You gentlemen have been very supportive of the ship and its crew."

Worthington rotated his cigar between his thumb and forefinger, he continued. "The coastwise and European trips have been profitable, but the owners are contemplating a much more aggressive and potentially more rewarding voyage."

Israel's interest had been tweaked. He replied, "Please, tell me more."

Worthington continued, "There is a growing leather goods industry around Boston, shoes, saddles, bags and the like. We have been told that the best source of cheap hides is the Pacific coast of New Spain."

Worthington stopped and let his previous statements sink in. He then continued, "We want to send *Setauket* around Cape Horn and take on a load of hides. Not only does this mean a voyage of maybe two years but having to establish business relationships with the Spaniards." Worthington leaned forward in his chair looking Israel in the eye. "This is an aggressive voyage; do you feel up to the challenge?"

Israel responded without hesitation, "Aye sir, *Setauket* and I are ready for the trip."

Worthington shook Israel's hand. "Then it is done. I will inform the owners." He leans back in his chair. "Now let's enjoy these cigars."

After Worthington's visit, Israel spent most of his time overseeing the work on his ship. The work on *Setauket* progressed at an acceptable rate, but there were invoices to be paid and instructions to be given. A ship, even while in port deserves the full attention of its Master. During this period, Zachary spent much of his time at the shipyard viewing the work and contemplating the sight of this massive vessel at sea.

After several repairs *Setauket* was re-floated, and the rig was tuned, and she was ready to earn her living at sea. Now, Israel had no time for the little skiff or other frivolities, he was into every detail of preparing his vessel for its next voyage. The day of the shakedown cruise approached, and all must be ready.

Mr. Bolton was also busy with preparations, in particular finding additional crew. At times *Setauket* sailed with as few as eight seamen, but for a trip as long and challenging as rounding Cape Horn, they would take twelve. Bolton made the rounds of the pubs and saloons, as well as along the docks looking for candidates.

Early on a Monday morning Israel stood at the taffrail and watched as Bolton had his eight new deckhands sign the ships log to become an official part of the crew. When Bolton had finished, and the new hands took their belongings to the fo'c'sle, Israel called him aft.

"Aye sir," Bolton responded.

Israel rubbed his chin, "Mr. Bolton, that is a pretty scruffy lookin' brood you have there. Can any of them sail?"

Bolton, "Well sir the pickin's were thin. The whaling fleet got most of the experienced hands." Gesturing toward the fo'c'sle, "only two or three of the lot have had any square rigger experience, the rest are fishermen or farmer boys who I scratched up in town."

Israel, "Well you have two weeks to whip them into a crew." Bolton, "Aye Sir, consider it done."

Israel, "Muster the crew."

At Bolton's shout of "Muster," the crew hustled aft lining up aft of the main fife rail. Zachary stood by the main shrouds to hear the address.

Israel addressed them, "Lads, as Mr. Bolton has told you we are traveling south around Cape Horn to California and back." There was some uneasy squirming in the ranks. "It is a challenging voyage, but a good crew can do it and do it safely. I expect every man to do his part as a member of the ship's company. And I expect to bring as many men home as leave with us." Gesturing towards Bolton, "Mr. Bolton will make sure that each of you know your jobs, how to do them well, for the safety of the ship and yourselves." Straightening his stance almost to attention, he ended with, "That is all, Mr. Bolton take charge of the crew."

Israel turned and strode aft and the crew turned their attention to Bolton. "Those lads who have sailed with the Capt'n before know that he runs a clean, tight ship and won't stand for no foolishness. He also looks after his crew as well as his ship." He waved at one of the fisherman, a newbie crewmember who was sitting on a bitt, "Get your frickin' ass up, you never sit when you're on duty and you never sit when me or one of the other officers is talking to you."

The newbie popped up, "Aye."

Bolton continued, "Some of you have sailed on sloppy ships that got people hurt and killed. For the next couple weeks, we are going to work together until we function as a real crew. As the Capt'n said, so we all come home in one piece."

Gesturing toward the main topsails, "When in the rigging you will declare yourself before laying on or off of a yard. Your mates will acknowledge you, before you step on or off of the footrope." His voice inflection emphasized the "will" in each statement. "For instance, 'On the Main Lower Tops'l layering on port.' Your mates on that side of the yard will respond, 'laying on, Aye.' When laying off it is the same only you announce, 'On the Main Lower Tops'l layering off port.'" Bolton looked over his less than attentive crew. "Do you have that?"

The response was a mix of half garbled "Ayes."

Bolton, "Stay alert, you sons of whores, it's your asses I'm lookin' after. And remember, one hand for the ship and one hand for yourself."

The slovenly mix of crewmen standing before Bolton had a distinct hierarchy, the existing crew stood in a group. Next there was a pod of the experienced sailors who were joining the crew and the last pod was the newbie land lubbers and local fishermen that had little or no square rigger experience.

Some were scarred; all had scruffy hair and needed clean clothes and a bath.

Stepping to the port rail, Bolton grasped the aft most shroud. "When climbing, you will only grab the shrouds and other firm standing rigging, not the ratlins or any of the running riggin'." Running his hand on the shroud, "You can tell the standing riggin' as it is black with tar. With a chuckle to himself, "You all will be familiar with that soon enough."

Motioning to the existing crew members Bolton waved toward the windward shrouds. "Coggins take the new lads on and up and over. Lambert, follow behind and keep them moving." "Oh, lads, you always climb on the windward side and you always ask permission before going aloft."

Zachary had been quietly listening to the directions. He stepped forward, "Mr. Bolton can I go too?"

Bolton, "Aye lad, but watch your step, I don't want to explain to your uncle how you managed to mess up his deck with your body."

He eagerly replied, "Aye sir, I'll be careful."

Zachary followed the last of the new crew up the shrouds, stepping on the ratlins, grasping the shrouds, just as Bolton had directed. Lambert followed behind. When the shrouds went under the platform at the first spar, short shrouds came out from the mast to the outer edge of the platform.

Lambert, "grab the platform and pull yourself up."

Having seen the men ahead of him do it, he had the concept. However, as he pulled himself on to the platform at the base of the second level of shrouds, his back and buttock were aiming down and for the first time he felt a chill of apprehension run through his body. Being young and strong he was up on the platform in a few seconds and followed the backside of the fellow ahead of him up the second level of shrouds. At the top of the lower section of the mainmast each crewman curled his leg around the aft end of the shroud, stepped on top of the mast and then stepped over to the leeward shroud and proceeded down. Stepping down onto one of the bitts and then the deck, the whole trip took less than ten minutes.

Bolton patted Zachary on the shoulder as he went by. "What did you think, lad?" Zachary replied, "That was good, it was fun. Thank you, sir."

Bolton, "OK lads, take a break and then we'll begin the day's chores."

As he walked away, he thought to himself, "That was not a big deal!" Then he noticed that his forearms were somewhat tight, and his hands were a bit stiff. He thought, "Maybe I was hanging on harder than I thought."

After about five minutes Bolton gathered the crew again. "Gather around lads."

He puts a cloth tar bucket up to his nose. "I love the smell of this stuff. Smells like me uncle's barbeque." Passing the bucket to the newbies. "Smell it lads. That's Stockholm tar, it's been protecting ships and their rigging for the last hundred years." Now that you are all climbers, we are going to tar the rigging starting on the foremast.

Zachary followed along as if he were a part of the crew. Bolton noticed, but said nothing, he was happy to have the lad's interest.

At the foremast was a line of tar buckets and a pile of rags and fleece.

Bolton, directed the crew members to tar the port side shrouds, starting high and working their way down. The experienced seamen went to the top of the 95' mast, showing their superior skills to the new crew. Zachary and the remainder of the crew started on the lower shrouds. The work method was to dip the fleece in the tar bucket, wrap the fleece around a shroud and then slide the fleece down the shroud squeezing the tar into the heavy rope.

Bolton had made it clear, "Woe be unto any swab that gets tar on the Captain's deck."

They worked in pairs, one holding the tar bucket and the other applying the tar. The day was hot, and it was not long before Zachary and the other crew had tar on their hands and arms, with an occasional smudge on their faces. By the end of the day, they were a tired, sweaty black streaked mass of humanity all smelling of the smoky scent of the Stockholm tar.

Bolton directed them to the turpentine in the paint locker to clean off the tar stains. He then dismissed them to go beyond the drydock and bathe in the Thames River. The old salts quietly dipped themselves in the cool brackish water of the river. The new crew, along with Zachary, though dog tired began splashing each other and carrying on, buoyed by the excitement of the new experiences of the day.

For the next two weeks the crew spent part of their day in training and part of the day performing maintenance. Particularly for the new crew members there was a new language to learn along with the names of the sails and place and function of the over 180 lines that comprised *Setauket's* running rigging. Among the new words that were part of the commands were: "Avast" which meant "stop everything until the next command," and "belay" which meant to secure a line to a "belaying pin." That first day there were shouts of orders and many Avast's, as the crew hauled and belayed in all the wrong sequences.

By the end of the second week, the sequences of events had sunk into the crew members, plus they had been assigned to the port and starboard watches and assigned to specific duties during the ship's maneuvers. Though not quite a ballet, there was a certain balance, a choreography that took place during maneuvers. They were acting not as a bunch of individuals who happened to work on a ship, they were acting as a crew.

At home, discussions of the upcoming cruise flowed around the dinner table. At first Zachary did not understand that the short shakedown cruise of a couple days would be a chance for Jessica, Emily and him to accompany Israel offshore. Israel proclaimed, "Jessica, you will have to bring some fresh meat and your special goods for the cook to prepare for us. There is no reason to eat sea rations on this outing."

"Emily, you can be accommodated in the officer's quarters. The Second Mate can spend a night or so bunking in the Day man's quarters. Zach, you will be berthed amidships."

It sunk into Zachary's mind what all the excited talk was about, a chance to sail on *Setauket*. He beamed from ear to ear. "Aye, Sir."

After two more days of preparation the day of departure was at hand. The sky was overcast with little wisps of clouds scooting along on the brisk northwesterly winds. As Jessica, Emily and Zachary boarded the *Setauket;* Israel kissed Jessica on the cheek and directed the ladies below before the approaching rains reached them. Jessica had kept Zachary in tow all morning since they left home and kept him close on the dock and now on board the ship. Zachary felt uncomfortable, he did not want to run afoul of his aunt, but he had trained with the crew and felt that he would be a wimp if he did not take part with them. Israel saw Zachary slowing his trail behind Jessica and his eyeing the crew who were busy preparing to make way. He decided to solve Zachary's dilemma, "Mister Bolton," Israel motioned, "Find Mr. Bower a slicker, he will be wanting to participate in our departure."

"Aye sir," was Bolton's only reply, as he motioned Zachary to follow him. Zachary was outfitted with oilskins and returned on deck to watch the activity.

Israel barked orders, each of which was repeated by the directed officer. The officers then gave the never-ending series of commands required to execute the Captain's order, causing action in all quarters of the deck. To ease the *Setauket* from its slip at the yard, one of the ship's anchors was lowered from the stern into a longboat. The longboat then rowed off the stern about 200 hundred feet and pushed the anchor into the water. Bolton ordered four crew to heave around the capstan," while he tailed the anchor rode. This cranked in the anchor rode, slowly pulling the ship out of its slip. Both the port and starboard number two dock lines had been run from the forward most hawsehole, as a spring lines, aft to pilings aft of the ship's stern. The remainder of the crew hauled on the heavy dock lines. Slowly the ship moved aft in its slip. Meanwhile, the longboat was joined by two more work boats owned by the shipyard. Lines were tossed to these boats, which rowed at an angle to the ship's bow turning it toward the entrance to the harbor.

Israel had waited for this day when the tide was going out and the northwesterly breeze would help push his ship away from the shipyard and other local docks. Getting the ship out of the dock was likely the most complex maneuver he would have to direct for some time, and nothing was more embarrassing and injurious to a captain's reputation than to run aground, or float into a dock, in one's own home port.

When a crewman hollered that the stern anchor had broken free, Israel ordered the unfurling of the inner and outer jib and all staysails. Then Fore and Main topsails. During the past week's training crewmen were assigned to a particular mast and had practiced a specific set of duties. With commands from the officers all hands sprang into action. Two hands, along with Zachary who had been temporarily assigned to the foremast crew, moved on to the footropes on the bowsprit, and moved onto the jibboom to loosen the headsails. Other crew hustled into the rigging, including:

- Two hands from the Main moved out on the fore crane lines to loose the main staysails.
- Two Mizzen crews moved out on the Main crane lines to lose the Mizzen staysails.
- Two other Mizzen hands moved out on Mizzen crane lines to unfurl the Spanker.

Once the jibs and staysails had been unfurled the crew moved up the shrouds to unfurl the square sails. The order of unfurling the Fore and Main sails is the lower topsail, the upper topsail and then the course. To do otherwise would put the upper topsail in the faces of the crew while they were unfurling the Lower Topsail. The hands worked out on the footropes. The first man out untied the gasket lines as he went out on the spar. The hands behind took up stations along the yard. They unwrapped the gasket and dropped the sail. Then the crew tied each line into a gasket coil, which hung from the yard forward of the sail. As instructed the hands chimed, "Laying On …" and "Laying Off…" as they moved about the rigging. The commands and calls continued for twenty minutes while the sails were loosed.

As planned, the tide and following breeze began to push the ship towards the harbor entrance. The longboat came alongside, and its crew scurried on deck and took up their stations to haul on the halyards, as soon as their mates were out of the rigging. The longboat was led astern and tied off, to bounce along in *Setauket's* wake.

As the hands came down the shrouds onto the rail using a bitt as a step on to the deck, they grabbed a scoop of water from a bucket at the foot of the masts. Climbing in the rigging is a thirsty business. They move quickly, looking to their officer for the next series of commands.

They did not have to wait long, Israel called to the mast officers, "On the Fore, Main and Mizzen, standby the headsail and staysail gear!"

The hands hustled to their stations. The officers responded, in turn, "Fore Ready!" "Main Ready!" Mizzen Ready!"

Israel commanded, "Set the Staysail!"

The officers responded, "Set staysails, Aye!" Their crew, "heave around the halyard!"

As the halyards drew out the staysails and the downhauls were loosed, the next command from the mast officers was"

Take a Sweat!" Two hands pushed in on the halyards and then leaned back with all their might, as the tailing hands took in the slack created by the "sweat." Looking at the stiff luff on the staysail the officer commanded, "That is Well, Belay!"

Sails are normally set from aft to fore, so the sequence of commands and responses continued for the setting of the Spanker, then the Fore and Mizzen Topmast Staysails along with the Main

Topgallant Staysail. Next the Main and Mizzen Topmast staysails and the Inner and Outer Jibs were set.

A light rain began as the ship passed the shoals on either side of the harbor entrance. The jibs and staysails were all set before reaching the entrance. As *Setauket* broke into open water the breeze which had been hampered by land affect, turned more to the west and freshened. *Setauket* was back in her home and began a gentle pitch and roll responding to roll off the waves.

Israel called his next command to the mast officers, "On the Fore and Main standby the Lower Topsail gear!" The officers responded as ready. Next, he commanded "On the Fore, Main and Mizzen, Sheet Home!"

The mast officers commanded "Heave around the Halyard!" The deck hands hauled on the halyards. The Shanty man sang his hauling song as the Upper Topsails hauled the topsails aloft.

Israel did not wish to set additional sails until he knew what magnitude winds would accompany the rains. He left the Main and Fore course unfurled but not set so that he could better see the seas around them. At this point *Setauket* was making six knots with fourteen of her nineteen sails set.

Israel gave the order to bare off on a southerly course, causing more activity as the crew hauled on sheets to set the yards for a starboard tack. He inhaled the brisk salt air and could feel a smile come over his face. Even though Israel had been glad to be home with his family for an extended time, he was equally glad to be back in his element with the feel of the ship's movement under his feet and the breeze in his face.

Zachary was exhilarated by the sense of adventure. His eyes were bright, and his ears were tuned, to absorb all that was happening around him. Neither the rain nor anything else could have tarnished this moment in his mind. He was at sea on a fine ship and in his mind, before him lay the whole world. His mind was not allowed to wander for long, as he heard the command, "Stand by to Come About!" This was the first time he had been involved with a real tack, thought the crew had many practice tacks over the past weeks.

The mast officers responded as "Ready" and then the sequence of additional commands began that were required to tack a square-rigged ship. Next Israel commanded, "Helms A' Lee," followed by "Spanker Amidships," then Ease headsail Sheets," and "Back the Headsails!"

Setauket came up into the wind, but lost momentum and stopped with her head dead into the wind. After a couple curses under his breath, Israel gave the command "Stand by to Wear Ship!"

Having muffed the tack, sailing through the wind on the bow of the ship, Israel called a Wear, which is passing the stern through the eye of the wind. Mr. Bolton knew that his Captain's pride had just taken a hit at not executing a proper tack. As he guessed there were many more tacks than necessary for the remainder of the shakedown. At the end Captain and crew were a well-greased team.

The shakedown cruise lasted three days before returning to its homeport. During this time, along with everything else Zachary, saw that his uncle whom he found to be a gentle, instructive man on shore was quite different at sea. People's personas change to fit their circumstances and as the captain of a significant vessel, Israel had a much sterner look about him; his comments were only to his officers.

They were short and direct, as if everything he said was an order. Israel attempted to lighten up when in the presence of Jessica and Emily, as if he did not want them to see his other side.

During the trip Zachary was a part of the family and called to join Jessica and Emily on the aft deck and to have dinner at the Captain's table. Jessica had brought food which she cooked in the small gallery in the officer's quarters. Israel and his officers ate much better than their normal sea fare.

Zachary felt a part of the working crew and wanted to learn from them. However, he believed that his mates were a bit standoffish from him because he was not really one of them, but a product of the gentry. With many of the gnarly old crew members his feeling was right. Anyone who could read and write was immediately suspect and not fit for the rigors of an ordinary seaman.

Lying in their bed two nights after returning from the shakedown cruise, Israel broached a subject with Jessica that he had been considering ever since Zachary started work on the ship. He started, "Did you notice how much Zachary has learned about seamanship?" He turned toward Jessica. "He seems to have a natural affinity for climbing in the rigging, and workin' about the ship."

Jessica responded, "He did seem to have a good time at it, but what young boy would not relish the chance to spend a couple days on a ship?"

Israel, "It's more than that, I think that the lad has knack to be a seaman." He rubbed Jessica's shoulder. I have been thinkin' about takin' the lad on the voyage with me."

Jessica had anticipated where the discussion was going and responded immediately. "That is not what I owe to my dear departed sister. She sent the lad to us to provide him with a proper education so that he might make something of himself." When Jessica heard Israel's grunt of displeasure, she back tracked, choosing her words more carefully. "I mean that I hope he becomes more than a common seaman. That is no better than the back woodsmen that his father and brothers are."

Israel, "I did not mean for Zachary to be a mere deck hand. I can teach him navigation and all the other disciplines to become a ship's officer." Poking Jessica's ribs, "I trust that you consider that to be an honorable occupation, since you married an old sea-dog."

Jessica turned and kissed his cheek. "I agree that you are the most honorable of men and quite charming as old sea-dogs go." She hesitated, "But in the case of Zachary, I have an obligation to give him an education and there is still a long way to go with that."

Israel, "You know once a lad gets salt water in his veins that it will never go away."

Jessica, "Yes dear, and in a couple years when he is old enough to make his own choices, if he wants to join your crew, he may do so."

Seeing that he was in a no-win discussion, Israel rolled over and went to sleep.

CHAPTER 5

FIRST LOVE

SAILING WAS NOT Zachary's only love that summer. A new minister had arrived in town with his family, which included Elizabeth, who in Zachary's mind was the finest young lady he had ever seen.

Elizabeth possessed all the attributes that would set a young man's heart afire. She was tall for her age, but well-proportioned still developing, high and firm youthful breasts. A freckled nose and sparkling blue eyes, her blonde hair was just beyond shoulder length.

Lizzie's father, Reverend Edmund Hopkins had been truly stuck in the middle, during the Revolutionary War. He was an Anglican Priest owing allegiance to the Church of England and the Archbishop of Canterbury. Also, in much of the colonies, many members of the Church of England, who were his parishioners tended to be loyalists, while the Congregationalists and other protestant sects tended to be patriots. In spite of this, Edmund was fiercely loyal to the patriot's cause and aided that cause wherever he could, though not to the point of actually bearing arms against the King.

After the war, the Archbishop of Canterbury ordered all of the Anglican priests out of the colonies leaving many empty churches throughout the new country. At this point Edmund had to make the toughest decision of his life and after much soul searching, he decided that he was after all a third generation American and that is where he would stay. Edmund believed that his mission to serve his God was more important than an obligation to serve an earthly King. The response to his decision was his excommunication from the Church of England.

Edmund continued to minister to the ex-Anglicans and perform the Holy Communion whenever and wherever he could. All became better defined in 1784 when Edmund along with other Connecticut clergy chose Samuel Seabury to travel to England and seek consecration as a bishop. English bishops would not consecrate Seabury, so he approached the Episcopal Church of Scotland which agreed to consecrate him with his promise to use their Prayer Book. Upon returning to New England, Bishop Seabury of Connecticut brought together Edmund and the many ex-Anglicans priests and formed the Episcopal Church in America.

Edmund was a short rotund man with a prematurely gray receding hairline. He looked very much like a man of the cloth. As an educated and well-read man he had that certain air of aristocracy that befits an English gentleman. One could tell his obvious education by the number of people, (who meant nothing to anyone but him), that he quoted during his sermons. Though he dutifully ministered to the local farmers and watermen, he kept his distance from those bumpkins, who were not his social equal.

Edmund arrived in New London to become an assistant to Bishop Seabury, at St. James Episcopal Church. Soon after their arrival, a reception was planned by the local congregation to welcome Reverend Hopkins and his family. This would be the social event of the summer. All of the parishioners would be there in the best attire to suitably impress their new Rector and of course partake in the fine food and spirits that had been prepared for the affair.

The evening of the reception Jessica was lining up her troops for inspection. "Emily you can make a better bow than that." On to the next victim, "Zachary Bower, I told you to clean those ears. Go back upstairs and don't come down until the wax is out and the dirt is gone from behind your ears."

After the short walk to the town hall where the affair was to be held, Jessica picked a piece of lint from Israel's uniform and lined Emily and Zachary behind her in the queue and waited to pass through the receiving line. "Zachary, quit fidgeting!" The line moved slowly; Zachary's stiff collar itched; he knew that this would be a miserable night. With luck he would get something to eat and then slip out of the hall.

When they heard the Senior Warden announce, "Captain Redden and family and Master Zachary Bower," Zachary snapped back to the mission at hand. He wanted to be on his best behavior for as long as possible.

Israel shook the minister's hand and introduced Jessica, Emily and Zachary. Zachary followed suit. shaking Edmund's hand. The process was repeated with Mabel Hopkins, the minister's wife. Then he saw her. Elizabeth was doing her duty with a repetition of "how do you do," and "pleased to meet you."

After Emily introduced herself and shook Elizabeth's hand, Zachary stepped up and stammered, "How do you do, Miss?" He was not sure that he should be so bold as to touch the hand of such a lovely creature, but Elizabeth thrust out her right hand and Zachary grasped it.

"I am Elizabeth Hopkins and you are?"

Zachary stammered, "Zachary Bower, the Captain's my uncle."

Zachary stood there a moment grasping Elizabeth's hand, until the next person in line politely bumped him as a clue to move on. He moved on following Emily across the room but kept one eye on Elizabeth. He was smitten.

"Zachary," Jessica motioned to him, "come get something to eat."

"Yes Auntie," Zachary moved to the assembled array of fine foods. He found a number of delicacies that met his fancy and returned to the side of the room where he could eat in peace and watch the reception line. He began to dig into his plate, but stopped, thinking a young gentleman would eat slowly, savor the foods, and most importantly, keep his hands off of his plate.

Zachary lost all his eagerness to slip out of the party early. He did not approach Elizabeth again.

He felt more at ease watching her from a distance. He could not explain it in his mind, but it was as if He was afraid of this young beauty. He couldn't remember ever being afraid of a girl before, though Emily was pretty spooky at first.

When the party was winding down, Israel had to actually coax Zachary to leave. On the walk home, Jessica complemented Emily's and Zachary's fine demeanor that evening. She joked, "I didn't know that Zachary had it in him to stay clean for that long."

In the days following the reception Zachary spent time at the shipyard watching the progress on *Setauket*, but he would also pass by the rectory and church in hopes of getting a glance at the object of his affection. He continued to have an approach/avoidance urge with regard to Elizabeth. He continually wanted to see her, but at the same time was troubled that he would appear too eager to be near her. How could he approach such a goddess? When he first met her, he was sure that he came off as a bumpkin. When they next met, he would have to be less intimidated than he was in the reception line.

In the small-town Zachary found plenty of occasions to view his heartthrob; however, the social morays of the time attempted to keep young persons of the opposite sex at a respectable distance from one another, unless appropriately chaperoned. Jessica marched the family to church each and every Sunday, an occasion, which Zachary once found painful and he now eagerly anticipated. There were brief meetings on the street, with pleasantries passed, but not much more than a few words.

A month after the reception Zachary's prospects took a turn for the better. Even though Emily was older than Elizabeth, they became friends and Lizzie, as her family and friends called her, came to visit Emily at home. It was somehow easier to interact like one might with an ordinary person, when this beauty was on Zach's home turf. Zachary was most comfortable when talking about his other new found love, sailing and the sea. He told Lizzie of the sailing lessons with Israel and the progress on *Setauket*, using as much of his nautical vocabulary as possible, to impress her.

Emily and Lizzie invited Zachary to participate in several of their outings and projects. When Elizabeth helped Emily and Zachary with their chores though she was raised to be very prim and proper, Zach noted an impish twinkle in her eye which warned of her potential for mischief. He noticed the way her nose wrinkled, and eyes twinkled when she laughed. He noticed things about her he had never noticed about anyone else. The more time Zachary spent with Lizzie the more infatuated he became.

Though Lizzie was not burning with the same puppy love fire that was consuming Zachary, she found him most interesting. Zachary was developing into a handsome young man in a town with few choices close to Elizabeth's age and intellect. She found his somewhat wild backwoods demeanor exciting. Unbeknownst to Zachary he had a mutual admirer.

The Reverend Hopkins had witnessed Elizabeth, Emily and Zachary together on a few occasions and was discomforted by his daughter's apparent friendship with a boy of her own age. He called Lizzie to his study. "Have a seat." Edmund motioned to the chair in front of his desk. "Elizabeth, I know that you have developed a strong friendship with Emily Redden and I am happy for that." He peered over his glasses at Lizzie. "Captain Redden and his family are fine people, but I have asked around town and found that their ward, Zachary, is from some illiterate backwoods stock." Edmund stiffened in his chair and looked Lizzie straight in the eye, "I want you to keep your distance from this Zachary Bower character. He is not your quality of person."

This direction took Lizzie by surprise. She was never at a loss for words and was incensed by her Father's snobbish assault on her friend. "Father, that is entirely unfair. You don't even know Zachary, other than to see him at Sunday services." Lizzie stiffened in her chair, her back ramrod straight. "How can you label him as some sort of backwoods bumpkin? Zachary is not illiterate; he came to study with Mrs. Redden after his Mother died and is doing quite well."

Edmund knew that his daughter was never an easy case. She was always ready to defend her position and was quick witted enough to hold her own in most debates. "Young Lady, this young man is just not our kind of people."

Elizabeth was even more incensed. She snapped out of her chair, stood in front of her Father's desk, leaned forward and stared him in the eyes. "Father, how can you preach that Christianity is the religion of love, when you hate half the people you meet?"

"That will be enough, Young Lady." Edmund had to regain control of this exchange. He wanted his direction to stand, but Lizzie had hit a nerve with her last comment. "And sit back down," He ordered, "I do not hate anyone, but I understand, and you should too that some people because of their breeding and education are better than others."

Emily was back in her seat, but sitting on the very edge, as if she were about to spring across the desk. "Father, Zachary fits your definition of the right kind of people." Lizzie's assault will be using her Father's logic, "He is Mrs. Redden's nephew and is becoming rather well read under her instruction." She added, "He is not some kind of bumpkin, as you would say."

Edmund felt that he had better compromise on his position to begin the end to this debate. "Now Elizabeth, I did not say that you could not see this young man again. I approve of your friendship with Emily and know that you cannot remain her friend and completely avoid the Bower boy." A renewed sternness was added to his voice. "I expect you to respect my wishes and maintain some distance from this young man and take the circumstances into consideration." Again, peering over his glasses, he ended, "Do I make myself clear?"

Lizzie was not quite sure what her Father's last statement meant, but it sounded like a compromise and it appeared that she would get little else from this day's negotiation. She stood and in a most subordinate voice said, "Yes, Father."

Lizzie left her Father's study still enraged by her Father's edict. She would have to re-address this issue with him. Next time she would not be caught unprepared. She might also work on her Mother to intercede.

Lizzie contemplated the direction, "taking the circumstances into consideration." She could not directly disobey her Father, but in a small town and considering her friendship with Emily, she could not help but see Zachary on a regular basis, and that would do quite nicely until she could renegotiate her Father's direction.

As his ship *Setauket* neared completion, Israel spent most of his time at the shipyard. There was no longer time for fishing and sailing lessons, but Zachary had learned well, and Israel decided that Zachary was ready to take the skiff out in the harbor by himself. Israel picked a fine sunny day with a gentle southerly breeze to announce to Zachary that he had purchased the skiff from the waterman from whom he had been borrowing the boat. He also announced that Zachary was authorized to sail the boat on his own, provided the weather and seas permitted.

Zachary heartily thanked his uncle and hurried to the little skiff for his first solo experience. He went through the process to make ready to sail, just as he had been taught. He named the lines on the boat. "Main Halyard, sheets, clew outhaul." He went on to the parts of the sail. "Leach, Luff, Foot" for the three sides of the sail. "Tack, Clew and Head" for the three corners of the sail." He assured himself that he was ready for this experience and castoff from the dock. Things did not go as smoothly as they had with his uncle in charge, but the sail was set, and the little skiff responded to Zachary's control of the tiller. He was off on his own with the sun, the blue sky, the freshening breeze. It was glorious.

Israel stopped to watch Zachary's departure from the afterdeck of *Setauket*. He was pleased with Zachary's progress as a sailor. He was pleased with his decision to let Zachary go out solo. It was a beautiful day and the progress on his ship was going well. He thought to himself, "What a fine day."

That night at the dinner table, Zachary recounted his day's adventure to Emily and Jessica. He again thanked his uncle and told Israel of his plans to do some fishing on his own, to provide fresh flounder for future dinners.

In the following days Zachary was very busy. Jessica continued Zachary and Emily's education. Jessica made sure that Zachary and Emily had daily chores tending the garden and the few animals that Jessica kept on the grounds. Zachary was also splitting his time between his two loves, the sailboat and being around whenever Elizabeth came to visit.

One afternoon while Emily was tending to the chickens, Zachary and Lizzie climbed into the loft of the little barn to push down some hay for the cow's dinner. After pushing several bundles over the side to the barn's dirt floor Lizzie leaned too far over the edge and began to fall. Zachary grabbed her arm in an attempt to save her, but her weight pulled him over the side of the loft. They landed in the pile of hay laughing and squealing with joy.

As their laughter subsided, they fell silent looking into each other's eyes, their noses almost touching. Lizzie playfully leaned forward and gave Zachary a peck on the cheek. Zachary was momentarily in shock. She had kissed him! He responded instinctively with a full kiss on her mouth. Lizzie stiffened in surprise, but then relaxed to enjoy the moment. Her mouth relaxed and their tongues touched. They both felt urges that they only previously touched upon in the deep recesses of their adolescent minds.

The moment was broken when Emily entered the barn and gasped when she came upon her two friends embracing in the hay pile. "My God," she sputtered. Not quite knowing what to do, Emily stood motionless for a moment and then turned on her heels and ran back to the chicken coop to regain her composure.

Elizabeth stood up, knocked a bit of the hay from her dress and followed after Emily. Zachary sat up in the hay pile, scratched his head and tried to make sense of what just happened.

Lizzie caught up with Emily at the chicken coop. "Emily that was not what it looked like." She grasped Emily's arm. "It was sort of an accident, though I cannot deny that I am fond of your cousin."

Lizzie did not want to tell Emily that she had been ordered to avoid her cousin as some sort of undesirable, but she could not let this incident become public knowledge. She grasped both of Emily's arms and turned her so that she could look Emily straight in the eyes. "Promise me, on our friendship, that you will keep this incident a secret." Grasping Emily, a bit tighter, "Promise me." Emily reluctantly agreed and beat a hasty retreat to the house.

The incident in the barn changed the relationship between the three young people forever. Lizzie still came to visit, but it was now more to see Zachary, than to do girlish things with Emily. Lizzie recognized her affection for Zachary but was mindful of her increased disobedience against her father's edict.

Emily could not overcome the feeling of being a third wheel any time the three of them were together. She still valued Elizabeth as a friend, but the relationship would never be the same.

Zachary was completely fired up; all of his male adolescent juices were flowing. However, Jessica continued to be present most of the time when the three teens were together. Zachary took every opportunity to be with Lizzie, and he would hold her hand or steal a kiss whenever there were no witnesses around.

One afternoon while the three were peeling corn for the night's dinner and Zachary was describing his adventures with the little sailboat, Lizzie responded, "I would like to go on your boat sometime."

Zachary beamed, "What a great idea. The three of us can go on a picnic. There is a little beach across the river, on the north end of the harbor that would be fine for our outing."

Emily felt uncomfortable with the relationship between her cohorts and made a lame excuse for not participating.

Zachary had invited Emily because he did not want her to feel left out but had hoped that she might decline. What could be better than an entire afternoon alone with Lizzie? The plan was set for the following day. Emily promised to keep their outing in strict confidence.

The next morning was warm and humid. Late summer was like that, and the heat had been building for the past five days. The breeze was light, but not as much as Zachary had hoped for to show off his skills. But, as his uncle always said when the breeze was light, "Any damn fool can make the boat go when it's blowing. It takes skill to make way in light airs."

Zachary took Lizzie's hand and helped her step out into the skiff. He stowed the picnic basket under the little foredeck. He raised the mainsail, loosed the dock lines and they were off. The humidity had caused enough haze to make the south shore of the harbor a slightly darker shade of gray. The sky above the hazy shoreline was clear blue with only an occasional cumulus cloud floating lazily above the harbor.

Israel came out of his cabin and observed the skiff heading offshore. He was busy and didn't take notice of a second person in the boat. Every time he saw the little boat heading out, he was self-satisfied that he had purchased it and that Zachary enjoyed it so much.

Even though the breeze was light, it felt good on the water, much cooler than it had been on shore. The trip to the beach took more than two hours, but they did not notice the time. The two young lovers talked and laughed and enjoyed each other's company.

Zachary guided the sailboat right up to the shoreline, until the boat's stubby keel scraped in the sand. He had stowed his shoes under the foredeck before they left the dock and had directed Lizzie to do the same. Zach vaulted over the gunwale carrying a small anchor. The water was barely knee deep. He led her up onto the beach until he reached the end of the anchor rode. He then returned to assist Lizzie, holding her at the right elbow as she splashed into the water, her dress held in a wad above her knees.

Zachary knew that they would both be in trouble if they were gone together for too long, but Zach had planned ahead. It was near low tide when he grounded the skiff and the incoming tide would ensure that they could depart in the afternoon. With luck they would return, and no one would be the wiser.

Lizzie opened the picnic basket and spread an old tablecloth on the sand. She produced some sandwiches made from leftover meat, a chunk of cheese and a flask of fresh water. They ate and made small talk.

Lizzie pointed out the most aggressive of the seagulls that had assembled near them in hopes of participating in the picnic. "He sure is a weathered old bird. He must have been here before the war."

Zachary replied, "Don't feed him or we will have the whole flock in our laps." With that he hollered and waved his arms causing the old bird and its colleagues to retreat a few yards.

As lunch was completed, Zachary stood up and ran toward the gulls waving his arms wildly.

The birds got the hint and took flight; although as they departed one of them dropped a sign of its disapproval on Zach's shoulder. Zachary waved a fist at the departing flock. Lizzie laughed at the comical episode, "Well, I'm not sure who got the last word in that debate."

Zachary sat back down on the cloth beside Lizzie. She used a napkin to wipe off his shoulder.

Being at close quarters, Zachary leaned over and gently kissed Lizzie's full young lips. She responded as he had hoped, pressing against him for a long, moist embrace. After a few moments he leaned to his left causing them to fall back onto the old tablecloth for a round of serious caressing.

Zachary slid his hand into the bodice of Lizzie's dress and grasped her firm aroused breast. She reacted by stiffening, but then relaxed to accept the pleasure of the fondling. After some time at this newfound pleasure, Zachary released her breast and slid his hand under Lizzie's skirt. Lizzie again stiffened, but this time she grabbed Zachary's hand pulling it from her thigh and placing it back on her breast. She whispered, "Me thinks that you are too eager, young man."

Zachary got the hint that the limits had been set. He nevertheless enjoyed the alternative, which she had willingly offered as a compromise. The two lovers enjoyed the afternoon in each other's embrace.

When the Sun was well past its zenith, Zachary reluctantly announced that they had better depart before it got too late. Lizzie picked up the tablecloth, shook the sand from it and placed it back into the basket. Meanwhile Zachary pulled the skiff into the beach, from the point where it bobbed on the now high tide.

The young lovers talked and laughed as Zachary sailed on a close reach back toward home. The breeze was dying and becoming light and variable. Zachary was not making the headway he would have liked. Zachary continually adjusted his heading and the sail to take advance of the occasional puff of air.

About halfway back to their home port Lizzie looked off to the south and said with a note of concern, "Zachary look at that!"

To the south was a line of churning dark gray clouds, with black linings. Lightning flashed from the huge column of clouds that towered to the heavens. A summer squall was approaching quickly, and they were directly in its path.

Zachary mentally weighed his options. It was too far back to the beach, so they would have to run before the storm. Seeing the look of concern in Lizzie's eyes, Zachary patted her on the knee saying, "Don't worry, my Uncle has told me what to do in storms."

A freshening breeze now came from the south. It began to push some building waves before it.

Israel had indeed instructed Zachary on the choices when confronted by stormy weather. He turned the boat into the breeze; it bounced in the short choppy seas. "Lizzie, hold the bow into the wind," he ordered, placing her hand on the tiller. He loosened the main halyard and quickly tied the sail to its boom at the second reef points.

He was hauling up the reefed mainsail when the first serious gust of rain hit them. The wind caused the waves to grow to three feet very quickly. The water, which had been a mixture of blues from the sky in its brown opalescence, turned a most ugly pea green reflecting the now ominous sky.

Israel had warned Zachary about the dangers of getting caught by a wave amidships, broaching and getting the boat swamped. Zachary took the tiller and ordered Lizzie to stay low in the boat.

Watching the pattern of the approaching waves and wind gusts, Zachary waited for a relative lull and then pushed the tiller hard over, turning the skiff before the wind. The little boat immediately sprang forward pushed by the building wind, charged up the backside of the first wave and speeding down its face.

Jessica had been in the house most of the day working on a sewing project. Hearing the first rumbles of thunder, she sought Emily and Zachary to get the animals under cover and otherwise batten down for a storm. Finding Emily, she asked, "Where is Zachary?"

Emily responded, "He took the sailboat out this morning."

Jessica replied, "Well, I hope that he gets in before this storm hits." She then enlisted Emily to prepare for the storm.

The Reverend Mrs. Hopkins was passing the Bower's house on the way to do some shopping when she heard the rumble of thunder. Seeing the activity in the Bower's yard, she decided to check on Lizzie. "Hello Jessica," she beckoned, "Is Elizabeth about?"

Jessica turned and gave a quizzical look at Emily, "Is Elizabeth here?" Emily responded, "No, I haven't seen her since this morning."

Mrs. Hopkins mused, "I wonder where she has gotten too?"

Emily could see that the day's secret outing was about to be uncovered and she was caught in the middle.

Jessica seeing Emily's uncomfortable look demanded, "Emily do you know where Elizabeth is?" Emily responded, "Yes ma'am, but I am sworn to secrecy."

Jessica would have none of this. "Out with it!"

Emily stammered' "She is on the boat with Zach."

As Emily spoke, the first gusts of the storm blew through the yard. Mrs. Hopkins looked at Jessica in concern, "We must see to the children."

Mrs. Hopkins turned and headed toward the shipyard. Jessica and Emily followed, and they marched through town headed to the water.

Israel, because of the scent of rain or some sixth sense, felt the approach of the storm and came on deck to see the black clouds rolling in. He also saw the skiff out in the open bay and Zachary shortening sail. He could see that Zachary was taking the proper steps in preparation, but he was no less concerned that Zach would have to face his first storm at sea, alone in a little boat. But he also observed a second person in the boat. This was very strange. He went below, fetched his oilskins and headed to the dock to meet the skiff.

Reverend Hopkins was working in his study when he looked out of the window and saw the formation of his wife followed by Jessica and Emily hurrying toward the water. He did not know what was happening, but there was an air of concern in their movement. He decided that he had better investigate. He departed his office, trailing the previous group by a hundred yards.

In the bay the weather continued to build. The winds reached thirty-five knots with gusts over fifty knots, blowing horizontal rain and pushing the waves to six feet, causing white froth on top of the green waves. The two lovers were low in the boat as the driving rain stung their backs. The rain briefly became mixed with marble sized hail, which stung even more. The skiff raced down the face of the swells at fourteen knots. In the trough of each wave the boat slowed to below six knots and climbed the next wave, to repeat the downhill sleigh ride. Zachary worked the tiller constantly to keep the boat before the wind. A broach in these conditions would be deadly.

Zachary squinted in an attempt to see through the rain and spray running into his eyes and the near zero visibility caused by the sheets of horizontal rain. In the back of his mind Zachary was thinking, "What happens if he runs before the storm and reaches the other shore at full speed? I guess we will face that prospect when the time comes."

He glanced at Lizzie who huddled next to him, "We'll be fine," he comforted.

On shore Israel met the three ladies at the base of the dock as the rains started coming hard, so he ushered them under the eve of a boat shed. "What are you all doing here?"

Jessica voiced the concern. "Zachary is out in this storm and Elizabeth is with him."

Edmund arrived at the boat shed dripping wet, for he had been just far enough behind the ladies to be caught in the full brunt of the squall. "What is going on?" He demanded.

Mrs. Hopkins grasped his arm and explained the situation. Edmund growled, "I knew no good would come of this."

Israel turned toward Edmund, "Come of what?" he questioned.

Edmund replied, "My daughter associating with that rapscallion you have taken into your house."

Israel fumed, "Reverend you should be more interested in praying for the safety of our young people, than making bigoted commentary."

Edmund moved toward Israel, "Sir, I suggest that you refrain from telling me when I should pray, and who are you calling a bigot?"

Jessica moved between the two men before the scene got any more confrontational. "Gentlemen, our concern here is the children."

On the water the wind began to abate. The eye of the storm had passed over and was now moving quickly to the north. It was over; the clouds to the south were beginning to break up with rays of sunbeams shining through the ragged holes in the gray clouds. Because of the great speed they had made during the storm, they were only two hundred yards from the dock. This was good since the breeze always dies behind a storm.

Lizzie and Zachary were soaked to the skin. Water was dripping from their hair. The storm had broken the week's heat spell, and Lizzie shivered slightly in the cool breeze. She huddled against Zachary. They looked at each other and laughed at each other's dripping windblown persona. All was well, the danger was over, they were safe, and they were together.

Zachary turned the boat toward the dock. As they headed in the greeting party emerged from under the eve of the boat shed and rushed down the dock. It looked to Zachary like a hanging jury. They were wet and they did not look happy. Zachary figured that this might mean the end of his boat use for a while.

Lizzie saw her parents on the dock and knew that the penalties for this adventure would be more severe. She was caught absolutely violating her father's edict regarding Zachary. But she didn't care, her teenage passion burned for this young man, and that was all that counted. She thought, "When caught red-handed and facing sure punishment, the only defense is total defiance."

As the skiff coasted into the dock Israel grabbed the bow and bowline to secure it. Zachary let loose of the mainsheet allowing the sail to luff while he secured the stern line. Edmund reached out and half helped; half pulled his daughter from the boat. Before Edmund could say anything, Mabel stepped forward and hugged her daughter. "Are you alright child?"

"I am fine," Lizzie responded, "Zachary did a fine job."

Hearing this, Edmund had to inject himself into the situation. "I am happy that you are safe." He grasped Lizzie and Mabel. "As for the rest of this situation, we had best discuss it at home."

Israel guessed what "the rest of this situation," meant and glared at Edmund.

Edmund guided his family from the dock and to their home. Lizzie glanced back and gave a little wave to Zachary, as she was ushered away.

Israel turned to Jessica, "You ladies ought to get on home and into some dry clothes. I'll help Zachary tidy up the boat and then we will be along."

Zachary worked in silence. He dropped the sail and tied it to the boom. Not knowing how much trouble he was in; he did not want to say anything.

Israel looking at the shrouds which had almost chafed through due to the rigors of the storm, started the conversation. "Not too much longer lad and you would have lost your mast." He patted Zachary on the back of his wet head. "I saw you reef the mainsail before the storm. You did exactly what you should have under the circumstances."

Zachary replied, "Thank you Sir."

Israel continued, "Other than your fine seamanship, you have certainly caused a mess with Miss Elizabeth. Reverend Hopkins seems more upset than the Lord ought to allow. I managed to almost come to blows with my minister. Whether you did anything or not, which I hope you didn't, this town will get wind of today's events and will question Elizabeth's virtue for a long time to come."

Zachary felt that it was time to respond. "Lizzie's virtue is fine. She wouldn't have let me do anything if I had wanted to."

Israel replied, "Don't be surprised if that pompous S.O.B. of a preacher makes sure that you don't get near his daughter anytime soon."

Zachary stammered, "But that's not fair. Lizzie and I love each other. No one can stand between us."

Israel gave Zachary another fatherly pat on the head, "As bad as that huh. We shall see, but I think the Reverend Hopkins will have no compassion for young lovers."

Edmund did not want to begin his interrogation in public, but as soon as he was in his house with the ladies secure behind closed doors, he began his tirade. "Elizabeth, you have directly disobeyed my direction and now this disgraceful act."

Never at a loss for words, Elizabeth still wet and cold, her hair limp and stringy, her sundress soaked clinging to her body. She in no mood to take her father's abuse. "There was no disgraceful act. Zachary is a fine young man and we went on a picnic. That is all."

Edmund stiffened into his take charge posture, "I specifically told you to stay away from that backwoods urchin and you disobeyed me." Waving his right arm toward the window, "I knew something like this would happen."

Mabel attempted to mediate the situation. "Now, Edmund we should just be thankful that the children are alright."

Edmund snapped back at Mabel. "Everything is not all right. Our daughter is sneaking around with a country bumpkin, who is most likely trying to take advantage of her."

Lizzie responded, "I only snuck around, because you chose to dictate who I should like and dislike. Zachary is my friend and I will keep it that way."

Grasping both his daughter's shoulders, Edmund stared into her eyes. "Did he touch you?"

Elizabeth pulled back. "What do you mean did he touch me?" She bristled and as much as she tried to hold them back, tears streamed down her cheeks. "Zachary would do nothing that I did not wish him to do."

Not knowing what was meant by Lizzie's statement Mabel sputtered, "Oh, dear." "Nothing happened," Lizzie snapped. She turned and ran from the room.

Edmund waved his arms. "Come back here young lady, we are not through."

Mabel grasped Edmunds arm. "Edmund you have been ranting and carrying on like a Calvinist preacher. I think that you have caused enough discord for one day."

Edmund still incensed, "What do you mean? Your daughter is out gallivanting around with this undesirable young man, and we have to put a stop to it."

Mabel responded, "Edmund don't you have it in your heart to feel compassion for these young lovers."

Edmund, "Love is what I am worried about."

Mabel grasped his arm again. "You know that you were a pretty aggressive suiter in your day."

Edmund retorted, "Yes, but I had a future to offer you. Our daughter deserves more that the affections of a backwoods ner-do-well"

Edmund would not be dissuaded. "I think that we should send Elizabeth to visit your sister until this whole thing blows over."

CHAPTER 6

OFF TO BOSTON

Lizzie lay in her bed trying to decide how what started out as one of the best days of her life could have turned out so awful. She wept quietly until she fell asleep.

It was late morning when Lizzie and Mabel arrived at the home of Aunt Beth after a hot and dusty trip via stagecoach. Beth was overjoyed to see them and eager to show them the sights of the city. Herding after them like a mother hen she had their bags carried to guest rooms and called her cook to prepare lunch.

Beth ambled on with a flurry of disjointed statements; "Oh, it is good to see you both." "You must be famished." "You ladies need to wash up and rest from your journey."

Lizzie and her mother went to their rooms and freshened up, had an acceptable lunch from leftovers, followed by an afternoon nap, followed by afternoon tea in the parlor. The discussion was quite gay, the ladies shared stories of the years since they had last been together.

Mabel finally explained as delicately as she could how she and Lizzie had been banished to Boston. She touched on Lizzie's scandalous outing with a young man, the storm and the judgment by Edmund that they should come to Boston as a means of defusing the issue. Lizzie sat quiet and sullen throughout her mother's explanation, feeling a mixture of shame and anger over the incident. She was afraid that her aunt, whom she had just met, a prim and proper Bostonian woman would consider her a wanton harlot.

But Lizzie did not know her aunt, who at times was known to be less than prim and proper herself. Seeing her niece's discomfort, Beth laughed and slapped Lizzie on the knee, "Good for you girl. I hope that he was a fine young man, for all the trouble it has caused."

Lizzie beamed at the unexpected support from her aunt. Mabel was not amused by her sister's support for Lizzie's actions, but she knew that her sister had always been the free spirit of the pair and there was little she could do to counteract Beth's fiery personality.

Beth: "I am so happy to have you both with me no matter the reason, but alas I am scheduled to sail for London in less than a month." Pouring another cup of tea Beth continued, "Before then you must enjoy your stay in Boston, but we must make some decisions before I depart."

Mabel: "We hated to come unannounced and catch you at such a bad time, but Edmund was insistent that we come."

Beth: "Nonsense, I am happy to have you both with me."

Mabel was two years older than Beth and always the more subdued and proper of the two.

Though Beth loved her sister she had been subjected to Mabel's steadfast compliance with the "rules" for her entire early life. Now as an adult, she could not help but take an occasional jovial poke at her older sister and the always stuffy Edmund.

Beth was a handsome woman, about five foot one, with a few strands of grey beginning to show in her chestnut hair. She still had that twinkle in her green eyes that most women lose after having children. Her skin was the opal white with freckles that is found on many people of Anglo-Saxon heritage.

Beth had married a Boston merchant and ship owner. She took her place in polite society during the early years of her marriage but was widowed when her husband Samuel was killed at the Battle of Monmouth in 1778. When Samuel left with the Massachusetts Militia, he left his manager Mr. Wyatt in charge of the business. Upon Samuel's death, Beth asked Wyatt to stay on and gave him a minority ownership in the firm. As it turned out, Wyatt did an excellent job and the firm prospered. Wyatt managed the business and only got Beth involved when absolutely necessary. Though she had several pursuers, Beth never re-married preferring to maintain her position as a butterfly flitting from event to event in Boston society.

Beth put down her cup. "We have so much to do ladies; I can't wait to show you both off." The next two weeks were among the most exciting in Lizzie's life. On their first full day in Boston, Beth had a seamstress take measurements of both ladies and within days returned with a lovely dress for Lizzie and one for her mother. Beth was serious about showing off her visitors. There was daily tea either at the homes of her friends or some days friends would call for tea with Beth. They went to two concerts, three plays and dined out on several occasions.

Lizzie was a most attractive young beauty, even by city standards and Beth made sure that her niece was introduced to several young men during their outings. After each introduction Beth commented on the young man's pedigree and would provide her assessment of his prospects, such as, "A fine looking young man, though the product of less than handsome parents. His mother is a dear friend. I can't believe that she has let herself gain so much weight. His father is a lawyer of some note, but I hope that Harvard College will make the lad less of a buffoon than his father."

At the end of the second week in Boston, Beth addressed a needed decision over breakfast. "The decision that needs to be made is whether or not you ladies accompany me to London. When I depart you are both more than welcome to stay in my house for as long as you like, but it would be oh so much fun if you both would join me in London. That would fix that stodgy old Edmund for putting you ladies under my care."

The discussion continued. Mabel who was not at all adventurous had no desire to pitch and roll on a ship for the better part of a month to cross the Atlantic. She made excuses about her duties in Edmund's church and how she could not be gone for an extended time. Beth countered with the fact that their father was so ready to send his wife and child to Boston he must not need the help. However, Mabel could not be budged in her opposition to the trip.

Beth changed her tactics and offered to pay the passage for Lizzie and pointed to the education Lizzie would receive after a couple of years in London society and most likely a tour on the continent. Lizzie had not only inherited her aunt's name "Elizabeth," but also much of her aunt's fiery personality. At this point Lizzie joined in the discussion, "Please mother, can I go?"

Mabel could not picture her flamboyant sister as a long-term mentor for Lizzie. She threw up a barrage of excuses about why Lizzie should not go on such a journey. Beth countered each of the excuses in order. Lizzie became more and more supportive of her aunt. Mabel was being outnumbered and out classed. When she ran out of objections, Beth summarized the arguments, "We have established that Edmund wants Lizzie to be away for some while. We agree Lizzie should become an educated young woman. Living in England for a while would aid that objective." Gesturing toward Mabel, "You will not go for whatever reason, but it is obvious that Lizzie is eager to join me on this journey."

Mabel sat quietly; her expression showed her defeat. Beth went for the close, "Then it is decided, Lizzie will accompany me."

Mabel nodded in acquiescence. Beth changed the subject. "Let us plan for our departure and the remainder of our activities in Boston."

At the end of the next week Beth and Lizzie boarded a ship for their voyage across the Atlantic. Mabel saw them off at the harbor and was then escorted to Beth's residence to pack her belongings for her return home. She could already hear Edmund huffing and puffing over his daughter being under the wing of his frivolous and flighty sister-in-law. She thought to herself, "That die is cast. Edmund will just have to get over it."

CHAPTER 7

OFF TO SEA

THE MORNING AFTER the debacle with Lizzie, Zachary awoke from a fitful night's sleep. He lay in his bed staring at the sun's reflection on the ceiling of his room. His only thoughts were of Lizzie. He had to see her, but it was obvious that Lizzie would not be allowed to visit their house. It was equally obvious that he would not be welcome at the Hopkins' house. He would plan a rendezvous, but he would have to somehow communicate it to Lizzie. Emily was the only possible go-between who might be able to visit Lizzie and not raise suspicions.

Emily was never an early riser. His room was next to hers', so he went out of his way to make some noise and hopefully awaken her without raising her dander. Around 9:30 he heard her moving around her room. He dressed and sped downstairs to wait for her to come down for breakfast.

After half an hour Emily pattered down the stairs, still dressed in her nightgown. Jessica was already working in the garden, so they would be alone long enough for Zachary to make his plea for help.

Without even saying "Good morning," Zachary made his request. "Emily, you have to see Lizzie for me."

Emily, never an easy touch replied, "I don't want to go anywhere near Reverend Hopkins. He was horrid yesterday."

"You most help me," he implored. "You are the only one I can trust to take a message to Lizzie." He became more emphatic, "I must see her, and find out how to make everything alright."

Emily was coming around, but still did not want to be viewed as being too cooperative. "I don't know."

Zachary grasped her hand between both of his. "Please, Emily. Have I ever asked you for anything before? You are the only hope for a go-between."

Emily relented, "Well alright, but Reverend Hopkins better not holler at me."

Zachary was elated. He squeezed Emily and kissed her on the cheek. "Thank you, I will make this up to you."

Just after sunup Reverend Hopkins awoke Mabel and announced that since her sister had repeatedly asked her and Elizabeth to visit; this was the time. He was sending them to visit Aunt Beth in Boston. Lizzie protested, but to no avail, Edmund's authority in his own house had been challenged and he was regaining control.

Mabel tried to broker a compromise with Edmund, but he would have none of it. Mabel helped Lizzie pack for the trip and made a feeble attempt at justifying her husband's actions.

Edmund hitched their two horses to the family's carriage. He hustled the ladies into the carriage and was on the road out of town by ten in the morning. Very little was spoken between the trio. There was nothing to say.

Emily went upstairs to wash and dress. After what seemed an eternity to Zachary, she came downstairs and headed toward the Hopkins' house. After the short walk, Emily knocked on the Hopkins' closed front door. It was unusual for it to be closed on a fine summer's morning. There was no answer. Emily went around to the back door, which was also closed.

Seeing a neighbor working in his garden, Emily went over to enquire about the Hopkins. The neighbor responded, "The Reverend asked me to feed his animals for a few days. They left earlier this morning. Seems they were going on a little trip."

Emily hurried home and reported the situation to Zachary. He was on the back porch when she arrived home. On hearing of the Hopkins' departure, he fell into a chair slouching forwards and staring at the ground. "My God, this is worse that I could have imagined. What are they doing with Lizzie? What did I do to cause this misfortune?"

Emily, not knowing what to say or do departed to the garden to tell her mother of the Hopkins' departure. She left Zachary to his moping.

For the next three days Zachary went through the motions of his chores but did little else. He sat on the back porch thinking of Lizzie and trying to come up with a plan of action but found none. He had plenty of frivolous thoughts about rushing to Lizzie and whisking her away from her evil captor but found no real-world answers to his dilemma.

Reverend Hopkins and his family met the coach to Boston. He placed Lizzie and Mabel along with their bags on the coach. When he returned home, he was alone. Zachary was tired but could not beg Emily to ask the Reverend what he had done with his wife and daughter.

Sunday morning Jessica came down dressed to go to church. Israel had already stated that he did not particularly want to see the stuffed shirt Reverend Hopkins. Jessica replied to Israel's position, "This is my church as much as anyone's and I am not about to let the skirmish with the minister dissuade my attendance."

Israel had noticed that Zachary had not visited the docks during the past few days, and the little sailboat had been left unattended since the events of the past Monday. Israel had been busy provisioning *Setauket* and preparing her for sea, since it was almost time to depart on the next voyage. He had not had time to talk to Zachary regarding the situation with Elizabeth, her father's intransigent position regarding the young lovers and the entire ugly mess.

Israel waited for Jessica to hustle Emily off to church with her before he went to the back porch to approach the still sullen Zachary. He started by beating around the bush. "Lad, you know we are going to have to work on the skiff's standing rigging after your little adventure?"

"Yes sir," Zachary replied. "I just haven't felt much like going to the boat since our mishap last Monday."

Israel took this opening, "I know this is tough; the Reverend whisked his daughter off to who knows where." He went on, "But you can't sit here on the porch for the rest of your life, so you better lick your wounds and get on with it."

"Yes sir," Zachary again replied.

Israel continued his side of the conversation, even if he was not gaining much of a response. "It is time that you learn a trade, and it is clear to me that you have taken to sailing and appear to be interested in the *Setauket*. I wanted to make this offer anyway, because the only trade I know is at sea, but now considering this situation with Elizabeth, it makes even more sense."

Zachary was now paying much more attention to his uncle, since he could sense where this conversation was heading."

Israel, "Many a sailor has set to sea because of an affair with a woman. Well, what I am offering you is to apprentice on my ship. Join us on this upcoming voyage."

Zachary was now looking intently at Israel. During the past few months, he had thought of going to sea, and had even thought about approaching his uncle on the subject. He was now getting the offer without soliciting it. This was great but, what about Lizzie?

"Sir, I am honored that you asked me, and would indeed like to join your crew, but I hate to leave Lizzie. I fear that I love her dearly."

Israel replied, "Well, the Reverend has fixed it so that you cannot see her anyway. If you two are truly in love, being apart for a while will not dampen the flame. This will be no ordinary trip. I have received instructions from the owners of *Setauket*. They want us to go up to Boston to take on cargo.

We will take a load to Charleston, South Carolina and then provision with trading goods for a trip to trade for furs and hides along the Pacific coast of the Americas. The voyage will take more than a year, possibly two. I have not yet been in the Pacific Ocean nor around Cape Horn. As much as I will miss Jessica and Emily, I cannot help but lust for this adventure. So, Zachary I would be pleased if you would join me on this great adventure."

For the first time in days Zachary's full attention was on other than Lizzie. Not only was he being offered a chance to become a real sailor, but also to visit faraway places that he had only imagined in his dreams. His old enthusiasm was returning, he could feel it flowing through his body.

After a few minutes of silent contemplation Zachary made his decision. "Yes Uncle, I would be pleased to join your crew."

"Excellent," declared Israel. "Of course, on shipboard you should address me as Captain." Zachary responded, "Aye, Aye sir."

Israel continued the point, "A sailor's life is not easy, and I cannot play favorites on the ship, so you will have no special treatment."

Zachary, "I would expect none."

"Good, then it is settled. We depart in two days with the morning's tide."

Zachary was elated, though his life had been shattered a few minutes ago, now it held new meaning and new objectives. He continued to think of Lizzie but was otherwise mentally engrossed in the upcoming adventure.

Israel knew that this means to solve the problem with Zachary and the current furor would not be popular at home. He waited until he and Jessica were lying quietly in bed to again broach the subject. "Dear, this is quite a kettle of fish, Zachary has gotten himself into."

Jessica, "Yes, the incident has made it all over town. I believe that nothing happened, but that is not the way it is being told on the streets and docks."

Israel, "I fear that both Elizabeth and the lad will be the subject of conversation for a long time to come. The old crones around here don't have much scandal to talk about."

Jessica, "It is rumored that the Reverend is going to send poor Elizabeth off to somewhere to get her out of the local eye. He is more worried about his own reputation than hers."

Israel, "That may not be such a bad thing to do. If both parties are away for a while, the locals will forget about the whole incident." Hesitating a bit, Israel continued, "If I take the lad on the upcoming voyage, by the time he returns no one will remember a thing. If it turns out that he is really in love, then the time away will prove his seriousness, one way or the other."

Jessica turned toward Israel, "We have had this discussion, and agreed that Zachary would continue his education, at least for the next year or so."

Israel, "Yes, but the current situation changes things. Zachary will not be much of a student if he is mooning after some young lady. He also does not need the abuse he will be getting from the Reverend and all the local wagging tongues." Israel took a deep breath, "Anyway, I talked to the lad about it and he is eager to go."

Jessica rose up on her elbow and her cheeks turned red. "You did what?" Sputtering in anger she continued, "You know that I have a duty to give him a proper education and my feelings on the subject. I cannot believe that you would absolutely ignore my wishes."

Israel raised his voice, "I was trying to do what was best for the boy under the circumstances." As she rolled over away from Israel, Jessica grumbled, "It is done."

Tuesday morning was overcast with an intermittent drizzle. Zachary was up before sunrise. He washed, dressed, and carried his duffle bag to the kitchen.

Israel rousted out the ladies so they could see them off. Before eight o'clock the family made the short walk to the dock.

After hugs and kisses from Jessica and Emily, Zachary and Israel boarded the waiting longboat and were rowed out to the waiting *Setauket*.

Jessica and Emily watched from the dock until *Setauket* had weighed anchor and was heading out to sea. Jessica waved and feigned a smile as long as the men were close to the dock, but she could not help an occasional tear rolling down her cheek.

Jessica declared, "Emily, this is the part I hate. As the wife of a seaman I knew there would be these departures, but I still hate them. I cannot keep your father from his chosen profession, and I don't think that anyone could keep Israel Redden from the sea." She put an arm over Emily's shoulder, "I always have this feeling of apprehension when your father departs on a voyage. It is silly, but all the troubling things that could happen run through my mind. It is for ladies to stoically wait for their men to return from the sea."

Upon arriving at the *Setauket*, Mr. Bolton welcomed them aboard. Israel asked him to show Zachary where to stow his duffle and put him to work.

Israel instructed Mr. Bolton that Zachary should be instructed as an apprentice seaman, which should include participating in and learning every aspect of the operation of the ship. However, Zachary should be berthed amidships opposed to sleeping forward with the seedy lot of seamen in the fo'c'sle.

When Zachary returned to the deck from below, he was assigned to winch up the anchor. Israel gave the command to weigh anchor. Mr. Bolton responded and then commanded the hands on the fore deck, "man the windless." Zachary and three other hands placed the two "T" shaped bars into the holes at the top of the rocker arm of the windless. One deckhand tailed the anchor rode, squatting low just aft of the windless. Bolton ordered, "Port down first." The two hands on the port side bar pushed it down almost to the deck, then Zachary and another hand pushed down the starboard bar. This sequence was repeated over and over for the next ten minutes. Bolton kept one eye on the rode while counting shot from the bow and announced when the anchor had broken loose from the bottom.

Israel had ordered the sails unfurled while the ship was resting at anchor. When coming off the anchor, he needed to make sail and gain way as fast as possible. All crew who were not involved in weighing anchor were at their assigned stations ready to make sail.

Israel, standing aft at the weather rail, gave the orders to loose the fore and aft sails. He called to the mast officers, "On the Fore, Main and Mizzen, standby the headsail and staysail gear!"

The officers responded, in turn, "Fore Ready!" "Main Ready!" Mizzen Ready!"

The sequence of setting sails from aft to fore began. The action continued everywhere on deck with orders being barked, and crewmen responding. As the ship began to make way the Main and Fore Topsails were set.

Israel to the helmsman, "Heading zero-eight-zero!" Helmsman: "080, Aye!"

The crewmen coiled halyards and other lines that would not be needed during maneuvering and hung them on the belaying pins. Sheets, tacks, and braces were coiled then capsized so that they would run clean.

Israel: "That is well!"

Israel to the helmsman, "Hold'er steady as ye go!" Helmsman: Steady as ye go, Aye!"

Bolton: "Go below the off watch!"

Upon this order the off watch went below and the duty watch relaxed a bit while awaiting further orders.

As the new swab on board, Zachary was assigned to take the bucket on a rope, drag the bucket to fill it and then wash the mud from the anchor. With this order came the warning not to let the bucket sink completely under the water or it would pull him overboard.

Zachary and Israel were too busy to see or acknowledge the final waves from Jessica and Emily. After the sails were set and *Setauket* was close hauled, the activity on deck settled down. Zachary went to the starboard rail watching the shoreline disappear into the summer haze. He thought of Lizzie and hoped that he had made the right decision in going to sea.

Zachary's interlude did not last long. Mr. Bolton saw him at the rail and knowing that most first-time seamen have misgivings as the land goes out-of-sight, immediately gave Zachary a chore to do. "Lads make those lines shipshape," Bolton bellowed. "Then clean the land dirt from her, ya sons of whores." Bolton was back in his element and just getting into stride. "O'Brien, show Mr. Bower how to Ballantine coil that line."

"Aye sir," responded a young sailor near Zachary. He moved to Zachary and began to demonstrate the proper coiling of the sheet.

There was little time aboard a ship when the crew was not kept busy with various chores.

Scraping and cleaning and painting were ongoing duties to counteract the continuous effects of salt and sea. Mr. Bolton especially planned to keep his new young charge and other neophyte crewmen extremely busy for the next few days, so that they did not have time to get homesick.

Mr. Bolton was prematurely gray, with tight curly hair and bushy lamb chop sideburns. His tanned complexion was deeply wrinkled from years of sun and salt air. He had been at sea since he was Zachary's age and was a good instructor and fine seaman. Bolton had never learned navigation and the other skills required to be a ship's captain. He was satisfied with his position in life, and proud to serve a respected skipper like Captain Redden. He was a fine teacher for the new apprentice.

Zachary lived his shipboard life with the officer's, his uncle and the mates Messrs. Bolton and Nimmo, but since he was learning his trade from the bottom up, he worked and spent much of his time with the crewmen. On a warship he would have been a Midshipman and had the defined role that came with that position. On a merchantman he worked a similar role, but it was much less defined.

In addition to Captain Redden and the First Mate Mr. Bolton there was the Second Mate Mr. Nimmo: he was tall, thin and rather quiet, especially when compared with the boisterous Bolton. The Second Mate is sort of a man in the middle. His berth is aft, adjacent to the Captain and First Mate's quarters, but when there is work to be accomplished, he usually works along with the rest of the crew.

Berthed amidships with Zachary were the ship's carpenter and the sailmaker Messrs. Stecker and Kimball respectively. These two crew members did not normally stand watch, but responded to the call for "all hands on deck." They were responsible for their specialties which were keeping the ship in good repair and running order.

The cook was a Negro called Callaway. He was a quiet man and berthed on a hammock hung in the small galley. No one knew for sure if Callaway was his first or last name. When he signed on to the ship, he made his mark and announced that as his name, which was all anyone cared to know. It also was not known if he was a freed slave or a runaway that had been aided by early New England abolitionists. No one cared much as long as he turned out the hardtack and salt pork or beef on schedule.

The ordinary sailors were an assortment of salty unkempt characters. Most had weather-beaten faces, wrinkled and permanently tanned by years of sun, wind and salt spray. Several had scars on their faces from past injuries or long ago fights in distance seaports. The ordinary crewmen numbered an even dozen counting Zachary. This provided for six on each watch. Many New England merchant ships would have carried less of a crew, but for his first trip around Cape Horn, Israel wanted the advantage of extra hands. Israel also knew that there was a good chance that all of the crew members would not survive the voyage, but in eighteenth and nineteenth century voyaging that was a cost of doing business.

Among the ordinary sailors was a hand called Howdy, a lifelong sailor. Years in the elements made him look much older than his forty-five years. He had been on ships of one sort or another since he was twelve. Though he walked with a limp, he was as fast as any man at scurrying in the rigging.

Another of the sailors was James Grant, a large hulk of a man in his early twenties. He was quiet and sullen by nature and tended to bully other crewmen frequently. Grant had a large chip on his shoulder due to several personal grievances. His parents were among the Tories who fled to Nova Scotia during the War. Their properties were confiscated and sold at a bargain price to a patriotic merchant who was building his fortune on the war for independence. Grant disliked and distrusted Americans but finding himself on an American ship was just the breaks.

Grant also had a basic dislike for the Irish. He had been taught that they were of some lesser Anglo-Saxon stock and the bottom of the barrel when it came to wit and ethics.

An exception to the rest of the seedy crewmen was Daniel O'Brien, an eighteen-year-old lad from Boston who possessed a bit of an Irish brogue mixed with a distinct New England accent. Danny as he was called was a short stocky lad with reddish blonde hair and pale blue eyes. He had shipped to sea as a cabin boy before he was twelve and worked his way up to skilled seaman. Danny was no less rough and tumble than the other ordinary seamen, but he was younger, therefore less weathered than his cohorts. He also had a spark in his eye that betrayed a keen intellect, though he had not been educated to take advantage of it.

It was obvious that Zachary had a close relationship with the Captain; therefore, the crew felt they had to be careful about what was said in his presence. For the most part, the ordinary crewmen kept Zachary at some distance from their discussions, not wanting someone who could snitch to the Captain and not then be properly dealt with for his infraction of the unwritten code of the fo'c'sle.
Zachary worked with the crew and maintained a position on the Starboard Watch, but the fact that he did not sleep in the fo'c'sle with the rest of the ordinary seamen showed his difference and consequently he had to be watched.

Danny O'Brien was not the least impressed by Zachary's relationship to the officers. Zachary was the only other lad aboard who was close to his age and Danny was eager to establish a friendship with Zachary. Mr. Bolton had encouraged that relationship from the beginning as a means for Zachary to be tutored without interfering with Bolton's other duties. Zachary and Danny were on the same watch. They had plenty of time together between tasks to talk and become friends.

Plunged into this new environment, Zachary was happy to have someone close to his age with whom he could talk freely. Danny taught Zachary many of the finer points of seamanship such as knots which were needed in a sailor's everyday work and he added to Zachary's nautical vocabulary. It was also from Danny that Zachary added new levels of profanity to his speech, which far out reached anything he had ever heard uttered by the hunters and trappers of his previous existence. Also, Danny was quite boastful of his prowess with the ladies who sold their favors in every port he had visited in his six years at sea.

It did not take long for James Grant to form a distinct dislike for Danny on several grounds. Danny was Irish for openers and relatively loud and jovial most of the time, just the opposite of Grant. Also, Grant did not like Danny's buttering up to Zachary, who was obviously the Captain's pet. Grant attempted to provoke the younger and smaller Danny by bumping into him and jostling him while they were working.

At the beginning of the voyage Grant was on the same watch as Danny and Zachary. About three days into the voyage the feud erupted. Danny and Zachary were scraping out the cracks between deck boards and filling the cracks with tar. The tar bucket was just forward of the kneeling Danny. As Grant passed by, hauling a line forward, he kicked over the bucket and splashed the tar on Danny and the deck.

Danny exploded, "You son-of-a-bitch!" He rose up and slapped Grant up the side of the head with his tar brush. Grant responded with a backhand to Danny's head sending him sprawling on the deck into the puddle of tar. This infuriated Danny. He rose up and grabbed a belaying pin and rushed towards Grant and waved it over his head. As he attempted to swing the marlinspike at Grant, it was jerked from his hand from behind. He looked over his shoulder to see Mr. Bolton backhand both he and Grant.

"You sons-of-bitches, I'll have none of your carrying on, not on this ship!" Bolton stepped between them. "I ought to let you bastards beat the shit out of each other, but I need you in one piece." Pointing to the forward companionway Bolton bellowed, "Grant, get your ass below, I'll not have you on this watch! O'Brien and Bower clean yourselves and this mess before your next chow!"

Bolton had watched this trouble brewing since they first set sail and had been waiting for it to erupt. He had already planned to move Grant to the Larboard Watch if necessary, to keep the two adversaries apart. Now the only contact between Grant and Danny were cold glares at mealtimes and when both watches were on deck together.

The passage to Boston was uneventful. The skies were mostly overcast with occasional breaks in the cloud cover, revealing a radiant sun by day and patches of brilliant stars at night. *Setauket* reached in a fair northwesterly breeze. After rounding Cape Cod, the breeze was on her nose, which forced some long tacks. *Setauket* clawed her way to Boston.

After *Setauket* was secure in its berth, Israel reluctantly allowed the crew to go ashore by watch.

He knew there would be no more harmony on board if the crew got this close to a major port city and did not get to kick up their heels a bit. He was reluctant because he knew that some crewmen might take this chance to jump ship by staying hidden ashore until they departed. He worried particularly about Danny O'Brien who was in his hometown.

Other crewmen were sure to overindulge, get lost in some brothel, and/or get thrown in jail. He needed all able bodies to load cargo so *Setauket* could head for Charleston and then on to the Pacific.

With a pat on the back Danny said, "Come on Zach, you need to see my part of town." Zachary had never seen a city as large as what he could see of Boston from the harbor. Zachary asked Israel's permission to accompany Danny ashore. Israel thought to himself, "*With Zachary along, Danny should return to the ship, or they could both jump ship, but no, they will both return.*"

Danny led Zach to the south end of Boston, which had many Irish immigrants, though nothing like the area would become in a few decades. The streets were a mixture of mud, water and horse apples. The houses were mostly roughhewn shacks with open doors and windows. The smell was a mixture of cooking odors coming from the various houses, horse apples and the contents of many chamber pots which were emptied into the gutters and ditches.

A number of people of varying ages recognized Danny as a long-lost resident and provided hugs and handshakes as they meandered down the street. They came to one of the few houses that had curtains on the lone front window and a small flower box under the window frame. Danny barged ahead into the door as if he belonged there. Zachary followed through the narrow door and could not see past Danny when he heard a woman's squeal. "Lord be, what a sight you are Daniel O'Brien." Zachary now saw an older woman with graying blonde hair, hugging Danny and kissing his cheeks. She held him out at arm's length and stated, "It is quite a young man that you have become in the last six years."

Danny broke away from her and gestured toward Zachary. "Mother, this is my friend and shipmate, Zachary Bower."

Zachary bowed a bit, "It's a pleasure ma'am."

"Any friend of Daniel's is welcome in our home." She turned again toward Danny, "Sisters are helping Mrs. O'Shanessey do the wash, but they will be delighted to see you."

After the pleasantries were over, Danny and his mother began talking about family and neighbors; and what had been happening during the past six years that Danny had been gone.

Zachary sat quietly at the table and perused the room. It was not that different from their cabin on the frontier. There was a large stone fireplace, which served for cooking. There were pots hanging over a cutting block and cooking utensils hanging from the cutting block. The table was more finished than the roughhewn table that his father had built; it may have been bought rather than homemade.

One thing that Zachary found interesting was the clean curtains hanging from the one front window. He commented, "My mother would have loved to have had such fine curtains in our cabin. Danny's mother responded, "Well as you can see, we don't have much to our names, but there are shanty Irish on this street who live in their hovels but don't wash and don't clean; and then there are the more respectable 'Lace Curtain Irish.' We are of the respectable variety."

Zachary didn't understand the significance of that distinction, but it was of obvious importance to Mrs. O'Brien. Before he could respond with a comment, two young ladies came through the open door; one of them carried a basket full of bedding. Upon seeing Danny, they rushed to him with squeals and tears of joy, along with hugs and kisses. Zachary watched in amusement.

Danny finally broke free from the girls long enough to introduce Zachary to his sisters, Kathryn and Bridget. They were comely young lasses, in their early teens. Both were a little over five foot with blonde hair, radiant blue eyes which sparkled from their recent tears and lots of freckles on their cheeks.

Danny's mother growled at the girls "Mind your manners." Heeding their mother's command, the older sister moved forward and curtsied in front of Zachary. "Pleased to meet you Mr. Bower." The second sister stepped forward and did the same. After which the merriment continued.

Danny's mother, again with an authoritative voice said, "Get a fresh chicken from the butcher shop and we will have a fine dinner tonight." She continued, "It will be crowded but we will make room for you lads tonight."

Danny interrupted, "Mother we may be able to stay for dinner, but we are expected back aboard ship tonight."

His mother retorted, "But it has been years since you've been here; we should at least be able to enjoy your presence for a day or two."

Danny replied, "You don't understand. We have a day or two to load and then we are off to the south around Cape Horn and into the Pacific. The captain was good enough to let us come ashore and visit you while the ship is loading, but we must go back for dark or there will be hell to pay."

Danny's mother's frown showed her disappointment, but she understood that her son was now a young man and had responsibilities. She responded, "Well, at least we can have a good dinner and enjoy the time we have together."

After eating on the ship for a few days it was in fact a good dinner. The chicken was fried and served with potatoes, turnips and some sort of greens. The evening was joyous, with much laughing and gaiety. Danny's sisters told embarrassing stories on their brother and he did his best to reciprocate.

Zachary enjoyed being in the company of two lovely young ladies who were around the same age. The whole group tried to keep Zachary involved in the conversation, even though they clearly needed family time together. If Zachary had known that only a half mile up the hill from the harbor his beloved Lizzie and her mother were encamped with Aunt Beth, he would have headed in that direction as soon as they left the ship that morning.

Meanwhile, back on the ship, Israel became increasingly nervous as the sun lowered in the afternoon sky. He queried Mr. Bolton on several occasions regarding the loading of the ship. What were the chances the crew ashore might be back on board in a timely manner?

After two or three hours of good food and much laughter, Danny and Zachary took their leave. There were hugs and tears from

Danny's mother and sisters, and God's blessings on the lads in their travels.

They had not walked but a block or so when Danny announced, "Let's stop at that pub over there and see if there is anyone in there that I know."

There were boyhood friends of Danny in the pub and after cheers and hugs and back slaps, a couple of those old friends bought drinks for the visiting sailors.

It was now dark, and Israel paced the afterdeck, his arms tightly behind his back. He again queried Mr. Bolton on several occasions regarding the loading of the ship and chances the crew ashore might be back on board in a timely manner.

After a couple of drinks at the pub, Danny and Zachary took their leave, while they could still navigate back to the ship. Zachary, with a little slur in his voice, "Danny, thank you for taking me to your home. I had a great time."

Danny replied, "I hope you enjoyed yourself, because we are going to be in big trouble when we get to the ship."

Israel saw them when they were about a block from the ship. He gestured to Mr. Bolton to join him aft. "Mr. Bolton please see to our prodigal sons when they arrive. I am going below."

Mr. Bolton met the lads as they came up the gangplank. "You boys are a bit late. Plan on half rations for a couple of days and tarring the upper hampers."

Though the young boys missed having some of their meals, tarring the upper hampers at the top of the main and fore masts was dirty work and sitting in bosun's chairs for hours is less than comfortable. But, the view of Boston and the surrounding countryside was glorious.

Two days later *Setauket* was unfurling sails for her reach out of the harbor when Lizzie and Aunt Beth passed by the harbor in a carriage. Beth pointed out the many ships along the wharf, but Lizzie stared at the barque that was a few miles offshore, as it looked strangely familiar, but then she thought, *"No it couldn't be."* She turns back to listen to her aunt.

The progress of *Setauket's* voyage to its destination of Charleston was not as swift as Israel had hoped. Due to a weak low-pressure front, the haze and rain at their departure was carried with them on a light southerly breeze. In addition, the Gulf Stream was close to shore, so they had to cross this adverse current before they could make any decent headway.

As luck would have it, soon after *Setauket* came out of the eastern edge of the Gulf Stream, the sun broke out of the overcast sky and brought with it a freshening northwesterly breeze. *Setauket* plowed through the seas on a broad reach and made up most of the time lost during the previous two days.

Zachary had many exhilarating experiences during his first few days on a ship at sea. While visiting the *Setauket* in the shipyard, Zachary had looked up at the mainmast and asked himself if he would be man enough to climb to its top. During the first two days of the voyage Zachary was assigned to hauling on sheets and halyards from the safety of the deck. On the third day, while resting on deck, Danny pointed up the mainmast and said "Zach, I'll race you to the top."

Zachary hesitated, "Well I haven't been to the tops before."

Danny responded, "OK, I'll let you off the hook. This time, we'll take it slow."

Danny jumped on the windward rail and swung onto the shrouds. "Come on lad," he beckoned with a wave of his hand Zachary followed suit and climbed onto the lower shrouds next to Danny.

When they got above the upper Topsail Danny encouraged his colleague, "Alright lad up we go.

Now don't look down and mind your footing on the ratlins, they get pretty narrow up here."

Danny scampered up the upper shrouds like the young monkey he was. Zachary moved along behind him at a cautious but respectable pace. At the crosstrees at the T'gallant yard, Danny reached out for the base of the topmast shrouds and pulled himself over the outer edge of the crosstrees.

Danny sat peacefully on the crosstrees waiting for Zachary's arrival.

Zachary hesitated staring at the bottom side of the crosstrees and the long reach to the base of the topmast shrouds. He definitely did not want to look down now or he would lose his already waning confidence, but his male pride took over. He could not lose face in front of Danny and the other crewmen. "*What the hell*." he thought and reached for the shroud, his back steeply angled toward the deck below. He pulled himself up onto the crosstrees with his upper body, just as he had learned to do on the platform down at the course yard. "Afternoon Danny," he panted, as a sign of his victory.

Danny let Zachary rest a few minutes and then announced, "Up we go, lad."

Danny hustled up the topmast shrouds. Zachary followed behind him. Up they went until they reached the top end of the uppermost shroud. They stayed at the top for a few minutes surveying the horizon in all directions. There was nothing but them and the endless ocean.

Danny gave the command, "Down we go Zach."

Danny then climbed down the shrouds at a quick pace. Zachary continued behind Danny at a more measured pace.

Back on deck Danny declared, "Zachary me boy, that was not a thing of beauty, but it will do." He poked Zachary in the bicep, "Truth be told, I almost peed me breeches when I first climbed up the crosstrees."

Zachary looked up the mast and grinned with his sense of accomplishment. He settled into a mellow state of self-satisfaction for the rest of the day.

In the coming weeks, trips up the rigging would become routine, as did the trips out on the yards.

However, like a first love, nothing could match the experience of that first venture into the rigging.

A second exhilaration that never lost its appeal was Zachary's turns at the helm. During each watch the crew took turns at the helm, each spending at least an hour at the wheel guiding the ship on its course. His first time at the helm, with Mr. Bolton nearby giving instruction, was a great experience.

Zachary could feel the power of the moving ship and its response when he moved the wheel. When Bolton moved away and left him to himself, he felt the sheer power of the experience, imagining that he could sail this ship anywhere and forever.

As the ship's company settled into a routine, Zachary was kept busy standing watch, and learning more about the workings of the ship. Jessica had sent books so that he could continue his studies, plus Israel had begun to teach him the rudiments of navigation. All of this activity left little time to contemplate Lizzie and the life he had left behind. On night watches or lying at night in his hammock, Zachary would picture Lizzie and his triumphant return from the sea to claim his lover from her tyrannical father.

When land came into view Zachary was excited at the prospect of seeing a new place. As they entered the harbor, he observed the low sandy islands on either side of the harbor's entrance. The city before them was situated on a peninsula between two rivers. He decided that the houses on the point of the peninsula were the finest he had ever seen.

At Charleston the crew was allowed to go ashore, though Zachary and Danny were not permitted to join them. After the incident during shore leave in Boston, there were certain things about a seaman's life that Israel did not want Zachary to learn too quickly. He did not want a repeat of the Boston event.

Several drunken crewmen returned to the ship. They announced to Mr. Bolton that three of their number had been thrown in jail after a fight with the crew of a visiting British ship. They also heard that another of their number would not return, for he had fallen in love or lust, or something like that, during the past three hours. They laughed and carried on as they stumbled to their berths forward.

Israel was not at all pleased with the loss of crewmembers. Since it would be months before the crew saw a civilized city again, he had decided to allow his crew ashore. He now second-guessed his decision. Israel dispatched Mr. Bolton and Nimmo to rectify the problem.

Mr. Bolton went ashore taking Zachary in tow. First, he visited the city jail and paid for the release of the three somewhat battered crewmen. He then made the rounds of several pubs and a couple of brothels in search of the missing crewman, who was nowhere to be found. Mr. Bolton replaced the errant crewman when he and Zachary came upon a sailor being ejected from a brothel who landed on his backside in the dusty street. He was out of luck, out of money and ready to go back to sea.

At Charleston, *Setauket* unloaded its cargo of farm implements manufactured in New England. The only part of the original cargo left onboard were axes, other tools and some cutlasses and muskets that could be traded for hides and furs in the Pacific. A large number of kegs of whiskey and other trade goods were loaded on board

Upon departing Charleston, *Setauket* sailed to the southeast. On the advice of local skippers, Israel decided to again sail across the Gulf Stream and east of the Bahamas rather than fighting the Gulf Stream for several hundred miles through the length of the Florida Straits. When safely east of the Bahamas, Israel ordered the heading to 180 degrees due south. The trade winds aided *Setauket* as she sped south in a broad reach.

The life of a sailor heading south on the northeast Tradewinds was easy. The only reefing of sails came when squalls approached. After reducing sail in anticipation of a squall the sailors would romp about the deck in the warm rain, like schoolboys, their bare backsides much whiter than the rest of their tanned hides.

The ship's company settled into its routine. At 06:00, four bells, all hands were called, and the decks were scrubbed and holystoned. The ship was cleaned above and below decks until 08:00 when breakfast was served to the crew. A half hour was given for breakfast and then the off watch would go below and the on-duty watch would be given its chores for the day. The ship required constant scraping, painting and repair. During good weather each watch was fully engaged in these activities when not tending to the sails or taking a turn at the helm.

During the night watches one crewman is at the helm, at least one is at the bow as lookout and the remainder of the men standby, out of the weather as much as possible, to tend sails when needed.

As all good things cannot last forever; one night the trades began to falter. By sunrise *Setauket* was barely making way on a glassy sea. They had reached the doldrums and were becalmed.

All hands were called to hang any scrap of sail they could out into the fickle light breeze. After days on the same course with the same sail set, the sails were trimmed several times in an attempt to take advantage of the shifting puffs and maintain way. The crew worked continually in the tropical heat. Water rations were doubled, but they sweat it out as fast as they drank it.

By noon the sail hung limp on the yards, flapping and luffing in the occasional puff of wind.

The ship was dead in the water. Captain Redden had done most of his sailing in the North Atlantic and Caribbean; he had only been south of the Equator once as second mate on the old brigantine *Oneida*. In that experience the ship bobbed in the seas for two weeks before it got enough breeze to make some way, and then it took another painstaking week to work its way to the southeast trade winds.

After a day and a half of floating in the heat and humidity the crew began to get short tempered and growl at each other over the most trivial of happenings. There was a sense of purpose and progress when the ship was making way, but all of that was now lost.

The *Setauket* made ten or fifteen miles per day mostly when the occasional squall would roll through and provide ten or fifteen minutes of breeze. On the morning of the third day with little progress, Israel had enough, and ordered both watches to the two longboats. Lines were led off the bow to the boats so that they could tow the lifeless *Setauket*. Zachary had thought that he had worked before, but this was a new level of exertion.

At first, they rowed and there was no movement, they may as well have been rowing an anchor. The mates cursed and implored their crews to bend into the oars. After a few minutes there was a bit of forward progress, which built until they were moving at one knot.

After an hour each boat crew took a five-minute break to rest and drink water, while the other longboat continued to row.

At eight bells, the sun was at its zenith and the boats were brought alongside so that the crew could be fed, and the crewmen could rest during the heat of the day. Israel knew the crewmen had to be used until they were expended, but he needed to keep them healthy enough to continue rowing until they made it south of the doldrums. Then he needed every hand to be available when they rounded the Horn.

After two hours rest the crewmen were ordered back to their boats. This time the mates took extra water and a bundle containing hardtack with them. After rowing all afternoon with the boats taking alternate five-minute breaks each hour, the starboard watch took a longer break to eat some hardtack and drink water, while the Larboard Watch continued rowing to maintain the forward motion. The boats continued to row into the dark. The cooling of the night felt good on the sunburned bodies, providing a bit of refreshment to the rowers. At six bells Redden estimated that his crew was spent and brought them back aboard to sleep.

It was obvious that it was less painful to row in the cool of the night. After four hours sleep the crew was rousted out to begin their toil anew. After being baked in the sun, the men now shivered in the cool of the night. When they finished a breakfast of hardtack and hot coffee, they manned the boats and began their labors anew.

Their routine went on the remainder of that night and all the next day with the exception of the rest period in the heat of the day and the four hours rest in the middle of the night. When the occasional squall would roll through, the Captain would helm the ship for the period that the sails were full. The crew would remain in their boats being towed along beside the ship. The cool rain felt good on their parched bodies. When the rain and accompanying breeze ceased, they rowed to maintain the ship's forward momentum.

Again at 02:00 in the morning the crew was rousted out of their bunks, had their meal of hardtack and coffee and began rowing to force the resting *Setauket* into movement. After no more than ten minutes of labor Bolton pointed to some cat's paws on the water breaking the glassy surface. The men could feel the blessed breeze on their cheeks, but they were ordered to continue to row, this might only be another squall line, and they did not want the ship to go dead in the water again.

After an hour of light breeze, Captain Redden called in the boats and had the sails trimmed. He had stayed on deck most of the time during the past three days of rowing, but he now stayed at the helm so that those on duty watch could rest on deck while the other watch hit the bunks.

The *Setauket* made a steady three knots during the night. With the horizon glowing red in the east, the Starboard Watch came on duty. The Captain gave over the helm and went below to flop into his bunk.

When the Captain returned to the deck five hours later, he found that the breeze had continued to build, and *Setauket* was now making six knots. They had made it through the doldrums and were now reaching south towards the Southern Ocean and Cape Horn.

It did not take long. After a few hours sleep and the return of progress along their route the spirits of the crew were lifted. The short-tempered snarling group which had languished in the doldrums existed no more. The lads kidded each other, and songs were heard while they worked. *Setauket* was once again, a happy ship.

As the *Setauket* approached the Equator, the old salts prepared for the ritual. Zachary, Danny and half a dozen other crewmen had never been south of the Equator and this required the initiation to mark their passing into the southern hemisphere. Howdy, the impish old Welshman from the Larboard Watch came from the fo'c'sle with a mop for a wig and a marlinspike in hand for his scepter. This makeshift Poseidon followed by his entourage of four similarly costumed crewmen went aft and queried the Captain regarding the ships position.

After being told that the ship was south of the zero latitude, Poseidon turned toward the bow and demanded that the candidates be brought forth. Zachary, Danny and the six other crewmen were led aft from the fo'c'sle, naked as jaybirds. Other veterans of the Southern Ocean heaved buckets of water on them. Poseidon made a declaration regarding the sacred properties of the southern waters. Fellow crewmen using dull razors shaved the heads and whiskers of each candidate. Poseidon anointed each candidate with a mixture of tar and molasses. Each candidate was given a foul mixture to drink. Danny and four of the other initiates dashed for the leeward rail and vomited out the foul mixture.

With the initiation complete, Poseidon deemed the candidates to be certified sailors of the Southern Ocean. Poseidon then turned to the poop deck and addressed the Captain. "Sir, I present to you these stout sailors of the Southern Ocean. With what shall we toast this noble crew?"

Israel knew that this request was coming and gestured to the cook who was also watching the ritual, "Cookie, double rum rations for all."

The crew cheered and the cook with a helper brought forth a keg of rum. That afternoon and evening there was not much work done on *Setauket* except for the crewman taking turns at the helm. The men partook of their added ration of rum, sang, danced and told stories of past voyages, of lovely women and past initiations. That night the course sailed may not have been as straight as normal, but other than that, all was well aboard the *Setauket*.

Within two weeks of making an average of 180 nautical miles a day, the breeze shifted westerly and was much cooler than the tropical airs that had been laid astern. Zachary continued to learn his trade. Israel taught him the rudiments of navigation starting with establishing a dead reckoning position and then to take a fix to verify the dead reckoning position. Israel explained methods for gaining the two or three lines-of-position required to establish a fix, by taking the lines-of-position from sighted objects along a coast. However, in the middle of the ocean celestial navigation was the only reliable means to fix the ship's position.

Zachary found celestial navigation to be almost magical and required the hardest math that he had ever faced. Zachary accompanied his Captain for the daily sun shots and late-night star shots. He took practice shots along with his uncle. Establishing the angle between a celestial body and the horizon while rolling on the deck of a moving ship was a major challenge. After the shots were taken, the calculation of the ship's position was daunting. With all of this precise activity, the sextant shots could be good, and the math correct, but if the ship's clock was not accurate the fix would be in error: one nautical mile for each minute of clock error.

Zachary learned his seamanship skills as a participating member of the crew. Even though Mr.

Bolton snarled and cursed, he was an accomplished sailor and imparted his knowledge on his watch with Zachary. Israel had also directed other crew members to aid in Zachary's instruction.

Mr. Stecker, the sailmaker on a small ship such as *Setauket*, was also the rigger, so he gave lessons on the construction and maintenance of the ship's many sails, standing rigging and running rigging.

The carpenter, Mr. Kimball explained the construction of the ship's hull and masts. He dragged Zachary from the bilge to the crosstrees of the mainmast showing him the intricacies of construction.

He gave lessons on how to construct a jury rig if the masts were damaged or partially lost overboard. He explained means of finding and plugging leaks if the ship was holed and taking water.

Kimball explained, "*Setauket* was rigged as a barque which meant that she has three masts: a fore, a main and a mizzen. She was built in 1785, on Long Island, with a stout New England oak keel and ribs and covered with pine planking."

In addition to Zachary's continuing education, he took it upon himself to teach Danny to read. He had come to greatly value Danny's friendship and recognized that his quick-witted companion had potential that had not been developed because of his rude upbringing.

CHAPTER 8

AROUND CAPE HORN

Now SOUTH OF thirty degrees southern latitude, the sea was a pallet of greens rather than the deep blues of the tropics. Now that *Setauket* had intruded into the higher latitudes, the color of the sea reflected the skies, which were overcast more days than not. The trade winds were replaced by light and fickle breezes. Progress was made in squalls and other periods when the breeze piped up enough to make way. The crew was busy doubling the hatch covers and re-securing the cargo, water casks and anything else that could come loose in the heavy weather that would soon be upon them.

Setauket entered the Roaring Forties with fore and main upper and lower topsails, jibs and staysails set. The winds were now from the west to west-southwest. Squalls became more frequent and more violent. The crew had to go aloft at least once every watch to either reef the sails as squalls approached or shake out previously reefed sails after the fast-moving storms had passed. The helm was now manned by two men to control the charging ship.

Israel had not rounded Cape Horn before, but in various sailors' pubs in several ports-of-call, he had heard all of the stories of the wild and treacherous seas at the bottom of the world. He had the best charts of the area he could procure and sought out what he could to study the oceans below fifty degrees south. He talked with whaler captains who had returned from trips to the Pacific. He and his ship were as prepared as they could be for the coming battle.

Setauket unceremoniously crossed fifty degrees south, the Furious Fifties. This marked the beginning of "Doubling the Horn" from fifty degrees in the Atlantic Ocean to fifty degrees in the Pacific Ocean. Gale force winds now blew from the southwest. *Setauket* proceeded south, sailing as close to the wind as she could. The waves continually broke over the bow sending salt spray most of the way to the poop deck. The spray coupled with the freezing rain and sleet ensured that no one on deck could stay dry for more than a few minutes. Since the decks were constantly awash crewmen did not move fore and aft without clinging to the lifelines that had been strung from the foredeck to the to the forward fife rail, from the forward fife rail to the fife rail at the main mast, to the steps to the aft deck.

The good news was that during this October rounding, it was spring in the southern hemisphere; the storms were not as violent as those of the southern winter that had just passed. Though none of *Setauket's* crew believed they were getting off easy, because they faced the meanest seas any of them had ever seen.

The most recent squall line had just passed; Zachary and his watch were aloft for the second time during this watch. The horizontal rain and sleet pelted them as they climbed the icy rigging.

Zachary thought to himself that he could not imagine being any colder. The only thing that provided any warmth was the strenuous activity. The glamour and adventure of voyaging had left him long ago; it was now just a matter of survival. A few stoic men struggling to keep their ship afloat, so that they might live to see a warmer and sunnier time and place.

Zachary had tied two ropes around his body in an attempt to hold his oilskin closed. One line was tightly under his armpits and the second around his waist. This worked better than his last attempt at rigging his oilskins to stay put, when he almost lost the flapping slicker as the wind tried to rip it from his body. He and the other crewmen wrapped scraps of cloth around their hands to make up for the lack of gloves. Mr. Bolton had directed his watch to change the cloth often, as a means of preventing frostbite.

Out on the footropes they loosed the reef in the upper main topsail to gain a bit more speed before the next line of storms forced them to reef the sail once more. The sturdy ship clawed its way southwest, fighting the wind and a two-knot current, which constantly attempted to push them from their intended course.

Though two of the whaling ship Captains who Israel had queried before the voyage suggested transiting the Horn via the Straits of Magellan, Israel was reluctant to be caught having to tack a square rigged ship into the wind in the sometimes narrow passage through the Straits. A square-rigged ship can only beat up to seventy degrees of the apparent wind; so, tacking back and forth into the wind made progress a long, slow process. Israel chose the longer route south of Tierra del Fuego allowing long tacks towards the Antarctic Ice cap. One of the whaling captains said that his ship had experienced a breeze from the east at sixty degrees south, to push them past the Horn. The danger with venturing to the sixty-degree latitude was the increased number of icebergs, which could rip the bottom out of a wooden ship. Israel did not want to challenge icebergs even with the promise of a favorable breeze, so he charted a course as close to the southern tip of South America as he could, considering the need to beat to the south to work to the west.

Setauket worked past Tierra del Fuego through the Strait of Le Maire leaving State Island to her lee. Now the ship could head west-south-west towards Wollaston Island. Depending on the wind and weather, Israel would make the decision whether to beat to the northwest around Wollaston and the other islands in the group and then beat southwest between the False Cape Horn and the islands, or take the still longer southern route around the islands past Cape Horn Island.

In the constant gale force winds tacking a square-rigged ship was no longer an option. Tacking involves changing course by heading up into the wind until the eye of the wind crosses the bow and then fills the sails on the opposite side of the ship. In light air or very heavy winds a square rigger cannot get its sails flat enough to maintain the momentum needed to bring the bow through the wind. In light air the ship merely gets stuck in irons, head on into the breeze. In heavy winds, the ship loses momentum as it approaches the eye of the wind and is blown back on to its previous tack.

The alternative to tacking through the wind is to wear ship, turning away from the wind until the eye of the wind passes the ship's stern then it continues turning until it is beating on the opposite tack.

This method is slower than tacking and requires the crew to constantly adjust the sails as the ship goes from a beat, into a reach, then a run before the wind passes astern, at which time it moves through a reach and back to a beat on the opposite heading.

After ten days of working into the winds and seas, some days only making twenty miles westering, *Setauket* had progressed to a position northwest of Wollaston Island and the order was given to wear ship to the southwest. The storm and associated heavy waves came at four bells in the middle of an already black and stormy night. It gusted to hurricane force winds pushing huge waves. The first wave pushed *Setauket's* bow over, the ship heeled over on its Larboard side, as the wind held it in a 35- degree heel and continued to push the bow off the wind. With its Larboard beam parallel to the waves Setauket broached, the next wave broke over its beam pushing the heel to 45 degrees.

The two helmsmen were thrown from the wheel by the force of the violent encounter. The leeward helmsman was knocked off his feet and slid on the canted deck until the Larboard rail stopped him from sliding overboard. Mr. Bolton acting as the windward helmsman fell off his feet and lodged against the wheel's housing, the wheel itself spun six inches from his head. Bolton crawled up the side of the wheel box and grabbed the wheel, which was now hard over.

Bolton hollered to the other dazed helmsman, "Get your ass up here or we'll all be goners."

The helmsman crawled up the deck until he could get his feet under him at the windward side of the wheel. Israel was rounded out of his bunk by the incident and also crawled across the poop deck to the wheel. The three men struggled to straighten the wheel, as succeeding waves broke over the starboard beam. The ship continued to list 30 to 35 degrees and roll to 45 degrees as each wave hit its side, but it did not roll any farther.

Israel shouted above the howling wind, "Hold 'er steady lads, we can't bring 'er up into this wind."

Israel saw that the first gust had sprung and split the main upper topsail yard. The windward half of the yard had split at the mast and was swinging wildly from a tangle of sheets, buntlines and remnants of the topsail that had been blown out and shredded by the incident. The jib, fore staysail and foretopsail were still holding together. If *Setauket* could continue to bear off the wind without plowing into a leeward wave and capsizing, it could be saved.

The off watch had crawled out of the fo'c'sle onto the deck without being called. The crewmen clawed their way to the windward side of the deck and hung on to anything that would hold them. The crew waited for orders, either they would be ordered into action to save the ship or they would meet their Maker in this cold desolate sea.

After ten minutes holding in its heeled position, which felt like an hour, the winds abated a bit and the gusts dropped below seventy knots. Israel saw the opportunity for which he had hoped. As *Setauket's* bow began to rise up on a wave that had just slammed into the starboard side, Israel gave the order, "Hard over lads, and pray."

The wave lifted and turned the bow. *Setauket* responded by rolling up towards an even keel. The next wave struck *Setauket* abaft the beam. When the maneuver was complete, *Setauket* was back under the control of its crew, running before the storm. The heading was now to the northeast, away from the False Cape Horn and back toward the north end of Wollaston Island. The crew cheered at their deliverance from disaster.

Even though James Grant was a hard case, he was a good seaman. Seeing the split spar swinging in the wind, as soon as the ship was on an even keel, he sprang into the rigging to secure it, though he had not thought about how he would do so once he was in the rigging.

Israel, still shouting over the scream of the wind in the rigging, gave his commands. "Mr.

Nimmo, have the Larboard watch, man the pumps and secure anything that has gone adrift. Mr. Bolton, do a damage assessment and head count." Gesturing toward the swinging main upper topsail yard he ordered, "Bolton secure that yard." Israel turned to go below, "I'll get my breeches and oilskins now."

The Starboard Watch had been huddled under the protection of the windward rail below the poop deck when the storm hit. Bolton stepped forward from the wheel to give his orders. Danny had heard Israel's orders and when Bolton looked in his direction, Danny sprang up before Bolton's verbal command could be given.

Grabbing the collar of Zachary's oilskin Danny prompted him to action. "Come on Zach, we have work."

The high winds caused the broken half of the topsail yard to swing out forward of the mainmast where it would catch momentarily on rigging lines that ran between the main and fore masts. When the bow of the ship would pitch up as waves of the now following sea passed under the hull, the broken piece fell back so that its lower jagged end, which was three feet below the main yard, swung aft crashing against the mast. This wicked pendulum had to be secured before it began tearing out standing rigging and brought down an already stressed mast.

Danny grabbed a line as they went forward to the shrouds and tied a large bowline in one end.

They scrambled up the shrouds, slipping through the lubber hole this time, so that the mast was between them and the pendulum. No one would question their seamanship this day.

Grant was already on the platform when Danny and Zachary arrived. He was leaning forward, attempting to grab the lines attached to the spar. As Grant grabbed a line, the ships' bow plunged down a wave causing the spar to swing forward pulling him with it. Danny reached out grabbing the back of Grant's breeches. The movement pulled Danny after Grant; Zachary grabbed Danny around the waste, dug his heels against the platform, and held on. The lines ripped Grant's right hand and swung away from him. As the bow rose on the next wave the three fell backwards on the platform.

Seeing Grant's bleeding hand Danny shouted, "Sit here until we've secured the spar!"

"Zach, up to the lower topsail yard and see if you can control this whore!" Danny directed as the broken piece again crashed against the mast.

Zachary proceeded up the starboard shrouds to the upper half of the lower topsail yard. As he climbed, he kept one eye on the swinging pendulum, in case it tried to get him. The ship's bow pitched up and rolled to starboard, the upper topsail yard end swung toward Zachary. He hung on to the aft side of the shrouds as the pendulum struck the leading edge of the shrouds shuddering the rigging. Zachary could not hear Israel cursing the helmsmen to keep the seas dead astern.

Wedging his body against the mast with his feet against the lower topsail yard, Zachary grabbed the lines to the broken yard. Danny tried to slip the loop of his bowline under the spar as it came back but missed it. As the pendulum swung forward the force almost pulled Zachary off his perch and over the top of the remaining yard. He was forced to let go of the lines.

Danny hollered up to Zachary, "Watch it lad. Next time we're goin' a get the bitch."

The second attempt worked. As the broken piece swung back against the mast, Zachary grabbed enough lines to dampen the swing. Danny slipped his bowline under the jagged end of the spar and got a wrap on the mast before the ship's bow began to pitch down the next wave.

After the broken spar was secured, other crew came up to assist Zachary and Danny. Zachary cut away the tangled lines and his mates lowered the piece of the yard to the deck and assisted Grant down the shrouds. Zachary then cut away the shredded pieces of the main topsail.

When the men returned to the deck Israel summoned them aft. "Well done Lads. Will the remaining yard stay put until we can find some shelter?"

Zachary responded, "Aye sir, she is still secure."

Grant came aft with a rag wrapped around his right hand. He reached out his left hand to Danny, "Thank you lads, you saved my hide."

Danny grasped the outstretched hand and replied, "You'd have done the same for me. That's what shipmates are for." This incident ended the feud between Danny and Grant. Though they would never be friends, they maintained a mutual respect from that point on, knowing for sure that each could depend on the other.

Setauket proceeded on a northeast heading until it could turn south and anchor in the lee of Wollaston Island. Israel knew that his ship and its crew had been pushed to their breaking points and he would need to rest and repair both before they could again challenge the Horn.

The *Setauket* rode at anchor for three days while the crew repaired their wounded ship. The remaining half of the main topsail yard was lowered to the deck. The two jagged ends were pushed back together, and a splint was lashed with whippings on either side of the break. The yard was lifted back in place and the rigging that had been affected by the incident was repaired or replaced. Israel ordered that all standing and running rigging be inspected and repaired as required.

On the gray morning of the fourth day the storms subsided the wind still came from the west but was reduced to thirty knots. All tools and materials from the repair work were secured and the anchor weighed. This time Israel would attempt the rounding by heading south of Wollaston Island transiting "Drake's Passage."

As *Setauket* worked its way to the southwest the lookouts were doubled to hopefully spot icebergs before the ship could collide with one and be splintered. As the ice flows became more and more numerous, no one snoozed while on lookout duty.

After two days *Setauket* had made seventy miles westering and then the wind died. Israel was fit to be tied. No one had told him that a ship could be becalmed in the Southern Ocean; this was the sea of big winds as they had been fighting for the last few weeks. The ship was now west of the Horn, but the two-knot current was now pushing *Setauket* back east.

If this kept up too long the ship would be pushed back east of the Horn, but the sea gods looked favorably on *Setauket* and after eight hours of drifting to the east a breeze began to build from the east. The east wind grew to twenty knots with higher gusts. Israel ordered up all the sails he dared. This was the chance to be done with the Cape.

For the next fifteen hours *Setauket* charged into the waves, which were made steeper by the east wind pushing against the opposing current. The waves had slowed progress, but one hundred miles progress to the west had been made. Israel was able to get sun shots with his sextant and establish a fix comfortably west of Diego Ramirez Island, the last landmass that could endanger their route.

Israel wanted to gain as much advantage from the fortunate east wind as possible. He gave the order to head to the northwest. The yards were hauled to a reach. Israel saw the mare's tails in the sky to the west which foretold a new storm approaching from the west.

Two hours later the east wind died, and *Setauket* was again becalmed. Israel knew what was coming next. He ordered the yards to be hauled from a starboard tack to a Larboard tack, and sails shortened. For another two hours *Setauket* rolled in the seas becalmed Night had fallen so the approaching storms could no longer be seen, but the seamen could feel its approach in their bones with the falling of the barometer.

The wind first reached the top of the masts, causing a howl in the rigging then the first full gust and associated large wave hit *Setauket's* Larboard beam. The gust did not heel the ship as much as push it sideways down the side of the wave. The two helmsmen immediately came to life and turned the Larboard bow into the seas. *Setauket* charged forward, under reefed topsails and stays. She could now make her northwest heading and do so at eight knots.

The storm blew steadily for two days allowing *Setauket* to make its passage from 56 degrees south, 73 degrees west to 50 degrees south in less than forty-eight hours. The doubling of Cape Horn was complete. The expanse of the Pacific Ocean was now before them.

CHAPTER 9

FAIR AMERICAN

SETAUKET MADE ITS way north, staying outside of Spanish territorial waters along the coast of South America. It was understood that the Spanish who had colonized this part of the world in the 1500s had restrictions on trading with foreigners and that their navy was less than hospitable to foreign vessels. Ever since Frances Drake rounded Cape Horn over two hundred years earlier, to pirate gold from unsuspecting Spanish ships and cities, the Spanish were wary of foreign vessels, especially English-speaking foreign vessels. The Spanish government had passed laws restricting trade with foreigners just to protect their own businesses from the competition. Also, in Catholic New Spain, Protestants were not particularly welcome. Captain Israel Redden and his ship met all of the criteria for not being welcome in South American waters.

Israel ventured into the major Spanish ports of Valparaiso and Lima, but was not allowed to trade, though the Spanish authorities were happy to have the gringos spend their scarce gold and silver in Spanish ports. Israel paid for water and minimal supplies and decided to continue north until he found a port, be it Spanish or not, that was willing to trade for his goods.

Because of Spanish restrictions on trading with foreigners, three ships had rounded the Horn to trade along the coast of the Americas: *Eleanora, Fair American* and *Setauket*. None were allowed to do business farther south. All three ships made calls at Valparaiso and Lima but were not allowed to trade. The captains of the *Eleanora* and *Fair American* also made the decision to venture farther north from the long-established cities of New Spain to the outposts along the coast of North America. They speculated that less visited towns would be in more need of their goods and therefore more willing to trade with foreign ships, in spite of the restrictions imposed by their mother country. After being rebuffed at South American ports, Israel made the same decision.

Already working the hide trade along the coast of California was the square-rigger *Eleanora* commanded by Captain Simon Metcalfe and the Schooner *Fair American* commanded by Thomas Metcalfe, Simon Metcalfe's son. In early December 1789, *Eleanora* and *Fair American* rendezvoused at San Diego in Alta California, a town that had grown up around the mission that had been established fifteen years earlier. The Metcalfe's had traded with the local Indians and Spanish inhabitants for almost a year prior to *Setauket's* arrival. The senior Metcalfe decided that this would be an appropriate place to trade and re-provision his ships for an offshore voyage. Metcalfe had decided rather than continue up the coast of the Americas, they would head west, for he had heard of a few ships that had done some profitable trading in the Sandwich Islands. Metcalfe figured that any place that was not frequented by many trading ships should be ready to pay a premium for anything they could get, and Metcalfe was always ready to charge a premium wherever he could.

Metcalfe informed his son of the plan and bid him to keep it to himself until they departed; for it was none of the crew's business and he did not want any other trading ships that might happen upon them to get the same idea. He told Thomas to fill all the water kegs and procure what supplies he could, for a voyage that would last three to four weeks depending on the weather.

In December 1789 *Setauket* rounded the point of land that marked the entrance to San Diego harbor. The harbor was actually a river entrance. The row of hills to the west provided a snug harbor, however the entrance was narrow, and a sharp eye was kept while entering. Two other ships were already anchored in the harbor. *Setauket* rounded up and the order was given to drop anchor.

Metcalfe was not wrong about other trading ships. Within days of arriving at San Diego, Setauket anchored in the harbor upwind of Metcalfe's ships. The only other ship in the harbor was a Spanish warship, the *Casa del Huelva*. The crews of the three merchant ships had been at sea for several months and were itching to go ashore and search for local sources of debauchery. The crews of the *Eleanora* and *Fair American* had been ashore, drinking, whoring and generally carrying on. Several of the crew had been thrown into the local jail, which was manned by a small Spanish army contingent.

Before the crew of the *Setauket* could go ashore, Israel was obligated to present himself and the ship's papers to the local authorities. Soon after the sun rose above the coastal range, Israel dressed in his best uniform and was rowed ashore in a longboat. The rowing crew had been cleaned up as much as possible to make a suitable impression on the locals. In the stern of the longboat sat Israel and Mr. Bolton, who spoke enough Spanish to act as the interpreter.

The town could not be seen from the anchorage. Despite this after Israel and Bolton were rowed to the beach; they were approached by a small dark-complexioned man. He offered to rent them horses. The deal made, Israel and Bolton rode over the rise and about a mile to the small village.

Under Spanish rule the area that would someday become California was divided into four districts: San Diego, Santa Barbara, Monterey and San Francisco. The Governor resided at the territorial capital of Monterey. Each district was administered by a commissioner or "*alcalde*" and an elected town council, the "*ayuntamiento*".

The local Commissioner at San Diego was not at all pleased with the prospect of three foreign ships full of rowdy sailors in the harbor at one time. He valued the revenue that visiting ships brought to the meager local economy: from trading for hides, as well as money spent on wine and women. Also, the government generated revenue when visiting skippers had to pay harbor fees and later pay fines required to get crew members out of jail. Of equal value were the trade goods that these merchant ships brought to this remote outpost. What was unnerving was to have three ships in the harbor at once. This had never happened before, and he was afraid that the band of rabble would ravage the town.

Israel and Bolton were ushered into the Commissioner's office. *Senor* Emmanuelle was seated behind a large redwood table that served as his desk. On one side of the Commissioner stood Major Castile, the commander of the local presidio and on the other side stood Captain Garcia, Commander of the *Casa del Huelva*.

Israel and Bolton stood before the Commissioner's desk stiffly, but not quite at attention, to show that they were not true military men. Israel nodded to the two military men and handed the ship's paper to the Commissioner. *Senor* Emmanuelle said nothing but opened the papers and read it for a full five minutes.

The Commissioner finally broke the silence, "Please be seated gentlemen."

The four uniformed men took chairs, the two Spanish officers still flanking the Commissioner and the two Americans seated in front of the desk.

The Commissioner went on, "Captain Redden, your papers seem to be in order." He handed them across the table. "What brings you to our little town?"

Israel was pleased that the Commissioner spoke English much better than Bolton spoke Spanish.

Not having to communicate through an interpreter would hasten the proceedings.

"*Senor*, Commissioner, we come to re-provision our ship and to trade for local goods." Israel addressed the Commissioner directly but cast a glance at the two officers flanking him. "We bring many fine goods from the eastern United States to trade for hides and furs."

"Very good Captain, we welcome you and your crew to our town." *Senor* Emmanuelle motioned toward the windows and went on. "However, we would ask that your ship's company not abuse our hospitality. We have already been forced to lock up crewmembers from the other two ships in the harbor. We do not want to have any more incidents." He motioned towards the two military officers. "If the situation should become unruly, I will be forced to have Captain

Garcia and Major Castile rectify the situation and use whatever means is required to restore order."

Israel nodded his understanding.

The Commissioner rose from his seat, as did Garcia and Castile. "With that understanding Captain Redden; enjoy your stay in *San Diego De Alcala.*"

Israel and Bolton stood, shook the extended hands of the three Spanish officials and departed the Commissioner's office.

On the way back to the *Setauket*, Bolton made his observation on the audience with the Commissioner. "Captain, those two Spanish laggards Garcia and Castile, looked like they'd have just as soon slit our throats and taken our ship as looked at us."

"True Mr. Bolton," Israel replied, "But it is in the Commissioner's best interest to promote trade with visiting ships, so he will keep his enforcers under his control." Israel stroked his chin, "However, it is best that we be on our best behavior."

The two young seamen back on ship were excited at the prospect of getting to go ashore for the first time in months. Danny was talkative as always. "Zach me boy, there are women of pleasure in every port where a ship can drop its anchor, and I'll be goin' to find me some." He went on, "Stick with me lad and me will get us both get one."

When Israel and Bolton returned to the *Setauket*, Israel went straight to the poop deck while Bolton called all hands on deck. Within three minutes the ship's company was assembled before the poop deck. They were jovial and boisterous in anticipation of their upcoming time ashore.

"Quiet down you buggers." Growled Bolton, "Pay attention."

As the group quieted, Israel addressed them. " Lads it seems that the local officials are in no mood for a lot of shenanigans, they have already thrown crew from the other ships in harbor into their brig and appear to be eager to add to that number." Gesturing toward the shore he continued, "I know that you men are eager to go ashore and kick up your heels, but you need to be on your good behavior or you may end up rotting in the Spaniards' jail."

"The crew will take shore liberty by watch." Taking a coin from his vest pocket, Israel flipped it in the air and caught it, then slapping it on to the back of his left hand he directed, "Mr. Nimmo call it."

"Heads, Sir."

Israel looked under his right hand, "It is tails. Mr. Bolton's Starboard Watch will go ashore first.

Mr. Bolton have them back on ship by 20:00 hours so that the Larboard Watch may go ashore."

From the crew's prospective both shore visits were a mixed blessing. The crew was of course eager to go ashore; so, the first watch ashore had that advantage. But it was always easier to pursue debauchery in the dark of the night, than in the heat of the day, so that honor went to the Larboard Watch.

Both longboats had been lowered to haul the crew to shore. The first longboat was crewed by the Starboard Watch and headed to shore with Bolton in its stern. The second longboat was rowed by members of the Larboard Watch and would convey Israel and the remaining members of the Starboard Watch ashore. Israel was intent on beginning trade talks with the locals. Mr. Nimmo would lead his men to fill the water kegs and return them to the ship.

"Zach hurry up into the first boat," Danny implored, "time's a wastin'."

Once on shore it did not take long for the crew to find the cantina. The Small adobe structure was stucco inside and out with a low thatch roof and dirt floor. A couple of industrious chickens pecked around the floor for refuse left by prior patrons of the establishment.

The Starboard Watch was seated on benches at a couple of long tables. Much to their chagrin, the establishment had no rum, but only a rugged form of whiskey and the local wine, which was made by the Indians, as taught by the missionaries.

"We had better go at this slowly, my boy," proclaimed Danny, the self-appointed tour guide. "We'll try the local wine and take it from there."

Not long after the arrival of the Starboard Watch from the *Setauket,* the cantina began to fill with crewmen from the *Eleanora* and *Fair American*. Soon after the arrival of crews from the three American merchant ships, crewmen arrived from the Spanish warship. The cantina was now filled to overflowing with drinking, singing, and boisterous sailors.

After three mugs of the local wine, one of the crew suggested that Danny and Zachary belly up for shots of whiskey. This sounded like a better idea to the lads than it might have earlier in the day.

Danny had been watching other seamen disappear out of the cantina and was sure where they were going. After the shot of whiskey began to take effect, Danny slapped Zachary on the back. "Come on lad, we need to do our deed before our lizards go limp."

Danny took Zachary by the arm and led him out of the cantina and behind the building. In front of them were four dusty tents and a number of sailors milling around more or less standing in line. The sailors were joking and drinking and carrying on.

Zachary was having an approach/avoidance feeling about the upcoming experience. He had often fantasized about making love to Lizzie and other attractive women he met, but this was a far cry from that idyllic fantasy. This was as the sailors would say pure fucking. This was merely dipping your wick without so much as a please or a thank you. But he had never done this before, and like all young men he was ready for his first sexual experience. Also, what would the other lads think if he chickened out? As the whiskey helped make the decision, Zachary thought, "What the hell, I can always do it for love someday, this is for fun."

At the head of the line of sailors was an old stoop-shouldered woman. She looked to be of the local Indian clan that Zachary had seen around the town. As Zachary arrived at the head of the line, Danny announced he should give the old woman money and she then directed him to the third tent in the line, one from which a sailor had departed only five minutes before.

Zachary staggered forward, threw back the tent flap and entered the tent. Before him was a cot, a small table with a single candle standing ready for the evening's business, and a three-legged stool containing a rumpled towel. Next to the stool were a washbasin and a pitcher of water, which were used to wash away the sweat and other bodily fluids left behind by the previous customer. On the cot sat a dark-complexioned girl of about twenty years, she was draped in a rumpled and stained sheet, the establishment's idea of a touch of intrigue. The girl dropped the sheet from her shoulders revealing diminutive tan breasts, a lean waste and black pubic hair that matched the long dark hair on her head.

She lay back on the cot motioning for Zachary to join her.

Zachary now stumbled around the tent trying to remove his breeches. Between the hurry caused by his arousal, the effects of the whiskey and wine, and the lack of anything solid to hang on to; he finally fell backwards onto the dirt floor. He kicked off his breeches and flopped on top of the young lady. Not only did he expect that he should arouse his female cohort, but the effects of the whiskey had delayed his penis from becoming fully erect. He gave the girl a long wet kiss as his opening act of foreplay. Before he could continue any additional foreplay, the girl grasped his penis and inserted it in her waiting vagina, this was business and there was no time to waste on the preliminaries. Having a female hand on his member caused immediate erection and her rocking motion caused Zachary's similar response. Notwithstanding the whiskey, Zachary came to climax within two minutes of insertion.

Zachary's first real sexual experience was over. He immediately felt remorse, for having experienced it in such a tasteless setting. He snatched up his breeches from the floor and put them on. He departed the tent without a word, thinking in his stupor that the entire affair had taken place without a word spoken.

Zachary reentered the cantina and was passing the tables containing the crew from the *Fair American* when a fight broke out. It is hard to tell what started the fight. One of the Yankee sailors making fun of the Spanish sailors' uniforms or somebody questioned the occupation of someone else's mother. Whatever caused it, it was on. The crew of the *Fair American* got up from their tables and charged the oncoming Spaniards. One of the Spanish sailors was pushed against Zachary who pushed him back into the fray. The Spanish sailor reacted with a wild swing with a backhand to Zachary's head. He missed, which left him completely open, so Zachary punched him squarely on the chin, causing him to fly backwards onto the floor.

Two of the *Setauket* crew stood up to join the fray. What was a good liberty ashore without a friendly fight? Bolton grabbed each of them by a wrist. "Not this time boys. It's time to get out of here before it gets ugly."

As Bolton hustled his crew out the front door of the cantina, the brawl was being pushed out the side door and into the sailors, both Spanish and American, who were waiting in line at the tents. These waiting sailors noted the sides taken in the brawl. Each chose an appropriate adversary and also joined in the fray.

Danny had just finished his deed in the third tent when a sailor crashed against the back of the tent knocking down the rear pole and collapsing half the tent. The girl that he had just dismounted, screamed, clutched the sheet to her midsection and ran from the tent. Danny grabbed his breeches and exited behind her. Danny had never been one to pass up a good fight, but even in his drunken state, he decided that entering the brawl with his nuts swinging in the breeze, was not a good thing to do. He hastened around to the far side of the cantina.

Fearing just such an outbreak from the visiting sailors, the Commissioner had directed Major Castile to station troops near the cantina to quell any riotous behavior. Now, if his fears came true, his investment in the cantina and brothel would be depreciated by the foreign hooligans. Seeing the fight burst out of the cantina's side door, the Sergeant assembled his squad and hurried to break-up the brawl with muskets loaded and bayonets fixed.

Bolton saw the approaching troops coming down the hill toward the cantina. He also saw Danny, breeches in hand, skirting the side of the building. Bolton motioned to Danny to join them. He then hustled his crew down to the longboats.

Though the crew of the *Eleanora* tried to join their brethren from the *Fair American* in the fight, their First Mate took the same action as Bolton and forced them to retreat. He had to pay to get some of his crew out of jail earlier in the week and was not about to have it happen again.

A squad of ten soldiers arrived on the scene and began swinging their musket butts into the fray. The fight went on, the soldiers merely adding to the confusion, until the Sergeant fired his pistol into the air. Everyone stopped. There was a brief moment of pure silence. Then the Sergeant growled at the Spanish sailors. All of them stumbled up against the cantina wall and fell into a rough formation. At the same time the soldiers pushed the Yankee sailors into a mass in the middle of the dusty street.

The Sergeant ordered the Spanish sailors to march up the hill toward the garrison. His soldiers pushed and prodded Zachary and the other Yankees up the hill.

Inside the garrison the two adversarial groups were placed in separate large cells to sleep off the effects of the spirits. Zachary crumpled in a corner and fell asleep.

Israel was coming from a meeting with a local rancher when he saw the fray at the cantina and Bolton ushering his crew out of the village. He hastened to join them.

"Good job avoiding that mess, Mr. Bolton." Israel then looked over his disheveled crew. "Mr.

O'Brien, please put on your breeches."

Danny blushed and responded, "Aye Sir." He shook out his pants and slipped them on. Israel noticed his missing nephew. "Where is Zachary?" He asked.

Danny replied, "I think I saw him in the fight, Sir."

Bolton added, "I fear the dagos have taken him to the brig, Sir."

Simon and Thomas Metcalfe had come ashore and were entering the village when they saw members of the *Eleanora's* crew assembled in a group outside of the cantina. They proceeded to query their crew.

Commissioner Emmanuelle viewed the fight and actions of his troops from the safety of his office window. Now that peace was restored, he was free to leave his residence and assess the damage. He headed down the hill with Captain Garcia close behind him. As he passed the cantina, he observed the collapsed tents out back and he could see broken furniture inside the cantina. His investments had suffered this day and he was not at all pleased.

The Commissioner continued to the two Captains. Seeing Israel, he motioned for him to join them. Israel strode over to join the group. He gave a nod to the other two Captains and turned toward the Commissioner and Captain Garcia.

"Your people have overstayed their welcome," bellowed Emmanuelle. "I want all of your ships out of my harbor immediately."

Thomas Metcalfe, seeing that his crew was not among the assemblage on the dock protested. "Sir, I believe that you have my crew in your brig."

Emmanuelle responded, "Fine, when you have paid for the damages and fines, you can have your crew back." He waved toward Israel and the elder Metcalfe. "In the meantime, you two will exit my harbor immediately."

Israel, thinking of his lost nephew protested, "*Senor* Emmanuelle" The Commissioner cut him off. "Silence," he shouted.

Emmanuelle turned to the Spanish Captain. "Captain Garcia if these two ships have not weighed anchor within the next three hours, you may consider taking them as your prizes."

The Commissioner turned and marched back up the hill with Captain Garcia still in tow. "Your Excellency, do you really mean what you said?"

Emmanuelle responded, "No Captain, that would be bad for long term business, but the Gringo captains do not know it."

"To the ship men," Israel ordered. We will comply with the Commissioner's order."

At *Setauket*, the Starboard Watch scurried on to the deck. The remainder of the Larboard Watch that had not been manning the longboats was assembled on deck, eager to go ashore. Upon reaching the deck Israel gave the order, "Weigh anchor lads."

Nimmo stood his ground. "What about the liberty ashore, Sir."

Israel replied, "Not now Mr. Nimmo, we must load the water casks and weigh anchor."

Within an hour and forty-five minutes of returning to the ship, *Setauket* was headed to sea into the dark night. The *Eleanora* not having to stow water casks was an hour ahead of *Setauket*.

After the sails had been set and the activity on deck was concluded, Bolton approached his Captain. "What are you going to do about Zachary, Sir?"

Israel replied, "It is a bit of a gamble, but the other ships are trading along the coast, as are we. We'll head north along the coast to the next settlement and await their arrival, then retrieve Zachary."

As the sun brightened the cell, Zachary awoke. His head was pounding from the previous day's mixture of wine and whiskey. His mouth tasted like a pickle. The smell of urine and vomit in the cell turned his stomach, but he swallowed hard and did not lose its contents.

Looking around the cell Zachary saw a number of sailors in various states of drunken stupor. Standing on wobbly legs he looked through the barred window at the harbor. He shook his head in disbelief. What had happened? How long had he been in this jail? There were only two ships in the harbor, and neither were the *Setauket*. Zachary crumpled to the floor to contemplate his situation.

Before Zachary could contemplate too long, a wrinkled stoop-shouldered jailer appeared flanked by four soldiers. Opening the cell door, he growled, "Out of here you swine."

The sailors rose, each in his own painful manner. Grumbling a mixture of oaths at the jailor, they departed the cell and were escorted out into the sunlight. Having paid the fines to have his crew released, Thomas Metcalfe awaited them outside the garrison.

Thomas addressed the assembled crew, "Well lads you did it this time. The authorities have thrown the lot of us out of their town. We must depart as soon as possible."

Zachary stepped forward. "Excuse me Sir, but I am from the *Setauket*."

Thomas stared at the new face a moment. "I have just spent a tidy sum to get you released from the brig, you are mine now." Thomas turned and walked away.

Zachary began to follow him. "But Sir."

Isaac Davis grasped Zachary by the arm and stopped him. "Face it sailor, you are now in the crew of the *Fair American*."

While in San Diego, Israel had learned of the other missions and villages north along the coast. He planned to continue trading at San Juan Capistrano, San Gabriel Arcangel and so on heading north along the California coast until he reached the northernmost mission town of San Francisco De Assisi. As Israel had planned, the *Setauket* made port near San Juan Capistrano within forty-eight hours of leaving San Diego despite fighting adverse winds and current. The local officials were courteous and the trading brisk since they were the first trading ship to arrive in some months. But other than that, the plan did not work. Neither *Eleanora* nor *Fair American* arrived at this port. Israel considered the alternatives, the two ships could have bypassed this port, or maybe they had completed their trading expedition and headed south around the Horn and home. What would he tell Jessica? He had lost Zachary and had no means to find him.

Israel had no clue that the Metcalfe's had already filled their holds with hides and were bound south and home. The Metcalfe's planned to head west out into the Pacific to take on provisions and do some trading in the Sandwich Islands and not up the coast of California. *Setauket* had lost contact with *Eleanora* soon after departing San Diego harbor, for they had headed north, and *Eleanora* took a south- southwesterly heading.

Upon departing San Diego harbor, Thomas Metcalfe followed his father's instructions and also set a south-southwesterly course. They would either overtake *Eleanora* at sea or rendezvous somewhere in the Sandwich Islands. Since the crew could tell by the heading that they were not continuing along the coast, Metcalfe assembled the crew and advised them of the destination.

Zachary was shocked: a destination somewhere in the Pacific, which he had never heard. He thought that he would never find the *Setauket* or a way home. He was lost and could not be found.

Fair American did not overtake *Eleanora* at sea. In any type of reach or beat the schooner would have sailed faster and pointed higher than the square rigged *Eleanora but* running before the Tradewinds the square rigger was at the advantage and actually increased her lead by two days during the passage to Hawaii.

Because of the small crew needed to sail a schooner, Thomas Metcalfe was not only the Captain and navigator, but also stood the Larboard Watch. Isaac Davis was the only Mate and he therefore was in charge of the Starboard Watch.

Davis was in charge of educating the new crewman to the layout of *Fair American*. "A schooner is rigged simpler than a square-rigged ship so it needs less of a crew, but that also means that every one of you buggers have to know more jobs." He growled, "Listen up you bastard, cause I'm only goin' to explain this once. The Pinrails are set up standard on schooners, taking the aft most belaying pin on the Main Pinrail and moving forward is the Boom topping Lift, then the Gaff Peak Halyard, then the Gaff Throat Halyard, the Gaff Topsail Outhaul, the Gaff Topsail Tack and the Gaff Topsail Downhaul. You got that?"

Zachary, "Aye sir."

"Good, see that you remember it." Davis then explained the forward pinrail and other specifics of the ship. Though as gruff as a mate should be, Zachary sensed a fair and honest man without the basic abusive nature of the Captain.

Zachary was assigned to be the third man on Metcalfe's Larboard Watch, which turned out to be a mixed blessing. Both Metcalfe and Davis ruled with a harsh hand, kicking and punching crewmembers they felt were not moving with the required dispatch. Thomas Metcalfe had learned his trade from his Father Simon who was known as a harsh and ruthless skipper. Thomas emulated his Father in many ways, so being on the Larboard Watch meant more physical abuse than warranted, and more than Zachary would have experienced on the other watch. Thomas believed in intimidating new crewmen to ensure that they would snap to and obey orders. He therefore made sure that he backhanded Zachary a few times and cursed him for being too slow or not paying attention. This was all part of the normal indoctrination on a Metcalfe ship.

Zachary was young and strong and after being kicked and punched for not moving quickly enough to satisfy Metcalfe, he learned to move at the first command and also to stay out of Metcalfe's reach whenever possible. The only good part of being on the Larboard Watch was that Metcalfe was no fool; he realized within the first two days that Zachary was not the normal barnacle that is usually shanghaied or otherwise acquired in strange seaports. It became obvious that Zachary had learned seamanship well and had the makings of an officer. Having decided that Zachary had talent, though he was not about to make Zachary the Second Mate, having Zachary on his watch allowed Metcalfe to leave the deck more often when Zachary was on watch. Though Zachary felt abused by the Captain, Metcalfe felt that he had better treat Zachary with a bit less severity and build some loyalty from the youth so that he could continue to rely on him.

CHAPTER 10

HAWAII

Late in January 1790, *Eleanora* made landfall and anchored at Honua'ula on Maui. Simon Metcalfe had dealt with the Indians along the coast of the Americas and although he had a strong distaste for all peoples that he considered savages, he found that they would pay dearly for manufactured goods, which meant that he could cut some good and profitable deals. Metcalfe was weary of the inhabitants of these islands. The people were on average huge, almost giants compared to the average Yankee sailor, and they looked fierce with tattooed bodies and faces, and many warriors carried spears, daggers and war clubs.

Though Metcalfe was weary he was here to trade. At a minimum the *Eleanora* needed water and provisions. The local chiefs visited Metcalfe's ship upon its arrival and immediately offered water and provisions, including hogs, in exchange for weapons. Metcalfe was definitely not opposed to giving weapons to the native people. These chiefs had seen *Haole* ships before and it was obvious to Metcalfe that they knew what they wanted; now he would see what they had to trade for these goods.

As soon as the *Alii* chiefs left the *Eleanora* some of the local girls swam or paddled boards and canoes out to the ship much to the pleasure of the crew. For the next two days the off watch frolicked in their bunks with the willing consorts.

Metcalf was taking no chances. He armed the anchor watch and always took an armed escort with him when venturing ashore to trade.

Metcalfe was right in staying alert, for the Hawaiians had lost the awe and respect they had first exhibited toward Captain Cook. They wanted the white man's metal items particularly firearms and would do whatever they had to, to get them. There had been recent incidents of attacks on shore parties from visiting ships to gain their weapons.

The trouble began during *Eleanora's* third night at Honua'ula. A perpetrator had swum out to the ship; climbed into a longboat and slit the throat of the crewman who was guarding the boat. He then cut loose a longboat and paddled it to shore. The missing boat and crewman were discovered at sunup with the change of the watch and the Captain was informed.

Metcalfe was irate, "Get all those heathen whores off my ship," He bellowed.

Crewmen dragged the mostly naked women on deck and pushed them over the side, some crew did so with great relish; others were quite reluctant to lose their willing companions.

Later that morning Metcalfe and crew fired at a canoe wounding and killing a few Hawaiians.

Later they caught a local man swimming under the *Eleanora*. Metcalfe was intent on hanging the culprit from a yard as an example, but his mates dissuaded him for fear of a general uprising and attack by the local warriors. Metcalfe released the swimmer but exacted his lesson by firing cannons onto the village and setting a number of huts on fire. It was certain that there would be no further business in *Honuaula*, so Metcalfe gave the order to weigh anchor. He would move further along the coast to complete watering and provisioning his ship.

Metcalfe anchored off of *Olowalu* and the local chiefs came out in canoes to parley. News of Metcalfe's actions at Honua'ula had spread up and down the coast; so, the local chiefs came aboard fully armed and flanked by several warriors. Metcalfe was reluctant to allow this armed force on his deck but kept several crewmen at the ready with muskets and pistols, in case the situation became ugly.

The chief offered to return the stolen boat and crewman in return for a musket, ammunition and some iron. Metcalfe agreed to the deal, but later in the day, emissaries of the chief returned with a burnt piece of the longboat's keel and two thigh bones. This time it was Metcalfe's officers who wanted to hang the emissaries, but this time Metcalfe released the locals in favor of a better plan.

That afternoon a number of trading canoes approached the *Eleanora*. Metcalfe had his crew prepared for the "savages". When the canoes drew close, the gun ports were lowered and the cannons, which had been loaded with grapeshot, nails and other bits of metal, sprayed the canoes. On deck, crewmen with muskets fired down at the victims. Between the reports of the cannon and muskets, the cries and moans of the men, women and children in the canoes could be heard. Within a few minutes the water around *Eleanora* was red with the blood and bodies of a hundred dead and wounded locals.

Vengeance having been taken, it was obvious that there would be no further business to do on Maui, so Metcalfe gave the order to weigh anchor and head for the next island to the south. Metcalfe thought, "Maybe the heathens at the next island will be willing to do business in a civilized manner."

The local chief Kameeiamoku promised that he would take revenge on the *Haole*s for the massacre at *Olowalu*, he just was not sure how or when.

Simon Metcalfe sailed *Eleanora* south from the site of the massacre, along the coast of Maui, through the Alalakeiki Channel past the island of Kahoolawe and along the leeward coast of the Big Island of Hawaii. He wanted to travel a distance along the island chain to hopefully move beyond the range where the natives may have heard of his massacre on Maui, so that he might continue trading for local goods. *Eleanora* dropped anchor in *Kealakekua* Bay, the domain of Kamehameha and the same bay where Captain Cook had met his fate.

The news of the massacre had reached Kamehameha before the *Eleanora*'s arrival. News had also reached him regarding the capture of another *Haole* ship. Kamehameha did not want to do business with Metcalfe and did not want the *Haole's* to find out that one of their ships had been seized and the crew killed. Kamehameha placed a kapu on the bay, so no canoes would go to the *Haole* ship.

After a day with no visits from the locals, Metcalfe sent a party ashore led by his Bo' sun John Young. Young and his men found the village to be emptied of its inhabitants. No chiefs could be found with whom they could make trading arrangements.

In searching for the local inhabitants, the party split up and spread out to search in the vegetation upland from the bay. At some point Young became separated from the rest of the crewmen. He subsequently met and was captured by Kamehameha's warriors who had been tracking the shore party waiting for just such an opportunity. As the sun began to get low in the western sky the shore party reassembled back at their longboat. The guards who had been left with the boat asked after their Bo' sun. The others in the party had not seen him since they entered the jungle. They waited until almost dark for Young's return, but he did not appear. Not wanting to be caught in this unnerving deserted village after dark, the longboat returned to its ship.

"Those stinking bastards!" Simon Metcalfe was livid, "So far in the Sandwich Islands, the savages have stolen and burned one of my longboats, killed a crewmember, and now they have my Bo' sun."

Metcalfe ordered cannons to be fired into the village in hopes that it would get the local chief's attention, but there was no response from the shore. During the next two days Metcalfe had the village randomly shelled and sent armed parties ashore in hopes of gaining Young's release, but there was no contact from the local residents.

Metcalfe finally gave the order to weight anchor. "The savages have probably et him already.

Mr. Young was a good Bo' sun, poor son of a bitch."

Eleanora sailed out of *Kealakekua* Bay and headed for the South Pacific. Metcalfe was tired of the hospitality of these islands. He had, had enough of Hawaii.

Aboard the *Fair American* the crew had noted the appearance of more sea birds during the past day or two. Late in the afternoon the lookout called "Land Ho!" The peaks of the major mountains *Mauna Kea* and *Mauna Loa* poked over the horizon. Just before dark the peak of *Haleakala* appeared on the horizon. By morning the landmasses were spread before the approaching *Fair American*.

Excitement ran through the crew at the prospect of a new landfall. All crewmen not actively working watched the approaching islands.

The *Fair American* first made landfall at Molokai. Fearing dangerous reefs, Metcalfe doubled the lookouts as they worked closer to the island. After finding no suitable landing along the cliffs of the north shore, they sailed around the western end of the island and found a somewhat protected anchorage, in the lee of the island, at the village of *Kaunakakai*. The local chief was cautious but hospitable. He wanted to trade, but the news of the incident at *Olowalu* had spread through the islands and all local populations were on guard.

This land was like no other that Zachary had seen before in the voyage. After the arid California coast, Molokai was completely different. Even though *Kaunakakai* was on the leeward and therefore dry side of the island, it was covered with palm trees and fragrant vegetation. The smell of flowers filled his nostrils and lifted Zachary's spirit. Though different from anywhere he had ever been, this place seemed mystical and wondrous.

Thomas Metcalfe traded with the local people of Molokai for two days, filled the water casks and lay on some provisions. The local girls amorously entertained the crew, though Zachary in a sober state was reluctant to partake in this free love with women who looked nothing like the ones of his native land.

Thomas Metcalfe had asked the local chief about seeing the *Eleanora*. He was told only that a *Haole* ship had been reported to be at the neighboring island of Maui. The next morning Thomas gave the order to weigh anchor and they sailed south along the coast of Molokai and then across the *Pailolo* Channel to the north end of Maui.

CHAPTER 11

CAPTIVES

KAMEEIAMOKU COULD NOT believe his good fortune another *Haole* ship approached upon which he could exact his revenge. He summoned warriors and led two dozen canoes out to the *Fair American*, which had just anchored off his shore. Kameeiamoku and a delegation boarded the ship and presented themselves to Captain Thomas Metcalfe. When it was apparent that the *Haole* crew was off guard, Kameeiamoku gave a signal and his warriors pounced upon the crew throwing them overboard. The Warriors in the waiting boats beat the *Haole*s with war clubs and paddles.

One of the skills that Zachary had learned while under his uncle's tutelage was to swim, a skill not possessed by many sailors of that era. Zachary hit the water next to Metcalfe and between the outrigger of one canoe and the hull of another. Metcalfe could not swim and grabbed on to the outrigger to stay afloat. A couple paddles from the adjacent canoe beat him across the head and face.

Zachary found that he could stay afloat with very little leg action and used his arms to deflect the paddles that were aimed in his direction. Instinctively, Zachary also attempted to deflect some of the blows to his Captain, until a war club came straight down upon Metcalfe's head splitting his skull, killing him instantly. Zachary was splattered with Metcalfe's blood and brain matter. Zachary dove under the hull of the nearest canoe coming up to breathe under the curve of its short bow. The warriors in the next canoe upon seeing him yelled to their comrades pointing to his location. The warriors swung wildly at Zachary's head but by remaining close to the canoe's hull he avoided direct hits, but this could not go on for too long. Zachary was getting exhausted. His legs were beginning to cramp from churning in the water, and the glancing blows to his head were taking their toll.

A chief in the canoe next to the one under which Zachary had taken shelter, commented about how the *Haole* defended his Captain and how long he fights. The chief jokingly referred to Zachary as *Koa Kai*, (Sea Warrior), but he then took pity on the exhausted *Haole* and ordered the assault to stop. They dragged Zachary's limp beaten body into their canoe.

On shore, Zachary was flopped on the beach. Not far from him the warriors piled the bodies of the other *Fair American* crewmembers. The Mauians cheered at their conquest of the *Haole* ship. A late canoe arriving at the shoreline laid the body of Isaac Davis next to Zachary. Davis was bleeding from several places on his face and head. His one eye was swollen shut, but he was alive. Davis was the only other crewman who could swim, and today it had also saved his life.

Zachary and Davis were carried on litters into the village. Davis appeared to be unconscious but was still breathing. Zachary was in pain, but otherwise alert. As Zachary looked up from the litter, he thought that he had fallen into hell. If he could not feel the pain of his wounds, he would have been sure that he had died in the fight and had been sent to hell, just as the Calvinist preachers defined it. Huge men with evil looking tattooed faces and bodies were carrying him. They passed numbers of other large brown people, all of whom seemed to be staring at him menacingly. There were women naked to the waste and children running around, also nearly naked. The litters passed a *Heiau* (a Hawaiian temple), which was surrounded by skulls on pikes and even more menacing looking wooden statues with gargoyle-like grotesque shapes and faces.

Zachary thought in his dazed state that if this were not hell, it must be close to it. He had heard stories about men captured by the American Indians of New England and thought that he and Davis were probably about to be tortured and killed for the pleasure of their heathen captors.

Zachary and Davis were placed on woven mats, inside a thatched hut. Two bare breasted women entered the hut and cleaned their wounds. Bandages were applied to the wounds and they were left alone. Zachary thought that he should make a break for it, but to where would he escape? He looked over at Davis who was now snoring. He could not leave without Davis. He rationalized; if they were about to be tortured and killed the savages would not have cleaned and bandaged their wounds. Maybe all was well for the moment. With that thought Zachary lapsed into a fitful sleep.

Before the prisoners had been brought ashore, The Kameeiamoku had already decided that the two prisoners might be of some value. His warriors had just captured a *Haole* ship, but they were not sure that they could sail it, and the ship carried cannons, and they were not sure how to fire them. As long as the two *Haoles* were of some service they were worth keeping alive. The chief ordered the two prisoners to be taken to a hut, ministered to, and treated with respect.

The next morning Zachary was half awake from the light of the morning sun entering the hut, when two large warriors entered carrying food. There was a variety of foodstuffs including kalua pig, bananas, and tender fish from a fishpond. Many of these foods would have been *kapu* (taboo) to women and people of the lower classes, but the chief had ordered that they be treated as *Alii*, so the best was offered. The variety was due to some question as to what the *Haoles* might eat.

Zachary sat up and fed himself heartily. Davis was awake, but still weak from his wounds, and had to be helped with his food by the two warriors.

When the prisoners had eaten their fill the two warriors left the hut. Zachary rose and went to Davis's bed. "Sir, do you think that we should try and make a break for it?"

"I'm in no shape for it Lad." Davis's voice was still weak. "Anyway, where would we go?' We couldn't get the *Fair American* underway before the heathens were upon us. It looks as if these bastards are going to keep us alive for a while at least." He raised his head holding it off the mat with the palm of his right hand, the elbow pushed into the mat. "Best we bide our time, regain our strength a bit, and then plan how to get out of this god forsaken hell." With that Davis settled back on to his mat. "What happened to the rest of the crew, lad?"

Zachary hesitated a moment and then responded, "All died, Sir." He paused, "We are the only survivors. I saw the bodies of the Captain and other men stacked on the beach before the savages brought us to their village." He paused again, "The sons-of-bitches were dancing around our men and parading around with their naked bodies, like they had just won a war."

Zachary looked over and saw that Davis was dozing off. Zachary lay on his mat and contemplated his misfortune.

After two weeks of recovery both Zachary and Isaac Davis were regaining their strength. They wandered about the village venturing further and further each day. They were always accompanied by warriors who were respectful, helpful, but always there.
Kameeiamoku wanted his guests to be made welcome, but he did not want them to make off with his prize ship or be able to escape if another *Haole* ship should appear on their shores.

Zachary and Davis were well fed and learning to enjoy the local hospitality. The warriors that attended to the prisoners had heard the chief refer to Zachary as "Koa Kai," and assumed that this name was conferred upon him out of respect from their chief, so they continued calling him by this name, even though Zachary had no idea what the name meant. They were offered the companionship of several women. Zachary was not sure that he was ready to have sex with a woman who was bigger than him. After declining the favors of several women, he was taken aback when a warrior offered him the companionship of a young boy.

Kamehameha was eager to gain possession of the schooner, its cannon and muskets.

Kameeiamoku was beholden to him, so negotiations were undertaken and concluded, Kamehameha gained control of the prize and its surviving crew members.

Zachary and Davis did not know it, but they had just been sold into slavery. They were told to prepare to have an audience with Kameeiamoku. Davis instructed Zachary to show proper respect when they were before the chief. Zachary was appalled at the thought and responded, "Sir, I'll not bow down to some heathen king." Knowing that Davis was British, his teenage impertinence forced him to add, "My brothers fought a war to settle that."

Davis slapped Zachary with the back of his hand. "You will do what you have to do to save our hides." Davis stood up straight as a ship's officer should and added, "If that means kissing the arses of these savages, you'll do it."

Faced with this symbol of authority, Zachary immediately replied reluctantly, "Aye, Aye sir."

Kameeiamoku told Zachary and Davis that they and their ship were to be taken to the island to their south and that they would be in the service of Kamehameha, the *Alii* king of that region. They were then paddled out to their ship for the first time since it had been pirated. A number of Kamehameha's warriors were already on board when they arrived, plus there were a number of outrigger canoes and two large double-hulled war canoes waiting to accompany *Fair American* to her new port.

The warriors were to learn from the *Haole*'s how to sail the ship, but included was their helmeted chief who was authorized to take appropriate steps if the *Haole*'s attempted to escape with their ship or otherwise interfere with Kamehameha's possession of the ship and its weapons.

Davis instructed Zachary to take some Hawaiians forward and weigh anchor while he took another group and prepared to make sail. Within a half hour the *Fair American* was underway with native canoes on both sides. It felt good to have the ship under their feet and stiff trade winds to carry them swiftly south. The little schooner charged south on a beam reach, heeling in the fresh breeze. The course was the same one *Eleanora* had taken three weeks previously, along the coast of Maui, through the *Alalakeiki* Channel past the island of Kahoolawe and along the leeward coast of the Big Island of Hawaii to *Kealakekua* Bay.

As they entered the bay, to their wonder they saw another ship. a British merchantman that had been trading there for several days.

After arriving at *Kealakekua*, Zachary and Davis were carried ashore and escorted to a hut.

When ushered inside they were surprised to be face to face with another white man, John Young. The two British seamen knew each other, since their ships had sailed together prior to the separation in San Diego. The two grasped each other heartily, shaking hands, not quite hugging, but as close to an embrace as a proper English seaman can muster. Zachary was introduced and they then told the stories of the circumstances under which they had come together.

Davis: "Did you see the other ship in the harbor? That may be our chance to escape from this hell hole."

Young: "The ship has been in the Bay for several days and is most likely to up anchor soon. We will have to keep watch on the ship and when it appears ready to make way, we will have to steal a boat and make a dash for it."

Davis: "This may be our only chance lads, but if we get caught, the heathens will do us in." The three captives took turns watching the ship throughout the evening and night. At 4:00 AM Zachary awoke his elders to report activity on the ship. Young speculated, "High tide is about an hour after sunup, they will probably want to ride the tide out of the bay." He scratched his chin, "That means we must grab a boat as soon as they start upping their anchor and row like hell."

The three did not sleep after that. Not much was said but each was picturing in his mind the dash for freedom they would make in just a few hours.

As the first signs of light came over the *Kona* slopes toward *Kealakekua* Bay; the three captives slipped out of their hut and made for the beach. Sure, enough there was activity on the foredeck of the merchantman. In the silence of the morning, the three escapees could hear the creaking of the windless; the ship was weighing anchor.

The three pushed a small outrigger canoe into the water and jumped in. The three began paddling, but they had been seen. There was shouting on shore, Zachary looked over his shoulder and saw several dozen men running to other canoes.

"Paddle like the devil's after ya, lads," implored Davis. The only sound for a bit was the constant splashing of the paddles digging into the water. The three kept up the pace for two hundred yards, but it was Davis still suffering from his wounds that began to falter.

They could see the ship's anchor break water, and unfurled sails being set. The ship was moving, and they were losing ground. The shouts of the pursuing canoes were getting closer. They got halfway from the shore to the ship before the fully manned canoes overtook them. The first canoe continued ahead of them and blocked their progress. The other canoes surrounded them. The Hawaiians brandished spears and war clubs, the escape was over.

The three remained captives and sat quietly, panting, the sweat running from their foreheads.

They were not sure if they had not just perpetrated the infraction that would bring about their executions. They turned their canoe and paddled slowly back to shore escorted by the other canoes.

The British ship paid almost no notice to the activity; except the mate made a comment to the Captain, "Look at those crazy savages sir, looks like they were going to make one more dash out here to trade." The Captain nodded and they then got back to the serious business of guiding their ship out of the reef strewn bay.

On shore the three were led to their hut and placed inside. Guards were placed around the hut to ensure that there would be no further attempts to escape.

Davis: "We may have done it lads. These savages may do us in like they did the rest of the crew."

Young: "Our only hope is that they still think that they need us." Davis: "May as well rest lads, there is nowhere to go."

The three lay on their individual mats but slept little as each of them contemplated their pending demise.

The next morning the three captives were led to an audience with Kamehameha and his leading advisors and chiefs. It was immediately evident this was a much larger and more organized society than the local chief and his attendants on Maui. Among the chiefs was one who spoke fairly good English.

They learned later that Kaiana had sailed from Hawaii to China in 1781 on a British ship where he learned the language. He told them they were to be advisors to the king who wanted them to teach the proper use of the cannons and muskets that were now in Kamehameha's possession. They would be free to roam the island at will, as long as they did not attempt to escape. If they were to make such an attempt, they would be dealt with most severely. Considering that the two older *Haole*s would be the more experienced teachers, Kamehameha stated, "The boy will be executed as the price for yesterday's attempted escape."

Zachary looked at Davis and Young in panic. Davis did not want to lose one of the few people who might still aid him in escaping from this hellhole. Davis stepped forward and bowed like a good British subject. "Your Excellency, Mr. Young and I are seamen and as such are knowledgeable with sword and cannon, but young Mr. Bower here comes from a family of soldiers and is skilled in the ways of muskets and infantry."

Kamehameha paused a moment and then commanded, "The boy lives." Waving his right arm, he added, "Take them away."

As they walked back to their hut without guards, Zachary broke the silence. "Thank you, Sir, I thought that I was a goner."

Davis replied, "I couldn't let those heathens have one of my only remaining shipmates, now could I?" He patted Zachary's back, "I hope to hell you know how to fire a musket boy, or we're both in trouble."

Zachary responded' "Aye Sir, my brothers taught me well."

After the captives departed Kamehameha took counsel with Kalima, his trusted advisor.

"Kalima, the *Haole*s are needed to teach our warriors to sail their ship and use their weapons. We must treat them well as long as they are of value."

Kalima: "Yes, Majesty."

Kamehameha: "The three will be given freedom to move about the village but must always be watched. If they attempt to escape again, we will execute one of them to gain the obedience of the others. The *Haole*s shall be given food, gifts and women, but for them to become comfortable in their new homes and therefore trustworthy advisors, they must be helped to assimilate into the society. Each of the *Haole*s shall be befriended by one or more warriors, who will help them learn our ways and the friend will also keep an eye on his designated captive."

Kalima: "Yes, Majesty, it will be done."

As promised the three captives were given the run of the island, but Kalima did not take any chances. He gave each of the three separate huts and kept them apart as much as possible. He figured that if they were not together, they could not plan another escape.

Kalima summoned his son Kaleo to his hut. "Kaleo, it seems that the gods have given us a great opportunity. With the *Haole*'s ship and weapons, the king may have the advantage needed to defeat his enemies."

Kaleo: "Yes, Father."

Kalima: "Kaleo, I called for you, because you must befriend the *Haole* boy who will teach you and the rest of us how to use the muskets and the ways of the *Haole*'s armies. You are close in age and should be good friends. You will aid him through training as a warrior. You will also aid him in learning the ways of our people so that he may become one of our own. This is an exceedingly important task. Can you do it?"

"Yes, Father." Kaleo responded to his father's command.

The audience was over and Kaleo left his father's hut to contemplate this important assignment.

As he saw it, this was a great way for him to learn the *Haole*'s military expertise and with that knowledge he could rise up in the ranks of Kamehameha's army. He murmured to himself' "*Mai kai*, this is a great opportunity."

In the morning, Kaleo hailed Zachary from his hut, "Oe, Oe, Koa Kai!" Kaleo introduced himself, but the differences in language met very little was communicated other than who he was and the name that he had heard for Zachary. Kaleo explained as best he could, that he would assist Zachary in training the troops in the art of firing a musket. It was also ordered that Zachary was to learn the Hawaiian methods of fighting so that he too would be a warrior.

Zachary perused his new acquaintance. Kaleo was also in his teens but was taller and stockier than Zachary. First impressions were that he was a somewhat quiet and amiable individual. Zachary accepted this at face value and the amiable relationship between the young men began.

Among Zachary's first lessons was to properly wrap and wear a *malo* (loincloth). Kaleo laughed at him as they walked along, and Zachary began to lose his drawers. Once Zachary had mastered keeping his *malo* in place he was ready to participate in the day's activities.

The first order of the day was a long run along the beach. Though a sailor's life was strenuous in many ways, none of a sailor's chores built the stamina needed for long distance running. It did not take long for Zachary to trail the pack of other trainees by quite a distance. He arrived at the finish panting and favoring his left leg which had cramped up during the run. The instructor who was an older warrior, waved at Zachary to continue walking out the cramp before he was allowed to join the others for water and a brief rest.

The instructor began to explain the Hawaiian form of martial arts, "*Lua*" to the trainees. The rest had all been in training for some time and were honing their skills. This form of hand to hand combat included boxing, wrestling, kicking, bone breaking and pressure points.

Zachary understood none of the briefing but could tell that the subject was wrestling. After the briefing, the students were paired off to practice several moves. Zachary's opponent, Kimo was much larger than him, even bigger than Kaleo. Kimo had decided that he did not like the strange looking *Haole* kid and would exhibit his dislike and show his dominance. As they practiced the moves Kimo made sure to jostle him when they were at close quarters, an elbow in the ribs, and a slap to the head.

Zachary tried hard not to be intimidated by this large and muscular brown man. He had roughhoused and wrestled plenty with his big brothers, but this was not for fun.

Zachary tried a move, but each time, Kimo waited for his aggression, countered the move and then responded with his own punch or wrestling hold.

Zachary had grown quite a bit while at sea and the rugged work of a sailor had made him strong and sinuous. Against the much larger Kimo he held his own with moves he had learned rough housing with his brothers, more than the ones taught that day. Slammed to the ground three times, each slam left him more angered and frustrated.

Kaleo watched Zachary when he was not engaged in his own wrestling bouts and regretted not going out of his way to be Zachary's partner. He noticed that Kimo was being overly abusive for a training session. He finally stepped in, "Hey Kimo, take it easy on my friend, Koa Kai!" Kimo: "Koa Kai my *okole*! This *Haole* needs to learn to respect a real warrior!"

Kaleo strode over to Kimo, stopping face to face with him. "The *Haole* is my responsibility and I'll kick your real warrior *okole*!"

Seeing the confrontation, the instructor pushed his way between them. The two antagonists parted, still glaring at each other, but it was over, at least for the moment.

Zachary sat down next to Kaleo and wiped the sand from his sweating body. A bit of blood had dried under his left nostril. Kaleo could tell from the glare in his eyes that he was angered at the abuse. Kaleo, "You OK Koa Kai?"

Zachary responded, "I am going to get that son of a whore!"

The day's activities ended without further incident. The instructor called Zachary and Kaleo to him. Using Kaleo as an interpreter, he explained that this group of young warriors had been training for several years and that he would have to work hard to catch up. He tasked Kaleo to work extra with Zachary to hone his skills.

After training, as Kaleo and Zachary walked back to their huts Zachary was still angered about the bullying. He finally spoke, "Thanks for defending me, but you didn't have to do it. I can take care of myself."

Kaleo: "Sure you can, but Kimo was overdoing it and I wanted to aid my friend. You had some good moves. You held your own and

Kimo is one of the best wrestlers I know." He added with an air of confidence, "Almost as good as me, and you showed him up pretty good."

Passing a stand of bananas Kaleo motioned toward a large banana trunk, "We need to roughen up your arms and legs. Pretend this is Kimo and show him that you are the real warrior."

Zachary punched the trunk. Feeling the pain in his knuckles, he shook his hand. Kaleo, "No, use your forearm and side of your hand."

Zachary struck the banana trunk again. He had never hit something with the side of his hand before, it hurt a bit, but not too bad. His hand became numb, so each time he hit, it hurt less, and he could hit even harder.

Kaleo, "That's it. Now kick that Kimo, *mai kai*. Good, good whale on him!"

Zachary finally stopped. He was panting heavily. He felt better, no longer angered. Beating on the symbolic Kimo had worked.

Kaleo, "All right, you sure showed that banana!" Pointing to the beach he said, "Let's jump in the surf."

Zachary followed. They splashed about and washed away the sweat and soil of the day's activities.

Zachary awoke the next morning with aching legs. He also had other aches in strange places due to the previous day's strenuous activities. Kaleo roused him out and they proceeded to the beach to assemble with the other trainees. Zachary hobbled on his aching limbs.

Zachary: "Oh Kaleo, do we have to run again today?"

Kaleo: "Every day, but it will hurt less once you get moving."

Zachary: "I don't know if I can make it."

Kaleo: "You must, or the instructor will be severe to you. After the first few days it will stop hurting."

As they ran that morning, Zachary was far behind the rest of the trainees. An instructor ran behind him prodding him on with a cane and whipping his back when he slowed down. He also hollered unintelligible oaths to spur him on.

The training continued each day, six or seven days a week. In addition to wrestling, the young warriors practiced distance combat throwing with the *pololu*, a long spear, blocking incoming spears, and throwing large pebbles with slings. They practiced close combat with the *ihe*, a short spear, war clubs and *Pahoa* which are daggers.

During training Zachary was paired off with many different warriors. He continued to be jostled around, but he persevered because he had no other choice. Kaleo attempted to protect his charge from undue harassment; however, Kimo and the other young warriors took every opportunity to harass the stranger. Kaleo tried to raise Zachary's spirits at the end of the day and continued to work on Zachary's skills.

Many banana trunks got kicked and pummeled by the pair. After a few weeks of this training, Zachary attacked unassuming banana trunks with great gusto. On a particular afternoon when Zachary was fired up, he beat on a banana trunk with grunts and growls until it broke in the middle from the repeated blows. It fell between Kaleo and him, covering them with its broad green leaves. He smiled with satisfaction and Kaleo exclaimed, "The banana is down, and the winner is Koa Kai!"

One afternoon, while Zachary and Kaleo walked from the training area on the beach to their huts, Zachary noticed an old man carrying a pololu spear, moving through the palm grove parallel to them.

Seeming strange, Zachary kept one eye on this unknown Kanaka. When they reached a clearing in the palm grove, the old man turned and hurled his spear at Kaleo. Kaleo quickly turned sideways and fended off the spear with his forearm. Zachary saw that the old Kanaka did not have another spear and charged him. The old man stood still, a look of disbelief as Zachary ran towards him. Zachary struck the attacker in the jaw knocking him to the ground. Zachary was about to pummel their assailant when Kaleo started shouting at him.

"Stop, stop!" Kaleo ran over to them. "It is OK!"

Zachary stopped his move to kick the old Kanaka in the ribs, but stood over him glaring with rage.

Kaleo, "Koa Kai, it is alright."

Kaleo helped the old Kanaka up, patted him on the back and said a few words of apology in Hawaiian which Zachary did not understand. The old man went to retrieve his spear.

Kaleo, "Koa Kai, Mahalo for defending me; but this is part of the training; so that we may always be alert and ready to defend ourselves." Patting Zachary on the back, Kaleo added, "The old Kanaka was just doing his job."

During the first weeks of training, Zachary was often chastised by the instructor for doing things wrong or for being at the end of the pack during runs. The Hawaiian method of military training was like that of all military history. It started by tearing down the trainee's definition of themselves and then rebuilding it in the image of that particular warrior class. After a few weeks, Zachary became stronger, faster and more adept; he began to feel the esprit de corps of a true warrior.

Zachary watched the other wrestling bouts when he was not engaged in his own training. It became evident that all of the trainees attempted to wait for their adversary to make the first move so that they could repel the move and follow with their own offensive move. The last section of the wrestling session was to square off and actually wrestle with each other's opponent of the day.

The instructor pointed for Zachary and Kimo to enter the circle of trainees for another bout.

Zachary had trained hard for this moment, to have a rematch with Kimo. They moved around the circle of students. This time Zachary held back and attempted to force Kimo to make the first move. Kimo circled looking for an opening, he finally lunged at Zachary. Zachary turned sideways and tripped his opponent as he went by. Kimo got up off his hands and knees. Kimo tried two more aggressive moves and each time Zachary slipped away. Kimo heard the hoots of his peers which only spurred him on.

Zachary was making Kimo look bad. Finally, Zachary waited for the enraged Kimo to square-off with him and then he faked a punch at Kimo's head and when Kimo stuck out his arm to block the thrust, Zachary grabbed Kimo's wrist, swung under the outstretched arm and pulled the arm behind Kimo's back into a hammer-lock. While behind Kimo, Zachary kicked him in the back of the knee and dropped him into a kneeling position.

Kaleo and all the other trainees hooted and hollered at the unforeseen outcome of the match.

Kaleo's grasps on English and Zachary's use of Hawaiian had also increased during the past few weeks. Kaleo cheered, "Koa Kai, you are going to earn your name yet!" Zachary still did not appreciate the name that had been given him.

This victory by Zachary broke the ice. He had proven himself and after that was much more accepted by the group as an equal.

After two months of training, the instructors held the trainees back at the end of the day's session and asked Kaleo and Zachary to select the trainees for the musket platoon. Zachary studied the group of his peers.

Kaleo: "Are you thinkin' what I think you're thinkin'?" Zachary: "You bet! Now it's my turn."

Zachary first chose Kimo and then made sure he included the other trainees who had hassled him amidst the dozen they selected. The instructors then released the other trainees and told the selected group they were under Zachary's command and to do as they were told. When there were some grumbles from the group, the instructors assured them that their disobedience would be dealt with harshly.

Even though he was still sore from the rigorous activities, Zachary asked Kaleo to form the chosen ones into two lines and inform them that they would be drilled every day after the regular training session. He then marched them up and down the beach for the next three hours, chastising them for their lack of ability to march as a unit and keep in step.

The next day the selected ones were given muskets with which to drill. There would be no more grumbling. Now they knew they had been selected for a very special unit and were honored that the *Haole* had selected them.

Zachary knew how to shoot a musket and had heard about soldiering from his brothers. He would explain the next day's lesson to Kaleo one on one. After he knew that he had successfully communicated it to Kaleo, he would present the same lesson to his musket platoon. Kaleo having already had the lesson would assist in the teaching, explaining in Hawaiian what Zachary could only gesture.

Among the lessons was an explanation of the proper gun sight picture to hit a target. Zachary pointed to the rear notched sight on a musket and then drew it in the sand. He pointed to the front blade sight and drew it vertically from the "V" of the notched site to the top of the blade even with the top of the notch. Kaleo helped, waving his arms while he talked and pointing at the parts of the sight.

After the lesson with the muskets, Zachary rested under a coconut palm with Kaleo. "Kaleo" he said while staring out at the blue ocean and breaking waves before them. "To do this right, I need a sword."

"Don't know that I can get a *Haole* sword, but I can get you a short *ihe* spear," Replied Kaleo. Zachary thought for a moment and said, "That will have to do."

The next morning Zachary formed his platoon into two ranks and marched them around on the beach. He used the commands he had learned from his father and brothers, waving his ihe spear as he had his wooden sword as a child.

Gunpowder was at a premium: Zachary was only allowed to have his troops actually fire their muskets at targets on a few occasions. The remainder of the days Zachary drilled his troops, teaching them to march and the manual of arms.

Zachary did not know it, but Kamehameha and Kalima observed the troops marching about and were very pleased, because they had seen Captain Cook's red-coated Marines acting in the same manner. It was obvious they had picked the right man to train their troops.

The three captives were treated as allies. Davis and Young became trusted advisors to Kamehameha. Zachary since he was much younger did not reach that stature, but he did participate in frequent audiences with the king, along with Davis and Young. Kaleo was always at Zachary's side and enjoyed his new stature in the middle of the seat of power at Kamehameha's court. The three were given Hawaiian names. Davis and Young were known as Aikake and Olohana respectively. Zachary remained known as Koa Kai (Sea Warrior). The name given to him because of the tales surrounding the valiant fight he put up during the taking of the *Fair American*.

Davis and Young enjoyed their newfound status. They had spent their careers as sailors aboard British and American ships and had never even considered being in positions of power. They now moved in the highest circles of Hawaiian society, though it was a society much different than their own. They received greater respect than at any other time in their lives. They were also well fed and given women whenever they chose.

Zachary was becoming accustomed to his new surroundings and the new roles which he must play. The weeks turned into months and Zachary learned his lessons in spear dodging as well as spear throwing. Being lighter than most of his fellow trainees, it was not long before he was one of the faster troops when they did long distance runs. When not in training himself, he drilled his troops. He was beginning to feel like a real warrior.

Zachary and Kaleo communicated more and more, as Zachary learned Hawaiian and Kaleo learned more English from Zachary. Kaleo took his responsibility for Zachary very seriously. He continued to make sure that Zachary was treated with great respect, though Zachary had gained the respect of the other young warriors due to his progress in training and his role as commander of the musket platoon.

Zachary found Kaleo to be a gentle giant. He was soft spoken and understated with a jovial personality. Zachary as a captive in a strange society needed a friend that he could count on and Kaleo was perfect for that role.

Kaleo offered Zachary female companionship on several occasions and Zachary declined. Even though like any other healthy teenage boy, his overactive hormones kept him obsessed with thoughts of sex, he was still taken aback by the thought of making love to a woman who was bigger than he and most of the adult women seemed to be close to his size or bigger. It had become obvious that these large women were considered to be things of beauty in this society. Zachary was not sure how to explain this to Kaleo, but once again, not understanding the state of affairs, Kaleo offered him the services of a young boy. Not being the first time, this had happened, Zachary felt that he had to clarify the situation.

While resting under a palm tree Zachary broached the subject. "Kaleo you have offered me the affections of many young ladies since I have been here."

"That is right my friend, almost any wahine on the island would be happy to enjoy making love with our young *Haole* warrior."

Zachary considered the prospects of this statement and not wanting to sound inexperienced he went on. "You see girls where I come from are much smaller than your local girls. This is what I am used to."

It was obvious to Zachary that Kaleo had enjoyed the pleasures of sex for some time. Zachary did not want to let on that his only real experience was in a drunken stupor in a shabby tent, so he was purposely vague. "There is a girl at the court of the king whom I have not met. She is always there, but on the edge of the activity. She is tall, but nice and slim. If you can arrange my introduction to her, I would be pleased."

"Owe" Kaleo replied, "I think you mean Pua Lani. She is my half-sister. She has a good face but needs some meat on her bones." Kaleo stood up and waved his arms. "She is also pretty ornery sometimes and very particular."

Zachary responded, "She is the kind of girl I like. Can you arrange a meeting?" Kaleo, still waving his arms, "I will see what I can do, my friend."

Kaleo had run-ins with his half-sister in the past. He had felt the heat of her temper and slash of her cutting tongue. Rather than approach Pua Lani directly, Kaleo decided to ask his father to intercede. The next afternoon after military training for the day was completed, he went to his father. Kalima was somewhat honored that the *Haole* was interested in his skinny daughter above all of the other village wahines which he would have considered more lovely. Kalima agreed to talk to Pua Lani, but he also had seen her hot temper and bade Kaleo to accompany him.

Kalima and Kaleo found Pua Lani at the edge of a stream. She was washing and pounding fibers between rocks. The fibers would later be dyed and woven into kappa cloth.

As Kalima approached Pua stood up. They hugged and rubbed noses. Kalima, never one to waste words, got right to the subject. "Pua, my daughter, the *Haole* boy, Koa Kai has asked for you to join him." Kalima and Kaleo braced themselves for the possible onslaught, but Pua stood there silently for a moment contemplating the proposition. She was flattered that the *Haole* was attracted to her, for she knew that her lack of meaty exterior made her less than beautiful in her society. Not only was she thin by Hawaiian standards, but her sharp tongue had discouraged several would-be suitors. She replied, softly, graciously, "Yes Father, I will obey your wishes and join the *Haole* boy." She chose the words "obey your wishes" carefully so that she might have a bargaining chip with her father, if this relationship did not work out.

Pua prepared herself for the meeting with Koa Kai. She bathed in the pool below a cascading mountain stream. She dried her long dark hair. She donned her favorite *kapa* skirt. She also placed two fragrant *puakenikeni* leis over her head, arraying them appropriately on her shoulders and they draped down over her firm breasts.

The sun was low in the west when the men should have finished eating in the men's dining hut. If her timing was right, she would make an entrance at Zachary's hut soon after he arrived there from dinner.

When Zachary had asked Kaleo to introduce him to Pua Lani he did so based on his western Judeo-Christian concept of courtship. He expected Kaleo to make an introduction and then he would attempt to arrange some future meetings between them. It had been a day and a half since he had made the request of Kaleo but did not mention it when they were together that day. He did not want to appear too eager.

Pua arrived at Zachary's hut just after dark. The *kukui* nut lamps and torches were being lit around the village. She called into the hut, waited a moment, but got no answer. She called two more times without response. He was not there. Her courage began to waiver, she turned to retreat to her hut. Then she heard Kaleo's voice. She hid behind a nearby hut.

Along came Kaleo and Zachary talking and laughing. Pua watched them and when Zachary's back was turned, she stepped out from behind the hut and waved at Kaleo to leave. Kaleo took the hint. "Koa Kai I am tired. We have had a busy day and I need some rest."

Zachary accepted that, bid Kaleo a goodnight and entered his hut. His attendants had already lit kukui nut candles in his hut. The glow danced on the thatched ceiling of the hut.

Pua waited a few minutes and then approached the entrance to Zachary's hut. She softly called into the entrance, "Koa Kai, are you there?"

Zachary responded, "Yes, please come in."

Pua stepped inside. The candlelight glowed over her bronze upper body. The fragrant leis filled Zachary's nostrils. He was not sure what was happening, but it couldn't be bad.

"You sent for me." Pua said in a soft and sultry voice.

Zachary stammered, "Well, yes, well, no, well. I did tell Kaleo that I would like to meet you."

Pua stepped forward rubbing noses with Zachary, the Hawaiian form of kissing. Still in a soft gentle voice Pua said, "My Father sent me to warm your bed."

Zachary looked into her deep brown eyes. Stammering he replied, "Oh, ah, I would hope that you had come of your own free will."

She rubbed noses again and responded, "Of course."

With that Zachary gave her a big kiss in the *Haole* manner and they fell back onto the pile of mats in the corner of the hut which served as his bed. Zachary enjoyed his first sober experience at lovemaking. He took his time exploring and caressing Pua's tall strong body. He nibbled her earlobes, her neck and her rigid nipples. When his hand explored the moisture between her thighs, she loosened his already slipping *malo*. As the *kukui* candles burned out, they made love, crushing the fragrant leis between their moist bodies. And after a brief respite, they again made love. Pua and Zachary fell asleep sometime after midnight, entangled in each other's arms.

As was his habit, Kaleo rose at sunrise, put on his *malo*, splashed some water in his face and proceeded to Zachary's hut to awaken him. Knowing that his sister might be there, he showed some tact and hollered into the hut rather than his usual brash entrance to raise his friend.

Zachary came from the hut, hair a mess and bleary eyed. "Oh Kaleo, it's early."

Kaleo replied, "Come Koa Kai, our day awaits." He added, "O'e my sister must have done you good. You better jump in the surf and wake up."

Zachary did as suggested. He ran down the beach and tore off his *malo* as he dove into the cool clear water. He swam out a few yards to get beyond the shoreline waves and their suspended sand. He was exhilarated, the sun was bright, the water was just cool enough to alert his senses and he had spent the night with a beautiful woman. What could be better?

Zachary could not concentrate on the day's lesson in personal combat. His only thoughts were of returning to Pua Lani. Still half asleep, she had kissed him when he rose in the morning to respond to Kaleo's call. All Zachary could think of that day was returning to Pua's arms. After the day's activities Zachary made an excuse to return to his hut rather than proceeding directly to the men's dining hut.

When he arrived at his hut it was empty, Pua had gone. Not knowing where she might be, Zachary proceeded to the men's hut for dinner and to query Kaleo regarding Pua's whereabouts.

Kaleo explained that Pua had her daily chores and probably joined the other women of the village so that they could perform their communal tasks. Kaleo stated that if Koa Kai had enjoyed Pua's company, he was sure that she would please him again. Zachary was confused by this straightforward uninhibited form of casual sex. In his society where premarital sex was considered sinful, if one had the significant experience such as he had the previous night it would be the start of a long-term relationship, most likely marriage.

Kaleo told Zachary that the women would be eating dinner in their dining hut so he should be able to see Pua Lani after their evening meal. Zachary ate hurriedly and then made his way across the village to the women's dining hut. He was waiting as Pua exited the hut.

He stepped forward and gently grasped Pua's arm as she exited the hut. "Come with me, we must talk." Zachary led her behind the hut. Three old wahines, seeing his approach, cackled and laughed at the moves of such an apparent young lover. Zachary paid no attention to them.

Zachary turned Pua toward him, holding her by both arms. "Pua Lani were you going to come back to my hut?"

"Only if you found me to be acceptable." She replied. "Acceptable?" He stammered, "You were beautiful."

Zachary felt that the only course was complete honesty with regard to his Judeo-Christian assessment of the situation. He continued, "Pua, among my people a man usually only makes love to the woman that he marries."

He struggled for words. "That is a respectable woman like yourself."

He quickly thought, "This is not going well," but he continued, "Pua what I mean is that I did not want to meet you for only one night of sex, you are very dear to me."

Pua Lani's grasp of the English language was minimal and Zachary's Hawaiian though coming along, was not up to this level of passionate and complex discussion. When Zachary finished his passionate discourse, Pua replied, "So you want me to return to your hut?"

"Yes!" Zachary replied, "But not for just this night, but for good."

Based on that statement, Pua Lani moved to Zachary's hut and they became an informal man and wife. As they learned to communicate more and more, they reached a middle ground: a way to make both people feel comfortable with their relationship and the mores of their separate societies. It was not uncommon for a Hawaiian to take a wife and it was not unusual for a man to have several wives. From Zachary's point of reference, he had chosen a wife and even though a Christian church had not blessed their union in the normal manner, he felt that God would understand that under the circumstances he was acting in a monogamous relationship.

And so, it was that Pua Lani came to Zachary's hut to stay and in effect, he took a wife. They were a good match; Zachary could quell the fire of anger that sometimes exploded from Pua. Pua was mature enough to keep their still teenage relationship on an even keel.

In his view of this world, Zachary was now comfortable with Hawaiian society. He had seen the most savage and grotesque aspects of these warlike people, but he had also seen their soft and gentle side, the spirit of aloha. He found these two faces of the people to be an oxymoron. They were the most barbarous pagan warriors that he could imagine and at the same time the kindest and gentlest people he had ever encountered.

Though he did not understand their driving forces, he was amazed that he had become one of them. He had now been trained as a legitimate warrior. He was capable of killing his foes either with a musket or in the more traditional and bloody ways of the Hawaiians. He served a king who endeavored to conquer enemies from other islands. Zachary did not understand the politics or the motivations that fueled the wars between the island peoples, but he was firmly in the middle of these actions and could not escape them. On the other hand, he no longer wished to escape these beautiful islands. He now had a loving spouse who looked after his needs and would most likely bear his child. Then there was Kaleo. He could never have hoped for a more devoted friend. Danny O'Brien had been a good friend and teacher, but Kaleo was one step beyond that, he was always there when needed. What more could a man ask for than devoted family and friends?

At first the islands were so different from his home in New England that Zachary felt like a complete stranger, but after a year he learned to farm taro and spear freshwater shrimp in the mountain streams. He learned to capture fish in the fishponds and learned the language and the customs. Like so many converts, he became more ardently a Hawaiian than the native people. This place had become home.

CHAPTER 12

ON TO MAUI

THE PLANS FOR Kamehameha's invasion of Maui had been set. The great chief would consult with the *Kahuna*s, pray to the war god Ku, and when the time was right -- launch his fleet to Maui.

Two nights before the fleet would sail, Kalima summoned Kaleo to his hut. "Kaleo, I called for you because you must have a clear understanding of your task during the upcoming battles."

"Yes, Father." Kaleo responded with gravity in his voice that mirrored Kalima's grave demeanor.

"As I requested you have befriended the *Haole* boy and that has been good. You aided him through training and taught him the ways of our people."

"Yes, Father, Koa Kai has learned well, he is ready to become a warrior. He has also become a true friend, almost a brother to me."

Kalima's face grew graver. "Being good friends will make your task even harder. Though he may have learned the Hawaiian arts of war and has trained a group of our warriors to use the *Haole* muskets, there is only so much loyalty that a stranger can have for our cause. King Kamehameha expects to have the full support of the *Haole*'s weapons for his conquest of Maui. You must stay close to Koa Kai and ensure that he does his duty in battle. He must hold his ground and command the firing of the muskets."

Kalima grasped Kaleo by his shoulders, "You must do this, and if Koa Kai tries to escape the battle or otherwise retreat from his post you must keep the muskets in the battle." He stared straight into Kaleo's eyes. "Even if you must kill him and take command of the muskets yourself."

Kaleo's voice wavered as he responded, "Yes, Father."

Kalima squeezed Kaleo shoulders tighter, "You must do your duty, no matter how hard it might be for you."

Kaleo again responded in the affirmative, "Yes Father, I will do what must be done. However, I am sure Koa Kai will also do his duty on our behalf."

Kaleo departed his father's hut and proceeded directly to the *Heaiu*. Tears filled his eyes as he contemplated the wicked task that had been assigned to him. He prayed to the gods that his friend would be a brave warrior. He prayed to the gods that if required, he would have the strength to carry out his mission.

The war canoes had been assembling for several weeks, awaiting the order to sail to the adjacent island of Maui which lay less than forty miles away. Appropriate sacrifices had been made to the Gods, there were no bad omens to force a postponement, and so the order was given.

Zach and Kaleo were awakened well before dawn in preparation to move out. Zach's emotions were mixed. Having mastered his new skills as a Hawaiian warrior, he felt invincible. He was excited at the prospect of an encounter with a real enemy. However, he had flashes through his mind that he could be wounded or even killed. Also, he did not know for sure that he could actually take another person's life, particularly using the savage weapons of the Hawaiians.

Zachary did not have much time for contemplation of his situation. He dressed in his *malo* and gourd helmet. He rousted out his musketeers and called them to attention in their ranks. He instructed them on the importance of keeping their allotted gunpowder dry during the upcoming voyage.

The sky was vibrantly blue. Beyond the shallows, the sea was dark, almost navy blue where the ocean sloped away from the island and plunged thousands of feet into the deep. The trade winds were brisk, kicking up white caps and breaking up the otherwise endless blue *Alenuihaha* Channel. Zachary's troops were far from the first to depart. Before Zachary were the lateen sails of more war canoes than he could count. The campaign was on and he was a part of this history whether he liked it or not.

Zach had not been to sea for several months and found the sail across the channel, between the islands of Hawaii and Maui, exhilarating. The trade winds were blowing fifteen knots with gusts above twenty. The large catamaran war canoes charged through the waves on a close reach. Zachary studied the skilled Hawaiian sailors and was impressed with their ability to control the canoes at twice the speed that could be mustered by a heavy displacement white man's ship.

As the fleet approached the southern coast of Maui, Zachary spoke to his troops and patted the left shoulder of his trusted friend Kaleo as a sign of their mutual affection. "Kaleo, this is a glorious day. I cannot tell you how excited I am to be here and be a part of this adventure with you."

Kaleo could not immediately respond to Zach's affectionate gesture. The possibility of having to kill his friend flashed through his mind. After a moment, to comfort himself more than Zach, he placed his right hand on Zach's hand and said, "We will both distinguish ourselves in the coming days and gain the approval of our families, our ancestors and the Gods."

This comment caused quick thoughts to stream though Zach's brain. He could be killed in this far off land and his family would never know what became of him. Secondly, he was about to go to war and possibly kill for Gods other than the one Christian God. Was he about to commit sins against a number of the Ten Commandments, and could he be damned for aiding a heathen people? The sound of the twin hulls of the canoe scraping the coral as they approached the beach broke the thought and brought Zach's attention back to the mission at hand.

The war canoe upon which Zachary and his troops were passengers landed at Hamoa near Hana on the south end of Maui. This had been the area of previous invasions by the Hawaiians on their Mauian neighbors. Many battles had been fought in this area, but to date the forces from the Big Island had been consistently repulsed.

This campaign was to be different in many ways. The Hawaiian forces established their camp on the southern coast of Maui, as was their practice in previous campaigns. The Maui chiefs dispatched couriers to inform Kalanikupule of the invasion. After the southern base of operations was firmly established, Kamehameha began the potentially dangerous strategy of dividing his army, sending large elements to perform amphibious invasions along the north coast of Maui. The strategy was developed to keep Kalanikupule and his troops off balance.

The inherent danger in dividing forces is that small elements may be engaged and defeated by superior forces. As it turned out the strategy worked. Kalanikupule remained at his capital of Wailuku with substantial forces. Kalanikupule instead dispatched his trusted chieftain Kapakahili with a significant army to track down and defeat the invaders.

As has been the case in military endeavors for thousands of years, Zach and Kaleo learned to hurry-up and wait. They were encamped at the original landing site at the south end of Maui and were not included in the several assaults around the island of Maui. Kamehameha did not wish to commit his cannon and few muskets until he was ready for a decisive battle.

Zach and Kaleo practiced their personal combat skills with the other warriors who were encamped at Hamoa. Zach drilled his musket platoon on a daily basis. He had them continually practice the sequence of reloading their muzzle loading muskets. Though gunpowder remained in short supply, the troops were allowed a few shots each at targets made from gourds.

When Kaleo first befriended Zachary, he had several tattoos on his body, like most warriors. He had leis around his biceps and ankles. He had a small design, which was unintelligible to Zachary, between his thumb and forefinger. As time went on Kaleo added to his body art. Although he was still much less bedecked than many of his colleagues, his appearance became more menacing with each addition.

One afternoon after their day's drills, Kaleo and Zachary were resting in the shade of a palm grove. Kaleo sat staring at his cohort in silence. After some time, he announced, "You know if we are going to make you into a real warrior, you need some decoration." He pointed to his tattoos. "Maybe we should get your face tattooed. That would make you fierce."

Zachary replied, "I don't think that I am ready for that."

Kaleo was undeterred. "Come on we can start small and worry about something spectacular later." "My family adopted you right?"

Zachary remained unmoved. "Yes, I guess so."

Pointing to a design on his upper right arm, Kaleo continued, "Well my family's *aumakua* (Family god) is *Mano* the shark. It is only fitting that you have the symbol of your *ohana* family on your arm."

Seeing that Zachary was now considering the proposition, Kaleo stood up and pressed the issue. "It is the proper thing to do. Come Koa Kai let us go see the *Kahuna*."

Zachary reluctantly followed Kaleo to the camp's tattoo artist for his initiation into this ancient Polynesian art form. Lying on mats Zachary was given a piece of awa root to chew while the operation was performed on his left bicep. The *Kahuna* used a needle made of sharpened bone repeatedly dipped in a coconut shell bowl containing an inky liquid. The needle was tied perpendicular to a small stick. The *Kahuna* tapped the head of the needle with a small wooden mallet while skillfully making the outline of the shark.

At the first tap of the needle Zachary flinched, raising a growl from the *Kahuna*. After that, he lay as still as possible, gritting his teeth on the awa root. The numbing effects of the awa soon helped the situation and the process continued. Kaleo stood over the operation, arms folded on his chest, watching with great satisfaction.

When the *Kahuna* was finished with this artwork; he bade Zachary to sit up and view the creation. Both Zachary and Kaleo were pleased with the work, but Zachary had a pang of guilt at the thought of wearing the symbol of a pagan god on his body for the rest of his life. He asked the *Kahuna* to do another tattoo on his right bicep. He drew a simple cross in the dirt beside the mat and then lay down for the added symbol of his past life, but continuing beliefs.

The orders finally came. Zachary and Kaleo boarded a war canoe along with the musket platoon.

Other canoes in the flotilla carried Isaac Davis and John Young along with their cannons.

The flotilla landed at Waipio Bay, to the south of Kahului and Wailuku. The troops and their weapons disembarked. The encampment was established before nightfall.

The next morning a runner from Kalima arrived at the encampment, bearing orders directing the forces to move inland with all haste. The air was electric with the heady feeling that this was it, a real military engagement after all the months of preparing.

The musket company and the cannons began the slow trek up the grade from the beach toward the mountains. Kaleo and Zachary moved well ahead of the column. "Come Koa Kai, we should move quickly and find my Father for further orders. If we cannot find him, we should find a place to assemble the weapons to support the coming battle."

Upon arriving at the *Opae-pilau* hill they saw the army of Kapakahili below them and the troops of Kamehameha's advance troops arrayed along the hillside. Among the red-cloaked *Alii*, Kaleo saw Kalima at the right hand of Kamehameha. He pointed to the brightly colored group of chiefs. "Koa Kai we cannot go to my Father, the engagement of the day is already set. All we can do is engage our troops as soon as they arrive."

The two young warriors stayed low in the hala trees and watched the spectacle unfold. The Mauian army was deploying on the plain below. Standing out from the warm greens of the valley, the *Alii* chiefs were arrayed in bright capes of red and yellow feathers. The chiefs were led by images of the gods on pikes and *kahilis*, which looked to Zachary like large bright colored feather dusters. The chiefs wore helmets, many of which were also adorned with bright feathers. The units of common soldiers were arrayed on the field in a crescent formation. They were dressed only in *malos* and carrying a variety of weapons. They marched to the cadence of drums and *ipu* gourds;

many had ankle rattles or bells, which added to the sound of their advance. On command the Mauian soldiers roared a taunting cheer at their adversaries.

After a flurry of drum beating and taunts by the Hawaiian invaders, Kamehameha stepped out on a rise and addressed the foe arrayed below.

Zachary did not understand the proceedings that were taking place. "Kaleo what is happening?" Kaleo replied, "It is traditional that the sides trade insults. The great king is now defaming Kapakahili's heritage." Kaleo points to the group of Mauian *Alii* below. "It is now Kapakahili's turn to throw insults."

After the second round of insults and the hoots and hollers of the two assembled armies, Kamehameha again stepped out to speak.

Kaleo whispered, "*A 'we* Koa Kai, the great king has challenged Kapakahili to fight to the death to decide the day."

Kaleo and Zachary watched as the two combatants first traded spears and rocks fired by slingshot at some distance. Then Kamehameha charged his adversary with a long *pololo* spear. Kapakahili fended off the spear with his short *ihe* spear. The two combatants were locked together for a minute or two before Kamehameha broke the stalemate. He pushed Kapakahili away. Then he grabbed his war club and struck his adversary in the chest. The shark's teeth of the club caused great damage. Kapakahili lunged forward and stabbed Kamehameha with his dagger. Kamehameha pushed him away causing him to stumble to the ground. Before his adversary could regain his feet, Kamehameha swung his war club on to the skull of Kapakahili. It was over. Both armies stood silently in awe of the spectacle that they had just witnessed. The silence was broken when a Mauian chief commanded his warriors to advance on their enemy. The soldiers of Maui shouted and roared as they advanced up the slope.

The Hawaiian troops responded with an equally ear-piercing roar. They rained slinged stones and spears down upon the advancing Mauians.   The time spent by the individual combat between Kamehameha and Kapakahili had allowed more of the Hawaiian troops to arrive from the beachhead and join the fray.

Kaleo grabbed Zach's arm, "Come quickly we must bring up the muskets or we will miss the whole battle."

The two young warriors sprinted down the slope toward the path on which they had left the musketeers and the artillery. "Hurry Koa Kai, *wiki wiki*."

Kaleo and Zachary caught up with their troops who were helping Davis, Young and several dozen kanakas pull, push and grunt the cannon up the hillside path. They joined in moving the gun toward the sound of the battle. They finally broke out into the open on the flank of the Mauian army.

However, the Hawaiian troops were engaged at close quarters with their adversaries and turned the flank away from the cannon and muskets before they could fire a shot. Though they did not gain a position to fire, their presence did not go unnoticed by the already wavering Maui formation. The end of the Maui formation pulled away from the position of the guns.

Kaleo, Zachary and the musketeers moved forward again to join in pursuit of the retreating Mauians. Soon the grizzly refuse of the battle slowed their advance. The field was strewn with the dead and dying. Due to the vicious weapons used in the fray, many of the motionless bodies were ripped open, intestines and other organs exposed to the afternoon sun. There were victims whose skulls had been cracked open by war clubs; the distorted expression of their last agony shown on their bloody faces. The ground was covered with mud and trampled vegetation, all of which was mixed with the blood of the fallen warriors. The distinctive smell of death mixed with the fragrance of the surrounding flowers and other vegetation, laced the air with a nauseating potpourri.

As Kaleo and Zachary came upon the grizzly scene, Zachary stopped in his tracks, aghast at the sight before him. Zachary felt the contents of his stomach rushing up his throat from below. He grasped his stomach and swallowed hard to keep from losing its contents.

Kaleo seeing his comrade's distress came to his side, "Koa Kai, keep moving and don't look, it is easier that way."

They continued at a jogging pace through the carnage, but the battle was over, their enemy was in full retreat. It was over and they had not engaged the enemy. They missed it. The realization came upon Kaleo and Zachary at the same time. They both collapsed against the side of the hill, panting from the exertion. Sweat streamed down their faces and torsos.

"Damn, Koa Kai, we have missed the battle." Kaleo exclaimed with a still panting breath. "A great victory and we were almost a part of it."

Zachary replied, "There will most likely be an engagement tomorrow to gain the final victory, and we will be there. We will be ready."

Kaleo playfully poked Zachary's arm. "You are right; this war is not yet over. We will have our taste of glory before it ends."

The platoon carrying their muskets finally caught up with Kaleo and Zachary. They were also panting from their double-time jog pursuing their leaders, who were pursuing the action of the battle. Kaleo bid the troops to stand down and rest for a while. After about twenty minutes, Zachary ordered his platoon into a loose formation and marched them back through the carnage of the battlefield to their encampment.

Zachary was overly optimistic; there was no battle the next day, the survivors of Kapakahili's army retreated all the way back to the capital city of Wailuku.

Kamehameha had waited most of his life for the opportunity to vanquish the armies of his archenemy Kahekili, but, the Mauians still had a substantial army at Wailuku; he did not want to move too quickly when he was this close to success and perhaps sustain a loss that could reverse his fortunes. He waited while reinforcements arrived from the stronghold near Hana.

Kaleo and Zachary were not the only ones disappointed that the cannon and muskets did not reach the battle until it was too late for them to be of use. Kamehameha knew that he suffered casualties in the battle because the *Haole* weapons were not there to turn the tide of battle in his favor sooner than had actually happened. The next battle would be different. The cannon and muskets would be placed in the center of the formations, where they would be most effective.

Zachary continued to drill his troops on a daily basis. He was pleased and saw no particular significance when authorized to expend some more of the scarce gunpowder in live firing exercises.

Within two to three days of the previous battle Kamehameha ordered an amphibious assault on the beach near Kahului. The reinforcements from Hana went directly to that point. Once the beachhead was secured, the cannon and musket platoon were moved to that beach. All was ready for the final assault.

On the morning of the advance toward Wailuku, eighty to one hundred troops were detailed to help pull and push the cannon *Lopaka* at a pace that kept in stride with the moving army. Zachary and his musket platoon moved inland just ahead of the cannon.

This time the remaining army of Maui commanded by Kalanikupule took the advantage of the high ground. They were spread out along the slopes of Ioa Valley, awaiting the advancing Hawaiians. They watched the spectacle as the rival army approached marching to the sound of opu gourds and drums. The red and yellow cloaks of the Ali'i warriors shone brightly in the morning sun. Following the *Alii* were their standard bearers who carried equally bright *kahilis* signifying their chief's rank.

There were also bearers of the Ali'i chiefs' family gods and the war god *Ku*. Hundreds of common soldiers, the *kanakas*, marched below them, most were clad in their *malo* loincloths, carrying their designated complement of weapons.

On the perimeter of the Mauian side of the battlefield were old men, women and children. They brought their lunches and came to watch the upcoming battle. Many of the Hawaiian chiefs brought wives, children, and other followers, who arranged themselves along the edges of the field.

As the Hawaiian units wheeled off to the left and right to form the familiar crescent formation, an uneasiness ran through the Mauian lines as they saw the platoon armed with muskets form up in the middle of the formation and move into position. Next to them was the cannon *Lopaka*.

Davis and Young gave the orders to load and aim the brass artillery piece. The command was given and the cannon belched fire and a ball that whistled upward tearing through the Mauian ranks. From their position below Zachary and Kaleo could see two of the Maui soldiers fly into the air and another couple slump to the ground wounded.

Lopaka belched destruction on the assembled Maui forces several more times before the Hawaiians began to advance up the slope. The muskets had yet to be fired, since the range was still long and the amount of gunpowder carried by each of Zach's troopers was limited. The order to advance was given and the formation began to move forward.

When the formation had advanced part way up the slope, Zachary gave the order to halt. They were now close enough to take incoming stones and spears. Zachary encouraged his troops, "Steady, Men!"

Another mass of incoming missiles rained down on the musket platoon. The Maui troops were attempting to inflict casualties on the gun bearers before they could do their damage. Zachary dodged a long spear; several hurled stones flew by. One of Zach's men moaned, as a spear nicked his side, but he did not fall to the ground. He held his position in the ranks. Zachary commanded, "Hold Your Fire men, just a little further!"

Finally, within forty yards of the enemy's ranks, Zach gave the commands, "Platoon Halt!" The two ranks of ten men each stopped in their tracks just as they had practiced for many months. "First squad present arms!" A pause, "Ready!" Zachary pointed his short ihe spear at the enemy, "Take Aim, Fire!"

The report of the muskets echoed in the box canyon of the *Iao* Valley. Several Maui soldiers dropped from their wounds.

As trained, the First squad dropped to one knee and began reloading their muskets. "Second squad present arms!" A pause, "Ready!" Zachary again pointed his short ihe spear at the enemy, "Take Aim, Fire!" Again, the Mauian line suffered casualties.

Ever aware of the mission proscribed by his Father, Kaleo was standing behind Zachary throughout the advance forward and the beginning of the firing sequence. "*Maikai*, Koa Kai you have done it, your weapons are truly magic."

After several more rounds of musket fire the center of the Maui line began to waiver. The Hawaiian units on either side of the musket platoon began to advance. The once clear air was now clouded by black powder smoke. In between the reports of the muskets and cannon, the air was filled with the shouts and curses of the two armies, mixed with the moans of the wounded and dying.

Slowly at first the Maui troops began to falter and were pushed back up the slope. As their flanks began to be pushed together, their retreat began to quicken. While the earlier advance and musket firing had been taking place, the cannon was moved to higher ground, to gain a clear shot at the Mauian flanks. The first shot from the cannon cut across the rear of the Mauian soldiers. Some of the troops began to run up the slope in panic. The rout was on.

The Mauians were in full retreat up the slope toward *Ioa* needle. Many had dropped their weapons and run. Zachary's musketeers fired at will, dropping the retreating foe and adding to the panic, until their supply of gunpowder was exhausted. Many of the retreating soldiers were clubbed from behind as they climbed away from the Hawaiians.

This day's engagement would become known as the battle of the Damming of the Waters because of the bodies that blocked the mountain stream running from Ioa. The war to conquer Maui was all but over. The chiefs of the defeated side retreated to the island of Molokai and then on to Oahu and the rage of Kahekili.

The Hawaiian troops stopped at the base of the *Ioa* Needle. There were still small pockets of mopping up action in areas below and to their right and left. Zachary was heaving from the great exertion he expended getting up the slope. His body was covered in sweat, dirt and splatters of blood. He looked at the carnage below them and passed that to the vista of the coastal plain which included the villages of Wailuku and Kahalui and beyond that to the beautiful blue ocean stretching to the horizon.

Kaleo felt a rush of elation. Not only was the battle won, but his charge, Koa Kai had performed admirably, which meant that he would no longer have the grave responsibility of shadowing his friend. He wrapped his big arms around Zach and squeezed him in a bear hug. "We did it. No, you did it, the muskets did their deed, the day is won, and you fought like a true Hawaiian *Alii*."

The two comrades stood silently for a few minutes, each with an arm over the other's shoulder, each contemplating the deeds of the day. They were brothers, brothers in arms, if not in blood.

Kalanikupule, some of the remnants of his army and his family members escaped over the western Maui Mountains and on to Oahu, to report their loss to Kahekili. After many years of struggle, Kamehameha had finally conquered Maui, though he had yet to defeat an army directly commanded by his archrival Kahekili.

Kamehameha had only a few weeks to consolidate his hold on Maui; when in the ever-changing tapestry of politics and power struggles, war broke out on the Big Island. With Kamehameha's army engaged on Maui, the old rivals on the Big Island could not help but try to add to their districts of the island. Keoua of the Red Cloak killed his ally of the 1782 campaigns Keawe-Mauhili, and began raids into Kamehameha's domain.

Faced with the prospect of losing control of his home district, Kamehameha had no choice but to again divide his army. He left some troops on Maui to discourage Kahekili's return, and took the remainder home to the Big Island to finally defeat his adversaries there and unite the island under one authority.

Zachary and Kaleo, along with the musket platoon, made the short voyage back to the Big Island. The entire village at *Kealakekua* ran down to the beach to greet the returning army. Those who had been left behind when the army departed: the old, the women, and the children lined the beach waving and shouting.

As Zachary's war canoe slid up onto the sand, Pua Lani rushed out into the water to meet Zachary's outstretched arms. Pua placed a fresh lei over Zachary's head. They rubbed noses in the Hawaiian fashion and then hugged and kissed in the *Haole* style. Zachary leaned too far and fell out of the canoe falling into the knee- deep water with Pua in his arms. They rounded in the water, laughing and splashing and hugging in joy. Other women ran past them to the canoes. There were people splashing in the water all around them, but they only saw each other.

Sitting up in the water Zachary spoke, "Pua, I can't tell you how good it is to be home!" He continued professing his feelings, "You are my love and my joy." Zachary and Pua finally stood up and waded from the water.

There was great rejoicing and feasting for several days to celebrate the victory in Maui and the return of the Hawaiian troops. Though Zachary still ate in the men's dining hut, he spent as much of the next two days as he could with Pua.

The Hawaiian plan to keep the three *Haole*s apart was relaxed early on. The three had to work together to coordinate their military activities. They ate at the men's hut, though not always together since they had made their own friends and acquaintances among their Hawaiian capturers. The three were also together at Kamehameha's court and became trusted advisors to the king. The two older men still took the central role as advisors. Although everyone, including Kamehameha recognized Zachary's skills as a warrior.

One afternoon three weeks after returning from Maui, the three *Haole*s were together. Davis started the line of conversation, "You know we couldn't have asked for more. We went from lowly sailors to advisors to a king. These people treat us as one of their own and do all they can to see that our needs are looked after. And Zachary, you have become a real family man."

Young replied, "And to think we tried so hard to escape this paradise."

Zachary responded to Young's comment, "You have to remember that when we were trying to escape, we thought that the Hawaiians were most likely going to kill and eat us."

Davis added, "Ya, well if they had not needed us to man their guns, we might have become dinner meat."

Young, "The way it has worked out, I don't see why I would ever want to leave this place." The other two *Haole*s nodded their concurrence, thus ending the discussion.

The village at *Kealakekua* had truly become Zachary's home. After the stresses of battle and the sweet return to the safety of his lover's arms, Zachary had not thought of his previous life in weeks.

Though Zachary interacted with the other *Haole*s, Young and Davis almost daily, they were now as much a part of his Hawaiian landscape as Kaleo or Pua.

CHAPTER 13

LIFE IN LONDON AND CALIFORNIA

LIZZIE AND HER Aunt Beth arrived in London during a late summer shower. Beth was expected, as her cousin had invited her some time ago. Beth and her cousin Linda had corresponded after the end of the war to plan this reunion. Linda was pleasantly surprised at the arrival of a young second cousin along with Beth.

As it turned out, Lizzie and her aunt spent over two years in England including trips from there to the Continent. Beth made provisions for tutors and pressed for her niece's higher education in a world that was yet to value the education of women. Lizzie studied literature, art and language, most especially French. As a young lady in London she was exposed to many educational experiences that she only would have dreamed of in New England.

As Lizzie's beauty continued to blossom through her teenage years, she was approached and pursued by several well-placed young men. Aunt Beth, although quite liberal for her era, knew what young men were after, and made sure proper decorum was maintained and that her niece's virtue remained intact.

In this exciting time of her life, Lizzie had only a few thoughts of the rough-hewn boy of the picnic outing, which now seemed so long ago. When she did think of Zachary it was brief. She supposed that he was still at home under the tutelage of his aunt.

After Zachary was separated from *Setauket*, Israel had no choice but to continue the voyage northward along the coast of California to trade for hides. Israel learned of a requirement to call at the capitol of Monterey to have their cargo inspected. *Setauket* sailed north to Monterey and submitted to the inspection, which took days, as the entire cargo was required to be unloaded, inspected by local officials and then re-stowed. *Setauket* collected hides at Monterey and then moved south to San Pedro to do the same, before sailing back to San Diego.

While at San Pedro, Israel heard there had been some upheaval at San Diego and the Commissioner. *Senor* Emmanuelle had been replaced. After his eviction from this harbor only a few weeks earlier, Israel was apprehensive as he approached the Commissioner's office to present the ship's papers for the second time. Israel and Bolton entered the office and found themselves in front of a weathered old man who had obviously spent most of his days in the dry hot climate of southern California. At his side was Major Castile, the commander of the presidio. When Israel nodded to Castile, he stepped forward to shake hands. With a pleasant smile and tolerable English, he greeted Israel. "Welcome back, Captain Redden, and *Senor* Bolton, I believe. May I introduce our new Commissioner *Senor* Ramos?"

Israel released Castile's hand and shook the Commissioner's. Israel's first impression told him the old man's steely gray eyes and strong handshake were those of a man of integrity.

Ramos gestured to the chairs, "Gentlemen please be seated." He spoke in Spanish with a local accent. Bolton had a hard time understanding the Commissioner, but did his best to act as interpreter.

The Commissioner went on, "Major Castile has told me of your last visit and was sorry to hear that you and your men were so rudely treated. Since you have presented your ship's papers previously, we can dispense with that formality."

Seeing Bolton struggle, Major Castile injected himself as the interpreter. Israel relaxed, for it appeared that the atmosphere had changed since his last visit. Placing the documents on his lap he replied. "Thank you, Senor."

Ramos continued, "The Governor asked that I leave my ranch and take the roll of acting Commissioner until a new one may be appointed. It seems that *Senor* Emmanuelle was more interested in his private ventures than in the honorable trade of the local merchants and landowners. I assure you Captain. " We are happy to have your business and will be most pleased to support your efforts. I have several dozen hides at my ranch that are available for trade. Might I suggest that you take advantage of our protected harbor and beaches to prepare your hides for shipment?"

Israel acknowledged the offer, "Thank you *Senor*."

The Commissioner waved a crooked forefinger at Israel. "Of course, Captain we expect you to keep your crew under control while in San Diego. Other than that, we are happy to do business."

"Thank you, *Senor* Commissioner." Israel replied, "We appreciate your hospitality and will act accordingly."

The meeting over Israel and Bolton returned to their ship and made plans for the remainder of the venture.

It took a total of nine months to fill the ship with hides and head south for home. The process of trading for hides on the beach at San Diego caused Israel to station four to six men ashore to work on the hides while the remainder of the crew performed their normal duties on the ship. Nimmo was assigned to oversee the work ashore.

A work area was built on a flat stretch of land just off the beach. Lean-to shelters were made using canvas hatch covers and sails that had been patched for the last time. Casks were used for brine to soak the hides. The dried hides were soaked for several days in the casks then scraped to remove the fur and any remaining scraps of meat and sinus, before being hung on stretchers and again dried. The work was hot and smelly under the glare of the desert sun.

After months at sea there were many benefits to shore duty. Mr. Nimmo was not a hard driver though he made sure that the daily quota of processed hides was met. When the quota was reached, the crewmen had time to wander the beach, rent a horse and ride to town, or just relish having mother earth under their feet.

Replacing the standard ship's ration of hardtack and salted meat was the least expensive ration on this coast: fresh beef. At first the sailors were overjoyed with the change in diet, but after a week or so of beef at every meal; many of them longed for their more familiar rations.

Most days were hot and sunny. The sailors worked barefoot with only their seediest breeches to cover their tanned bodies. Since the desert air became cool at night, the sailors built a fire next to their sleeping lean-tos. They would sing and tell stories for some time before going to sleep.

Over time Bolton rotated the entire crew through the shore duty. At first every man was eager to have time on terra firma, but after a few day of the new drudgery: hauling heavy hides and splashing inthe brine: they were happy to be aboard ship again and their sailor's routine.

The process of tanning hides had several steps. First the goods that had been brought from New England were traded with the local ranchers and missionaries to gain hides. Secondly, the hides were scraped, soaked in brine, and then dried. The dried hides were stored until enough were accumulated to load the ship for the voyage home. While the onshore processing was ongoing, *Setauket* moved up and down the coast accumulating more hides.

While sailing along the coast, Israel hoped to find the whereabouts of the *Eleanora* and/or *Fair American*. The two ships were known along the California coast since they had been in the hide trade in previous years, but they were nowhere to be found. It appeared they were loaded from their previous activity and were now headed south, around the Horn and home.

Before heading to its homeport, *Setauket* went to Boston and unloaded the hides. While there, Israel met and dined with Mr. Worthington and the other owners. All were in high spirits over the conclusion of the successful voyage and the profits generated by the valuable cargo. After fine cigars and several brandies, it was decided they would have to do this profitable voyage more than once.

Returning home after two years at sea, Israel would have to explain to Jessica that he had lost Zachary. Sailing in the eighteenth and nineteenth centuries was understood to be a dangerous business. If Zachary had fallen from a yard or had been washed overboard, he could have more easily explained this to Jessica, and they would have grieved but had closure to the issue. Not knowing what happened to Zachary made it worse.

It was a sunny June day in 1791 when word reached Jessica that the *Setauket* had been sighted and was heading up the river. She was jubilant. After summoning Emily, they washed, primped, and put on their best dresses to meet their returning husband and father.

Setauket anchored. Israel, along with Mr. Bolton was rowed into the dock. As they climbed onto the dock Jessica decided she was not about to stand on ceremony or withhold her emotions in the stoic New England fashion. She wrapped her arms around Israel's neck and gave him a big kiss. Israel reached out and pulled Emily to them, hugging both of his women at once.

When the round of joyful affection was over, Jessica looked around and not seeing Zachary asked, "Is Zachary still on the ship?"

Israel not knowing how to tactfully explain responded, "I'm afraid that we lost him." Jessica's joy turned to shock and grief. "You mean he is dead."

"I don't know! We lost him." Israel grasped her shoulders.

"What do you mean you lost him?" said Jessica with tears running down her cheeks. Israel tried to defuse the situation and replied. "Jessica let's go home; I will explain."

When they got home, Israel sat Jessica and Emily on the couch and as unemotionally as he could, explained the circumstances under which Zachary was lost. Minimizing the mention of the cantina and making no reference to brothels, Israel explained that Zachary was separated from the ship's company and they were ordered from the harbor without him.

Israel ended his story with, "he was a fine lad and I have prayed every day since that he is alive and well."

Israel then hugged Jessica and Emily. Their sense of loss bound them more tightly together as a family.

During the remainder of 1791 and all of 1792, *Setauket* was engaged in the coastal trade with only one voyage to England and back. Israel was happy to have more time at home, but knew that the real profits were to be made with another extended voyage to the California coast.

In July of 1793, Mr. Worthington made another visit to Israel and Jessica. Jessica knew that the visit would likely mean another extended voyage for her husband. She was reluctantly pleasant to Worthington.

It was a cold rainy day when Worthington arrived and boarded *Setauket*. In the captain's cabin, Worthington took off and hung his oilskins and as usual started with the good news. "Israel, the owners and I as always, are happy with your work. We have decided to offer you the opportunity to purchase a ten percent share in the ownership of *Setauket*."

Israel responded, "Thank you very much. That is completely unexpected and greatly appreciated."

Worthington moved on to the point of the discussion. "We have decided that the hide business is as successful as anything we have pursued and wish to continue and expand that business. We want you to take *Setauket* back to New Spain to accumulate another cargo of hides. We are looking for a second ship to join you in California so that it might continue to accumulate cargo after you are loaded and heading for home. If you are agreeable, we want you to depart within the next two months.

The business concluded, Worthington enjoyed a fine dinner, spent the night, and headed off in the morning. Once he had left, Israel explained the preceding day's discussions to Jessica. He was excited at the chance to become a part owner in his ship. He explained to Jessica, "This not only shows the owner's great confidence in me, but ensures that I can command *Setauket* for as long as I choose."

Jessica replied softly, "Israel, I am happy for you, but I am not happy at the prospect of losing you for the next two years."

Taking her hand, Israel replied. "I know dear, I do not relish that part of it, but if I do one more trip, I may be able to buy the *Setauket* or a similar ship outright. If I can do that, I can then decide what trips to take, or if I want to hire a captain to take some of them instead of me."

Jessica reluctantly agreed, knowing that she had no choice or real input. In Mid-August 1793 Setauket departed south again loaded with a cargo of metal goods, cloth, and whiskey to trade with the people of California. It was the beginning of spring in Patagonia and the rest of the Southern Hemisphere. By the time *Setauket* arrived at Cape Horn it would be early Summer.

The crew for the second voyage around the Horn included the Mates, Bolton and Nimmo. The carpenter and sail maker remained the same, also. Much of the ordinary crew had changed since the first voyage; however, Danny O'Brien remained. The *Setauket* had become Danny's family and he was hopeful that on the second trip to California they might find out what happened to Zachary.

Setauket rounded Cape Horn in October of 1793 and arrived in Monterrey in December, where they began collecting hides. As Israel had learned on the first trip, foreign vessels must have their cargoes inspected at the capital of Monterey before trading along the coast. Being that far north along the coast, Israel decided to sail north to San Francisco to begin accumulating hides and then to work south to San Diego, making stops at the mission villages and presidios along the way.

One afternoon, several weeks after his return from Maui, Zachary's thoughts turned briefly to his previous life. A ship entered *Kealakekua* Bay. It was a brig with dimensions similar to the whalers and smaller merchant ships which he had seen back home. Seeing the ship brought back additional memories of his past including Jessica and Israel and of course Lizzie. He had not thought about "Back Home," for weeks. It all seemed so long ago and far away, as if they were in some other world. Of course, culturally speaking they were in another world.

Kaleo, who was always eager to explore *Haole* things, sought out Zachary. "Come Koa Kai, we should go out to the *Haole* ship. You can be my interpreter."

Kamehameha was attempting to get powder and additional *Haole* weapons from any ship that visited his waters. A large war canoe carrying Kamehameha, Davis and Young was headed to the anchored ship before Kaleo and Zachary left the shore in their outrigger canoe.

Kaleo speculated as they paddled out to the ship, "Maybe we can trade for a *Haole* sword or something else really good."

As they approached from the downwind side of the ship, Zachary inhaled a distinctive smell that he recollected from ships he had seen in New England. "Kaleo, there will not be much trading here, it is a whaler."

Kaleo responded, "Ah, too bad, but let us go on it anyway."

Zachary tied the canoe to the side of the ship and the two lads scrambled up the side and onto the deck. Kamehameha and his *Haole* advisors were already talking with the Captain.

The mate saw Zachary and Kaleo as well as other locals climbing on to his ship and came toward them. "Off my ship you frickin' savages."

The mate waved a belaying pin toward Zachary and Kaleo. Zachary blocked the belaying pin and replied, "Who the fuck you callin' a savage?"

The mate was stopped in his tracks by the sound of an English-speaking native. He saw the two Englishmen accompanying the king, now he meets another with a clearly Yankee accent. He exclaimed, "How many of you mother sons are there?"

Zachary replied, "How many what?" As the mate relaxed the belaying pin, Zachary let go of it and went on. "If you mean white men, there is Mr. Young from the *Eleanora* and Mr. Davis and me from the *Fair American*." Zachary leaned back against the main shrouds, "We are warriors in the service of Kamehameha the king of this and other islands."

The mate now relaxed and leaned against the starboard rail and remained inquisitive. "How the hell did that happen?"

Zachary replied, "It's a long story."

The mate reached out his right hand, "I am Billy Buckingham." They shook hands. This is the *Ester Lee* out of Nantucket. We have been whaling for the best part of two years and are heading home with all our barrels full." He waved toward the raised main hatch. "If you got the time, I'd sure like to hear more of how you got here."

Zachary agreed and for the next two hours he conversed with Billy Buckingham. He explained how he had been separated from the *Setauket* and came to be on the *Fair American* when it was attacked.

Billy responded, "*Setauket*, a pretty, three mast'd ship? I think I seen it once off Orient Point."

While this discussion was going on, Kaleo was becoming bored. His grasp of English was only good enough to understand fleeting parts of the conversation and he had nothing to add. Like most Hawaiians he was ready to abscond with any metal objects that were not bolted down. Kaleo picked up and was exploring the strange looking whaling paraphernalia.

Billy picked up his belaying pin pointing it at Kaleo, "Get away from that shit, you heathen."

Zachary responded to this move, "Kaleo is my friend and brother. Please treat him with respect."

Billy replied, "At the last island we visited the savages stole us blind and I'm not going to have it happen again."

Zachary all of a sudden felt less bonded to this fellow sailor and more in defense of his adopted brother. He asked Kaleo in Hawaiian not to disturb or take anything. He then said to Billy, "He will not take anything."

Billy snarled, "He better not or I will have his hide."

Zachary was again offended. "Be careful my friend. Kaleo has killed more men that you would care to count." Feeling the distancing from his fellow Yankee, he added, "We probably should be going, anyway."

Billy replied, "It has been a pleasure hearing your story. Is there anything I can do for you?"

Zachary thought a moment and then responded. "As I told you my people have no idea where I am and if I am alive or dead. Do you think that you could get a note to them when you get back to Nantucket?"

"Sure thing, I'll get you some writing paper and a pen."

Billy proceeded below decks and returned with the writing implements. Zachary looked around and found a flat place to write which was out of the wind so that his paper would not be carried away or flapped during his writing. He started slowly, for it had been years since he had attempted to write something. He started and stopped many times not knowing what he should say. He wrote:

Dear Aunt Jessica:

I am pleased to have this opportunity to write to you. I trust that Captain Redden and you are well.

I was grieved to have lost contact with the Setauket while we were in New Spain, but I have survived, and I am safe. I am on the island of Hawaii in the Sandwich Islands.

I am in the company of two British seamen, Messrs. Davis and Young. We are in the service of a local king, and are being treated well.

Zachary stopped and thought if he should mention that he was a soldier, but thought better of it.

No reason to make them worry. He went on.

Though I miss you folks, I have become accustomed to my new surroundings and remain well and strong.

He stopped again and wondered if he should tell them of Pua, but decided not to do so. He felt a pang of self-incrimination because he did not know if he would not mention them because he was ashamed of his native family or if it was just that they would not understand.

He finished the letter with no additional explanations.

Give my regards and affection to Emily. May God be with you all. Your loving nephew,
Zachary Bower

Zachary folded the letter and wrote his aunt's name and town on the backside. He handed it to Billy.

Billy took the letter in his left hand and shook Zachary's hand with his right. "I will be sure that your letter gets to your people. It has been a pleasure talking with you."

Zachary and Kaleo scrambled over the side of the ship into their waiting canoe and paddled to shore. Zachary was silent as he paddled. He thought of his American family and missed them. He thought that he had not addressed anything in the letter to Lizzie, but of course he did not know where she was. Anyway, he should not think of Lizzie, for he was now a married man.

Kaleo, seeing his friend's pensive reflection, felt that he should break the silence. He stopped paddling. "Koa Kai, look at this."

Reaching into his *malo* Kaleo extracted two iron bolts and four nails. "These will make good fishhooks, ya?"

Zachary responded, "Kaleo you shit, I told you not to take anything. I should make you take them back."

Kaleo's jaw dropped. "You wouldn't do that to me. Those *Haoles* might string me up."

Zachary sat quietly for a moment, looking as if he were weighing the alternatives. He then smiled and said, "No. I guess I couldn't let them get my brother."

By the time Kaleo and Zachary reached the beach, Zachary was again at peace with his new home and culture. He smiled to himself at the thought that the mate on the whaling ship had at first taken him as a Hawaiian and not a *Haole*.

In the coming months Zachary was involved with his wife and extended family and thought very little of his former life. The need to participate in additional skirmishes and battles were again to become his major preoccupation.

After several weeks at home, Zachary and Kaleo along with their musket unit were rotated back to Maui, so that other troops might come home for a spell.

It was three and a half years from the return of *Setauket,* from its first Pacific voyage before the letter arrived from Zachary. Billy Buckingham faithfully carried it back to Nantucket and then paid the postage to have it delivered to Jessica.

Jessica received the letter and recognized the handwriting and rushed to open it. She could not believe it; the joy that she felt equaled the sorrow she felt when she heard of Zachary's disappearance. She let out a whoop that caused Emily to come running.

When Emily entered the room and before she could say anything, Jessica hugged her and spun her around. Letting Emily go, Jessica exclaimed, waving the letter, "It is from Zachary, he is alive."

There was joy at the Redden house that night and throughout the town. In a small town the news of Zachary's disappearance had spread quickly. The news of his reappearance spread equally fast. Lizzie heard of Zachary's whereabouts from Emily within an hour of Jessica passing the news to her.

Jessica knew of the plan to send a second ship to California to replace *Setauket*. She knew that the second ship was to depart Boston in February of 1795. She had already sent a packet of letters to Mr. Worthington to forward to Israel. The morning after receiving Zachary's letter, Jessica wrote and posted a letter to Mr. Worthington in Boston telling him that Zachary was alive and asked him to forward an enclosed letter to Israel.

In Boston the Brigantine *Impatience* was upping anchor when Worthington was rowed out to her through a February snow squall. His mission was to get the letter from Jessica onboard before she departed. As he left the *Impatience* and was being rowed back to the dock, he felt warm in spite of the snow. He thought, "Within six- or seven-months Captain Redden will have a chance to find the lad."

CHAPTER 14

WAR ON THE BIG ISLAND

Since Kamehameha had made it clear that he intended to continue his campaign until all of the islands were in his domain, his old adversary, Kahekili planned a diversion so that he might rebuild his armies after the costly defeats at Maui. Kahekili called upon his ally on the southern end of the Big Island, Keoua of the Red Cloak to invade Kamehameha's home territory, thus making him pull his armies back to the Big Island.

The reports came to Kamehameha that Keoua had captured Hilo and was moving north: pillaging, raping, burning crops, and tearing up fishponds in the *Hamakua* district. The next rounds of reports said the invading army was moving into the Waipio Valley, the middle of Kamehameha's home territory. Keoua was supplying just the diversion that Kahekili had expected.

Kamehameha was faced with the dilemma of possibly having to fight on two fronts. He did not want to give up the territory that had been gained through many hard-fought battles, but he could not continue on and have Keoua capturing his homeland and biting at his backside. After taking counsel with his chiefs at *Kaunakakai* and Molokai, Kamehameha decided that he must split his forces. He would leave a holding force on the conquered islands of Maui and Molokai and take his best troops along with the *Haole* weapons and try to make short work of Keoua and his army, before Kahekili could mount his own offensive.

The runner found Pua at the stream above *Kealakekua* Bay pounding *kapa* into softer fabric. He informed her that one of her favorite aunts, Pili, was gravely ill at her home village of Kauai-hae and was asking for her. Pua immediately returned to her hut and prepared for the journey north.

Pua hurried back to the village and to the hut of her favorite uncle. Uncle Kimo who was too old to be with the army in Maui, but still had a swift outrigger canoe that he had skillfully sailed for most of his seventy years. Pua gained his assistance to take her to Kauai-hae.

Kimo immediately went to his canoe and prepared it for the trip. He was never a man to take chances, so he loaded fishing tackle, including fishhooks that he had carved from bone, his spears, and his war club into the canoe. On top of these items he placed his and Pua's traveling gear, which were carried in two *lauhala* baskets.

Pua was eager to get under way, but Kimo insisted that she go to the women's hut to eat before the journey. "Eat well," he said, "if we depart while the sun is high, we will be at Kauai-hae before dark."

At the women's eating hut, the older wahines rattled on about Pua's upcoming trip. A few of the women were praising Pua for being so willing to go to her aunt's bedside. Other women warned of traveling north as there were reports of invading armies to the north.

One old wahine warned, "There are evil warriors of Keoua invading our lands. They burn and they kill, and they will have their way with a pretty like you."

Pua replied, "I will be fine, the reports are from far away in Hilo." She shrugged, "anyway I have Uncle Kimo to protect me."

Pua left the hut and proceeded to the waiting canoe. She would do her duty for her beloved aunt, but shivered for a moment at the old wahine's warning. Then she thought to herself, "Oh well, if anything ugly is afoot; we will head home in Uncle's fast canoe."

The voyage north to Kauai-hae was uneventful for Kimo who had made similar trips to the north many times. When he was at the tiller of his canoe, he was in his mind, young and strong and master of his destiny. Kimo told stories of his youth and the glories of his campaigns as a great warrior.

As they skirted along the coast, Kim pointed out villages and landmarks as they glided past in the swift canoe.

Pua was thrilled at the speed of the outrigger. She had been on the large war canoes on several occasions, but had never been on a small outrigger canoe, out beyond the shelter of the reef. She loved her jovial uncle and listened to his stories as intently as possible considering the movement of the canoe.

As Kimo had promised, they arrived just as the last rays of the sun were disappearing in the sea. As they approached the beach, a couple of young boys ran down to greet them, helped them out of the canoe and helped to pull the canoe above the high tide line. Standing up on the beach after hours of the sea's motion, Pua lost her land legs. She swayed for a moment and almost fell. Kimo, who would not admit it if he had the same feeling, made jest of his niece's dizziness.

Once the brief bout of dizziness passed, Pua hurried up the beach to the village with one of the boys who led her to her aunt's hut. Inside it was quiet except for the whispers of the two *Kahuna*s who were attending to Pili. The only light was from two kukui nut lamps that flickered near the frail form of Aunt Pili. Pili's three attendants sat quietly at the foot of Pili's sleeping mats.

Pua moved to her aunt's side, kneeling next to her, taking her hand. The old woman opened her eyes. Her eyes were glazed from age and illness and not the flashing, joyful eyes that Pua remembered. With tears pooling in her own eyes, Pua hugged her aunt while rubbing cheeks and noses.

"Do not cry my child; it is as it should be," came the weak voice of Pili. "I have lived a full life.

I have loved and been loved by many." She squeezed Pua's hand, "Give my aloha to all and ask that they remember me."

Pua released the hug and sat up, "Pili, do not talk that way. I have come to aid in your recovery, not to attend your funeral." Pointing to her *lauhala* basket she continued, "I bring some special medicines from the *Kahuna*'s of *Kealakekua* to aid in your recovery."

Pili whispered, "What will be, will be child." Rolling on her side, "Now let me rest a bit and we will see what tomorrow brings."

After her long and eventful day, Pua was physically and mentally exhausted. Soon after Pili fell asleep, Pua followed, with her head on her aunt's side.

Kimo had followed Pua to her aunt's hut, but on seeing the two huddled together, he thought it best to wait until tomorrow to pay his respects. He was sore and tired from the day's events. With his spear and war club over his shoulder and his sleeping mat under his arm, he walked away with a slight limp from an old war wound which was aggravated from sitting on that leg much of the day. He sought out an old friend whom he knew would offer to share his hut for the night.

The first rays of the sun were lighting the eastern sky, when Zachary was awakened by the commotion outside his hut. Putting on his *malo*, he went to the entrance only to meet Kaleo, coming in the doorway.

Zachary, "What's happening?"

Kaleo responded, "We have orders, we are moving to the boats." Zachary, "We can't be moving inland this soon."

Kaleo, "Rumor is we are going home." Zachary, "I don't understand?"

Kaleo, "Don't have to, we've got orders."

On the beach there were masses of troops hurrying back and forth. All of the bedlam associated with moving a large army was in full tilt. It was evident that the loading of the cannons would take most of the day. Zachary and Kaleo were eager to go home to their families and enjoy the peace of being home. To that end Zachary ordered his riflemen into the first two war canoes which were ready to set sail and he and Kaleo headed past the reef into the deep blue open ocean and south towards home.

The trade winds were brisk, and the catamaran war canoes sped through the waves at a good pace. Zachary was exhilarated with the breeze in his face, the smell of salt air, and most importantly, the thoughts of being home with his beloved Pua. Kaleo smiled back at him. They were both engrossed in their anticipation of home.

The two lead canoes raced each other, attempting to demonstrate their respective sailing skills.

In the meantime, other war canoes loaded and departed Maui heading for their home shore.

The army of Keoua of the Red Cloak having captured Waimea, moved to the north and west.

Keoua sent raiding parties as tentacles out ahead of his main force to scout for the possibility that there was a body of defending forces ahead of them or that Kamehameha and his entire army had returned to defend their home turf. In most cases, the small villages were not defended, and the raiding parties could pillage and burn at will. The raiders would take foodstuffs and any women and children worth enslaving back to the main army for their consumption.

Two of Keoua's raiding parties met about one mile east of Kauaihae in the early evening. They could see the village down the slope from their position, but it was late, and they decided to rest for the night, dining on the day's plunder. They would raid the village in the morning.

The leader of the raiding party was an older *Alii* warrior who had not arisen in the chiefly ranks due to his lack of savvy in the ways of court politics. He was scarred from many battles and tattooed over half of his body, imitating his distant uncle Kahekili. His nickname among his troops was Koa Ilio, (War Dog). He always volunteered to lead such raiding parties, as pillaging and raping were his specialty. Also, he won favor by sharing his captives and other booty with his superiors.

The raiding party woke an hour before dawn and formed up into two groups. They did not expect much resistance, but just in case there were warriors in the village, they would move to the edge of the banana grove on the eastern edge of the village and wait for the rising Sun to be behind them.

After an hour the Sun was high enough to serve their purpose. On a signal from Koa Ilio, the fifty warriors let out a war whoop and charged the village. The first couple of people who came bolting from their huts were clubbed down by the attackers. The marauders pushed into huts and dragged out the occupants. After taking anything of value, they set the huts afire.

Pua began to waken with the morning's first light. She saw that her aunt was breathing softly, still fast asleep. Pua moved a bit away from her aunt on the mat; and faded back and forth between sleep and being awake. Pua was fully awakened by the first war whoop and the following screams of the villagers.

Kimo was also awakened by the commotion. Grabbing his war club and spear, he and his friend exited their hut to see mayhem coming their way from the east end of the village. Kimo's friend instinctively turned toward the battle, swinging his war club over his head.

Kimo turned the other direction calling to his friend, "I must save Pua!"

Kimo ran to the hut where he had left Pua the evening before. Looking behind him, he could see the raiders close behind him. Upon entering the hut, he beckoned, "Come Pua we must run for the canoe!"

Pua pulled on her aunt. "Come we must go!"

Kimo, "No Pua, leave her, I must get you out of here!"

Aunt Pili was now struggling to comprehend what was happening and arose from her mat. Before Kimo could make another plea, two marauding warriors burst into the hut behind Kimo.

Kimo swung around with his war club, but his assailant ducked and thrust his short spear under Kimo's rib cage piercing Kimo's left lung and heart. As Kimo crumpled to the floor, the warrior pushed his body away with his foot, to extract his spear.

Pua screamed at the sight of her uncle's murder. She was enraged and charged the two warriors swinging wildly. One of them grabbed her flailing hands while the other grabbed her around the waste, lifting her off her feet.

Aunt Pili was now up and attempting to come to her niece's aid. One of the marauders growled, "She's too old to take."

His colleague swung his war club against the old lady's head, killing her instantly.

Pua again screamed and kicked and scratched her attacker, but to no avail. The larger of the two assailants dragged her outside and threw her to the ground.

All around was bedlam, bodies of dead villagers and the carcasses of some of their animals which were not worth taking. Huts were burning and the marauders were carrying away anything of value. There were screams of women and children who were being dragged to the center of the village. The assailants held women on the ground so that their colleagues might perpetrate their rape in an efficient manner. If all went well, the holders would also get their turn at the victim.

Pua, a young and comely woman, would be a fine conquest. Her two assailants argued for a moment over who should have their way with her. However, she was obviously of a high class and touching an *Alii* of the highest caste, let alone having sex with an *Alii* woman could mean death at the hands of their own chiefs.

Before they could decide if the risk was worth the pleasure, Koa Ilio strode up behind them and seeing a young, beautiful *Alii* woman, he announced, "This one is for me!" Pulling her to her feet by her hair and pointing toward the center of the village he directed, "Take her with the rest."

The two soldiers obeyed their orders and took Pua to the center of the village. Even as captives, the caste system was in place and Pua was told to squat down with a group of the village leaders.

Koa Ilio was making decisions as to which captives were worth taking as slaves and which were disposable. Warriors with blood-smeared clubs were seeing to the disposables. There were continued screams and wales from the huddled groups.

Koa Ilio glanced over toward Pua and thought to himself what a fine lay she would be. He thought, "After this ugly business is done, a little to eat and then I will have my reward."

A soldier came running from the seaside of the village, waving toward the west and hollering, "Boats are coming!"

Koa Ilio's mental diversion was thus ended and seeing the sails in the distance began to bark orders. "Bind up the captives!" Pointing to another group of his troops, he ordered, "Take all the food and prizes you can carry." "We will move inland before those pigs can spoil our fun!"

The two lead canoes were making good headway to the south. Zachary was thinking of being back with his beloved Pua. "Kaleo, if this wind holds, we could be home in *Kealakekua* before dark."

Kaleo sat up to respond to Zachary, but he saw several pillars of smoke rising from the shore to their east. "Koa Kai there may be trouble." He waved at the helmsman to steer toward the shore. He then waved at the other canoe to follow.

An hour and a half later the two canoes had negotiated through the surf and slid up on to the beach. Kaleo ordered a dozen men to guard the boats and the other dozen to follow Zachary and him to the village.

In the village the remains of huts were still smoldering, the stench of death was everywhere. Kaleo, Zachary and their troops split up to search for survivors. After some searching, they found a mortally wounded woman who with her dying breaths cursed the vermin and pointed to the east.

Kaleo's face showed his rage at this atrocity. "Koa Kai, they have probably taken prisoners and cannot be moving very fast." Gesturing to the east, "If we hurry, we should be able to overtake them."

Zachary having grown weary from his months at war was less vehement about the pursuit. "We don't know how many of them are out there." We could go charging into Keoua's whole army."

"Koa Kai, some of them are my Ohana and they must be avenged."

Zachary, "We have only two dozen men. We have our muskets, but the munitions are on the later transports." Waving toward the sea, "We should wait for reinforcements."

Kaleo was fired with emotion rather than logic, "Koa Kai, I am going after them. You can come if you want."

Zachary, not wanting to leave his adopted brother in this time of danger, replied, "Shit, let's go see what we can do, without getting killed."

They sent a troop back to the canoes to bring more weapons. Kaleo, Zachary and the eleven remaining men started heading inland following the fresh tracks on the trail. They moved at a brisk jog.

After an hour on the trail towards Waimea, Kaleo signaled for them to slow down before breaking out of the protective vegetation into an open clearing. Ahead of them, going up a rise on the other end of the clearing was the slow-moving procession. A number of warriors had several strings of tethered captives in tow. About a quarter mile behind the main group, was an afterguard of ten warriors.

Kaleo, "We cannot overtake them from the rear, but they will have to rest soon and then we may have a chance to free the people."

Kaleo, Zachary and their squad worked to the right of the slow-moving procession. Kaleo's intent was to keep them in sight without being seen while executing a flanking maneuver, to gain some advantage with their minimal force.

Koa Ilio was furious at the slow progress, but pushing and beating the captive marchers did not increase their speed. He thought, "But the prizes were good, and I still have not had a good meal and the even better dessert that I owe myself for this day's work."

Koa Ilio knew that the remains of a settlement which they had plundered earlier in the week was only a mile or two ahead. He thought, "Even if Kamehameha's army is coming ashore it will take them time to organize, so we should be safe there tonight." As an afterthought, "Maybe the dogs will have dragged off the bodies in the village so that it does not smell too bad."

Arriving at the settlement, Koa Ilio gave the orders to bivouac for the night. His troops were tired from the day's strenuous activity, but they went about their assigned duties. Some began to prepare food from the new day's plunder. Others tied the captives to palm trees to limit the numbers of men needed to watch them. Still others took up stations to guard the perimeter of the encampment.

Having left this work to his lieutenants to oversee, Koa Ilio found the remains of a hut in which he decided to nap before the evening's festivities.

All was settled by dark. Torches were lit and the cooking was done. *Opus* and drums began beating. A few of the troops began to dance the traditional hula. Koa Ilio appeared from his nap and his troops cheered knowing that it was now time for the festivities to begin. First Koa Ilio and the *Alii* chiefs would be served and then the rest of the troops.

Kaleo, Zachary and their squad hid in the bush beyond the perimeter guards. They watched the party building before them. Kaleo sent a runner back to find the other squad and lead them to their location. The food smelled good. They had not eaten all day; but more important business was ahead before this night was over.

The dancing continued as the *opus* and drums beat louder and louder as the hulas intensified.

There was laughing and joking among Koa Ilio's troops. Their bellies were full, and they felt fresh from the day's victory over an enemy village.

Kaleo and Zachary watched silently from their hiding place in the foliage. They saw that the perimeter guards were more interested in watching the festivities than watching for threats from the darkness.

Koa Ilio had eaten his fill, had chewed some Ava root and was in high spirits. He stood up and hollered to the two men guarding the captives, "Bring me the wahine!"

The guard knew whom he meant; they all knew his taste for young beautiful women. They untied Pua and pulled her to the center of the encampment.

Upon seeing her, Zachary started to blurt out her name, but Kaleo grabbed his mouth and whispered, "Easy my friend, we can do nothing until the rest of the troops get here."

Zachary watched in horror, his mind racing, "How did she get here, why is this happening?" Koa Ilio commanded, "Dance for me!"

Pua spit in his face, whereupon he cuffed her with the back of his hand. "Dance for me or I will sic the dogs on you."

Upon seeing Pua go to the ground, Zachary tried to rise up, but Kaleo pulled him back down. "We must wait." He whispered.

Pua got up and clothed only in a *malo* began a slow hula to the beat of the *opus* and drums. The audience cheered at the entertainment and began clapping, shaking rattles, ankle bells, anything that would make a noise to beat in time with the *opus* and drums.

"Faster!" Commanded Koa Ilio.

The cadence increased, as did Pua's hula.

Kaleo had increasing problems holding Zachary in place. The sight of his beloved being humiliated in this way was too much to bear.

The closest perimeter guard hearing some rustling in the bush looked briefing over his shoulder, but not seeing anything he returned to watch the party, as he knew what would come next.

The dance of a young woman always enthused Koa Ilio. He felt a bulge in his *malo* and arose, ripping it off, his erect penis bared for all to see. His troops had seen this before, whenever they had some fair female captives. Koa Ilio would pick the wahine of his choice and rape her in front of the cheering troops. Afterwards the troops would have sport with all the captives. In such orgies anybody became fair game in the frenzy: old women, young boys, even the occasional old man. One of the troops cheered, "There will not be a dry hole this night!"

The revelers knew that this was going to be a great night. They laughed at the exclamation and cheered for their leader. Two soldiers grabbed Pua's shoulders and arms, one pulled off her *malo*. Forced to the ground, she kicked and twisted in vain. Koa Ilio strode forward to have his pleasure.

This was too much; Zachary broke away from Kaleo, grabbing his war club and spear. Venting his rage, he let out a blood curdling war whoop. The nearest perimeter guard turned at the sound of the scream, just in time to get Zachary's war club up the side of his neck. The shark's teeth cut his jugular. Spurting blood, he fell to the ground.

At Zachary's bolting forward, Kaleo Exclaimed, "Oh shit!" and then let out a similar war whoop.

The rest of their squad followed suit and charged into the encampment.

Zachary continued his charge straight at Koa Ilio. As he got in striking distance, he swung his club up at Koa Ilio's crotch, the shark's teeth ripping his scrotum and penis. Koa Ilio let out a squeal as he grabbed at his groin. Zachary drove his spear into Koa Ilio's throat.

The squeal became a gurgle as he fell backwards on the remains of his dinner.

The second squad of their force was close to the encampment when they heard the sounds of battle. They ran forward coming into the camp on the opposite side from Zachary and Kaleo's assault.

The much superior force of Koa Ilio was in disarray. Their leader had just been killed in front of them and they were under attack on both flanks. A few found weapons and attempted to fight, but most broke and ran into the night.

When the brief battle was over, Zachary helped Pua to her feet. They stood in the middle of the encampment, hugging intently for two or three minutes, both were crying with a mixture of relief and joy and love.

Kaleo, "Come, we must free the others before those dogs can regroup."

Pua released Zachary and grabbed her *malo* from the dirt. They freed the captives and moved off in the night to the west. But there would be no counterattack from Koa Ilio's troops. They did not stop their retreat until they reached Keoua's camp at Waimea. They feared retribution by Keoua for their defeat. Most had run off without their weapons, some naked having prepared for the orgy before they were attacked. The most vocal of the troops stepped forward and told Keoua how they were attacked in the middle of the night by Kamehameha's army and that they only retreated after putting up a stalwart defense. The other troops silently nodded in agreement with the story. Keoua hearing that his adversary was closer than expected retreated east to find a more defensible position.

Upon reaching the coast at the remains of Kauai-hae, Zachary and Kaleo found that Kamehameha's main force was in fact coming ashore. The campaign against Keoua of the Red Cloak was about to begin.

After seeing that Pua was sent safely back to *Kealakekua*, Zachary and Kaleo reported the encounter to their superiors, including the loss of two troops and the wounding of two others. They counted eleven enemy killed because they saw it fit not to take any live prisoners.

The returning army had to attend to business. Kamehameha began to plan his campaign against Keoua of the Red Cloak. Keoua had increased his forces with troops of the now deceased Keawe-Mauhili. Kamehameha on the other hand was fighting with only a portion of his army. It would be hard for either side to gain a decisive advantage.

There was not much time for planning, since Keoua was raiding villages around Waimea.

Keoua did not hold any of the invaded land. He was taunting Kamehameha to action.

Kamehameha gave the order and his army moved along the Kona coast of the Big Island to confront Keoua's army at Waimea. The army moved slowly at the rate it could move the cannon, *Lopaka*.

The two armies met briefly at Waimea but only a skirmish ensued before Keoua ordered his troops to retreat toward the eastern coast of the island. Keoua's army retreated until he found a place on the plain of Koa-papa to make his stand. When compared to Kamehameha's sweating lumbering troops pushing and pulling the cannon; Keoua's troops were fresh having executed an orderly retreat and now rested while awaiting their enemies' arrival.

Keoua arrayed his army on the plain in the normal crescent formation. Kamehameha's army moved down the slope through a wooded area to the edge of the plain. The strategy for the modern weapons had changed somewhat since the campaign on Maui. Zachary's troops complained about the hot refuse from the squad firing over them while they were kneeling to reload. To overcome this, the squads would be arrayed next to the cannon and after firing, the first squad would retire behind the second to reload. Zachary had learned the hard way that he had advanced his troop too close to the enemy at Ioa and had taken needless casualties from spears and stones. This time the weapons would be fired from beyond the range of the enemy's conventional weapons.

Kamehameha's army arrayed itself through a grove of coconut palms with the cannon and muskets in the middle of the formation. Davis and Young had convinced Kamehameha to dispense with the customary name-calling and other precursors to the battle and begin at long range with the weapons.

As soon as the army was spread before its opposition, the order was given and the cannon *Lopaka* fired a ball across the field into the middle of the opposing line. Then volleys from the musket squad followed; first from the right side of the cannon and then from the squad on the left. The weapons took their toll on Keoua's troops.

Keoua had heard the reports of the devastation caused on Maui by the cannon and muskets. He calculated that the only way he could survive in the face of such weapons was to capture them and use them to his advantage. Zachary was about to learn, just as Captain Cook had learned the hard way, that the Polynesians of these islands were never willing to falter due to a few casualties. Keoua was willing to stand still while the artillery and muskets chewed up their lines as long as he could advance and capture them.

Instead of retreating, Keoua's troops unleashed a round of stones and spears. However, the conventional weapons fell short of the Hawaiian's lines. Keoua had not anticipated weapons that could yield death and destruction at such a distance. The cannon and muskets were reloaded and again ripped through Keoua's ranks. He gave the order to advance. With a deafening war hoop his troops advanced across the open field.

In the middle of the field, Keoua's troops unleashed another round of stones and spears. Most of the projectiles were blocked by the palm trees which were interspersed throughout the Hawaiian formation. This time, the cannon loaded with grapeshot ripped a mean hole in the center of Keoua's line.

As the cannon was being reloaded, John Young called to Davis to bring more powder and shoot. Davis replied with a fit of expletives that the powder wagons had not made it to their position. They had been in such a hurry to engage the enemy; they had not waited for all their powder and shot.

As the muskets fired their last powder, Keoua gave the command to advance on the guns. He had selected elite units that were on either side of the center of his formation to charge and capture the guns. These troops gave another war hoop and charged up the slope.

Zachary and Kaleo knew that the weapons were out of action until more powder was brought up.

At the sight of the charging warriors converging on their position, Zachary felt a surge of fear run through his body, an uncontrollable feeling that he had never felt before. He backed up to run, but in doing so tripped over the foot of his friend Kaleo, falling to the ground. Kaleo helped him up and in as calm a voice as he could muster under the circumstances said, "Be careful brother, you could hurt yourself."

The soft confident words of his friend calmed Zachary to the task at hand. Kaleo added, "It is time to fight the old-fashioned way."

The musket troops were standing in disarray since they had no powder. They awaited orders.

They saw Zachary and Kaleo brandish their conventional weapons and they did likewise.

The Hawaiian warriors began the war chant and beat their weapons and ankle bells. Zachary took up the chant, waved his short spear in one hand and his war club in the other. Now at close range, the enemy spears and stones were able to inflict casualties on the Hawaiian troops. Then the opposing forces met in a clash of sweating muscles. There was a groan as if the colliding armies had knocked the wind out of each other. There were wildly flaying weapons, shouts of anger, curses, screams from the wounded and the moans of dying. It was mayhem.

Zachary was wildly swinging his war club and spear, not in the orderly manner taught by his instructors, but with a reactionary swing at anything or anybody that came close to him. Kaleo was now at his side. There was no need to worry about Koa Kai's courage at this point. He would either be a courageous warrior or die.

Zachary parried a spear with his own spear and swung his war club against the head of his adversary. Another adversary began an overhand swing of his shark tooth studded war club at Kaleo. Zachary instinctively drove his short spear underhanded below the ribcage of the assailant. The spear sunk so deeply into the falling body, Zach had to let it go, as the body fell away from him. He now had to rely on his war club and his dagger, which he pulled from his *malo*.

The Hawaiian units on either side of the musket platoon were equally engaged in the fray.

Seeing the frontal assault on his valued weapons Kamehameha signaled for reinforcements to join the melee in the center of his formation. The reinforcements, along with Kamehameha and his staff, including Kaiana and Kalima, advanced on both flanks of the group around the cannon.

Keoua's troops pushed Zachary and the Hawaiian forces back away from the cannon. Several of Zachary's troops had been wounded and had lost their muskets. Others of his troops had dropped their weapons to engage in hand-to-hand combat. Keoua's troops who had achieved their objective began picking up the muskets and turned the cannon toward the retreating Hawaiian line. But with no powder, controlling the cannon was of no advantage.

Meanwhile, Davis had gone to find the missing munitions wagon. It had bogged down on the trail. Davis ordered the troops struggling with the wagon to grab bags of powder and proceed to the battle line.

With the influx Kamehameha's reinforcements, the knot of battling foes moved back around the cannon. Zachary faced an adversary who was defending himself with a short spear, but was unbalanced because he was carrying one of the muskets in his other hand. He blocked the first spear thrust with his war club. The weight of the club opened the foes midsection. Zachary ripped across the exposed abdomen with his dagger. As his adversary fell, Zachary grabbed the musket from his hand and threw it against the wheel of the cannon's carriage.

Finally, after ten minutes of furious fighting for control of the cannon, Kamehameha's forces pushed their foes twenty yards away from the gun. Davis and his powder bearers arrived at the recaptured cannon. Davis pulled a limp body off the gun's barrel and the crew maneuvered it back around.

Zachary picked up the musket which he had left near the cannon and grabbed a bag of powder.

Six of his platoon still possessed their muskets and also filled their powder bags and loaded their weapons. Zachary told them to fire at will, and then took aim on an enemy troop and fired. The remnants of the musket platoon also found targets and fired. The loud report of the weapons gave heart to Kamehameha's troops who were already pushing the enemy back. The sound had the opposite effect on Keoua's forces. They had not held the cannon and knew that it was about to do its damage.

Davis had ordered a load with a ball for the first round and aimed to minimize friendly casualties among the still fighting masses. The ball ripped into the middle of a knot of Keoua's troops. They wavered and retreated down the slope to reform into a unit for another assault on the gun, but a second round from the cannon, this time grapeshot at point blank range blew a hole in the middle of this formation.

Keoua's forces began to retreat down the slope under a hail of spears and stones. Zachary saw a retreating soldier carrying one of his muskets. He took aim and dropped the foe.

As the remnants of Keoua's assault troops arrived at the line of the main force, the cannon fired into them. Keoua formed his line, awaiting the charge of Kamehameha's forces, but it did not come.

Rather than a traditional assault, Kamehameha preferred to let the *Haole* weapons do their work. The cannon and the muskets continued to inflict casualties on Keoua's troops until all the powder was spent. The survivors in Keoua's army retreated to the beach where waiting canoes carried Keoua and his chiefs away from the battle scene. A few miles down the coast. Keoua joined his retreating army and marched back to the southern end of the island. Most of the army, along with the women and children who had followed the army north now had to retreat overland back to their homes in the Ka'u district.

During the ferocity of the battle, Zachary had lost contact with Kaleo. Now that the day's fighting was over, he searched the battlefield for his friend. The field was scattered with the dead and dying. The now too familiar stench of death was in the air.

When he did not immediately find his friend in the area where the heavy fighting had taken place around the gun, Zachary feared that Kaleo may have become a casualty or captured by the retreating army. Zachary's eye surveyed down the slope from the gun position, but found only the bodies of enemy soldiers. He did find the remaining two muskets that were almost captured by the enemy. He picked up the weapons, having to wrench one of them from the grasp of a fallen soldier who stared blankly at the late afternoon sun.

Having satisfied himself that Kaleo was not among the bodies on the field, Zachary speculated to himself that Kaleo might have been wounded and taken to the rear for treatment. He returned to the position of the cannon and found eight of his musket platoon sitting in a group. Kaleo was not with them and he learned that two of his platoon had been killed. Kimo plus two others were severely wounded. Zachary took a few minutes to lament the losses with his troops, but his growing concern for Kaleo caused him to move on.

As he moved through the coconut palms, which had been behind the lines, he recognized the form of Kaleo kneeling on the ground, huddled in a ball. Zachary rushed to him, while thinking "Kaleo must be gravely wounded."

As Zachary grasped his friend, Kaleo let out a blood cuddling moan, "*A 'we, A'we!*"

Kaleo sat up, tears running down his cheeks. Zachary could see that it was not Kaleo who had been wounded. Instead he knelt beside the body of his fallen father, Kalima. Kaleo leaned back forward again. Zachary hugged his back and they wept together for the death of Kalima and for the anguish of the day.

Kamehameha and the remainder of his staff came into the grove of coconut palms. Upon seeing the body of his old friend and advisor the king came to add to the lamentation. He bid that Kaleo and Zachary rise and announced that he would build a *Heaiu* (temple) to the war god Ku, in honor of his friend and great fallen warrior, Kalima.

Finally, in the evening's fading light, Zachary and Kaleo returned to their encampment and fell on their mats in an exhausted sleep, not even cleaning the blood of the day's business from their bodies.

The next morning the two young warriors awoke and bathed in a stream to remove the caked blood and determine if any of the blood was their own. Luckily other than a few minor cuts and bruises, neither combatant had been wounded. They did however have aches in strange places from the previous day's hand-to-hand combat. They remained subdued because of the loss of Kalima and their comrades in the musket platoon.

The day's activities would be to see to the dead and accumulate the weapons from the battlefield.

Zachary stayed close to his friend to provide comfort if needed.

Kaleo asked in a muted tone, "Koa Kai I need you to help me break out my pointed upper teeth." Zachary was taken aback by Kaleo's request. "What do you mean?"

Kaleo: "I must break these teeth as I lament the loss of my father. I do not know if I can do it by myself."

Zachary had seen many Hawaiians with missing teeth and severe scars, but he assumed the wounds were either from fighting or some malady. He had never thought that part of the grieving process in this society included self-mutilation. He responded, "There is no need for that."

Kaleo: "I must. It is my duty, but I do not know if I am brave enough to do it by myself. You must help me."

Zachary: "How can I do such a thing to my beloved friend?"

Kaleo: "Because I am your friend you will help me do my duty."

Kaleo led Zachary to a *Kahuna* who provided a narrow chisel shaped stone and another larger stone for a mallet. Kaleo lay on a mat and motioned Zachary to him. Zachary knelt next to Kaleo's head; his eyes glazed with anguish at the thought of the deed he was about to perform.

Kaleo: "Please my friend you must be brave."

Zachary held the chisel against Kaleo's left eye-tooth. He raised the stone mallet and closed his eyes as he struck the chisel. He heard Kaleo's muffled moan. After, Kaleo sat up and spit out the pieces of tooth along with blood and spittle into a bowl. He lay back down. Zachary moved the chisel to the right eye, the tooth and repeated the process. A *Kahuna* then rushed forward and helped Kaleo sit up and spit the remnants of the second tooth into the bowl. The *Kahuna* then had him gargle with salt water to reduce the bleeding.

Zachary, appalled at what he had just done, rushed from the hut and deposited the contents of his stomach in the bushes behind the hut. Shaken by the experience, he forced himself to return to Kaleo to help him to his hut. There were so many things in this society which appeared so savage to him, that they were beyond his comprehension.

In a strictly class-based society, the common soldier's remains were treated commonly, but a great leader like Kalima was given much attention. The Hawaiians believed that *mana* (spiritual power) resided in one's bone marrow: the higher the class, the greater the *mana*. When a chief like Kalima died, an *imu* (underground oven) was prepared and the body was baked to expose the bones. The bones were collected and then a most trusted friend or relative would hide the bones in a cave or crevice in the pock marked volcanic mountains, so that the deceased's enemies could not capture his bones, and therefore his *mana*.

Kalima's body was prepared in this way, with ceremony and great lamentation. The next day the *Kahuna*s prepared the bones and packaged them so that Kaleo could do his duty and hide them. Kaleo prepared himself for the day's journey. He bade Zachary to accompany him, "Koa Kai will you accompany me on this journey to the mountains?" He added, "Though you cannot come the entire way."

Zachary replied, "Of course my friend, I am honored to assist you."

The two traveled a trail through the jungle toward the northeast quadrant of Mauna Kea, one of two thirteen thousand foot mountains, which dominate the landscape of the Big Island. A local *Kahuna* had given Kaleo directions to lead him up the side of one mountain to an appropriate area to deposit the bones.

Being on the windward and rainy side of the island, the mountain was shrouded in low hanging clouds. As they moved along the path, they were veiled in a warm mist that occasionally became actual rain. The sun broke through the jungle canopy in places showing a rainbow in front of the climbers.

The path became continually steeper until Zachary and Kaleo were working their way along narrow ledges and forced to climb on their hands and knees. After several hours Kaleo stopped under an overhang and motioned Zachary to join him. Both were panting and they drank from their water gourds.

"Stay here my friend." Kaleo added, "I must do this last part on my own."

Zachary moved into the crevice formed by the overhang to be out of the mist and rain. He shivered a bit, for he was not used to the cool temperatures that accompanied mountain altitudes.

Kaleo put the pack over his shoulder and departed the shelter heading farther up the slope. He continued for another forty-five minutes before encountering an area that was packed with many caves and crevices. He selected an opening that was four feet high and crawled in. Not far inside he hit a package, in the dark. Rolling over to let the low light enter past his body he saw that this cave had been already used for several burials, possibly a single family or families of the windward side of the island. Feeling that this may not be an appropriate place for his father's remains, Kaleo backed out to explore other caves.

Finally, Kaleo saw a small lava tube that was roughly one foot high and three feet wide, just enough for him to squeeze his massive body inside. He crawled as far as he could while pushing the package before him. He then pushed the bundle as far as he could into the crevice, chanting prayers to his family god. He thought that he heard the faint beating of drums and gourds and the chants of his ancestors greeting the famed warrior to their realm.

After the ritual was complete Kaleo shimmied back out of the hole and proceeded back to Zachary's position. It had been two hours since he had left Zachary at the overhang.

On hearing his approach Zachary called out, "Kaleo, I was afraid that you had gone over the side."

Kaleo responded, "Come my friend, I have done my duty."

The return trip going downhill was much less strenuous. Once the two young warriors got below the narrow mountain paths, they jogged down toward the encampment. They were now below the mist and the afternoon sun shone brilliantly, before lowering behind *Mauna Loa*, the other great mountain on the Big Island.

That night at the men's dining hut Kaleo and Zachary ate heartily. Each of the chiefs and *Kahuna*s spoke to Kaleo to honor his father.

Keoua had retreated so there was no immediate threat of another battle. Kamehameha put further hostilities on hold while the *Heaiu* in honor of Kalima was built. The entire army, from slaves to the king himself, carried rocks to build the temple.

Meanwhile, the remnants of Keoua's army moved south through the moonscape-like area to the southeast of Kilauea crater. The landscape was black volcanic rock as far as one could see. The going was slow because of the many old lava flows, which had been broken by earth tremors and later flows, making for a maze., The army was spread over a mile snaking to the south over hundreds of acres of jagged black rocks.

The earth began to quake, and an eruption spewed forth a river of lava which flowed down the slope toward the soldiers below. Keoua's troops ran but the flow cut through the ragged column. Those to the south continued to run, many dropping their weapons while running for their lives. Those to the north of the flow were forced to run back further north, tangling with Keoua's oncoming troops and the camp followers at the rear of the column. The converging soldiers stalled in a mass when the eruption spewed forth a cloud of sulfur and gas. The cloud rolled down the slope and extinguished their lives.

When word of the deaths on the slope of Kilauea reached Kamehameha's encampment there was rejoicing. It was obvious to the, always religious, Kamehameha and his troops that the fire goddess *Pele* recognized that Kamehameha's cause was just, and exacted her vengeance on his enemy. The building of the *Heaiu* was pursued with added relish.

Keoua was devastated by news of the deaths of his troops as well as the many women and children. His army had suffered a defeat at the hands of Kamehameha and his new weapons. Now the gods had turned on him and his people. After this event Keoua suffered from fits of depression and resigned himself to his defeat.

During the months following the incident at *Kilauea* there were several skirmishes between the troops of Kamehameha and Keoua, but no major battles. Kamehameha's troops continued to win the engagements, reaffirming the fact that Keoua's bid to control the island of Hawaii was over.

After finishing the *Heaiu* near Koa-papa, the main portion of Kamehameha's army returned to *Kealakekua*. Kamehameha began the building of another *Heaiu* at Puu-kohola on the northwest coast of the island. He wanted to keep the gods on his side while he planned his next campaign.

Though Kamehameha's armies had been victorious on Maui and again against Keoua; the outcome of the wars was not certain. Keoua still reigned on the south end of Hawaii and having pulled his army out of Maui to fight Keoua had allowed his enemy Kahekili to regain control of Maui. As far as Kamehameha was concerned, he was winning battles but maybe not the war.

The news was bad when the rumors reached Kamehameha that Kahekili and his half-brother Kaeo had combined their fleets and armies on Maui so that they could invade the Big Island and lend their support to Keoua.

CHAPTER 15

WAR AT SEA

KAMEHAMEHA HAD BEEN busily trading for guns and gunpowder and now in 1791, only a little over a year since the capture of *Fair American*, the King had a much better supply than during previous campaigns. However, the arms race was not one sided. Word reached Kamehameha's court that Kahekili procured some cannons and muskets, and had employed some *Haole*s to manage his new weapons. It was reported that Kahekili's fleet now included some war canoes mounted with small cannons.

The traditional tactic would have been to wait for Kahekili's invasion and then engage his army on the landing beach. The intelligence reports did not include any mention of Kahekili having secured a sizable ship such as the *Fair American*, so Kamehameha opted to engage Kahekili's fleet in a sea battle before they could land on his island.

Fair American had been anchored in *Kealakekua* Bay for some time while the armies clashed on other parts of the island. Davis and Young along with Zachary were busied rearming the ship with cannons including the much-traveled *Lopaka*, and planning for a sea battle. They would have to determine who would perform what function during the battle. They had trained some Hawaiians to act as crew on the ship, but in the heat of battle the three of them would have to stand ready to control any aspect of the ship's armament or maneuvering, especially if one of them was wounded or worse during the engagement.

The delegation of responsibilities was as follows: Davis having been the Mate on *Fair American* was the most familiar with its sailing characteristics so he would command the vessel. Young would command the cannons and Zachary would as usual command the muskets. If any of them were incapacitated the other two would cover the responsibilities, assisted by their Hawaiian seconds in command. Zachary assured his two elders that Kaleo could most certainly stand in for him by taking command of the musket platoon.

Once the *Fair American* was outfitted with its weaponry and all running and standing rigging inspected and repaired as needed, the ship was taken out for a shakedown cruise and to train the crew. As always, the Hawaiians sent enough chiefs on the voyage to take command of the situation if the *Haole*s decided to make a break for freedom.

The three sailors relished the chance to be back at sea. Day after day they felt the fresh trade winds blowing and could not take advantage of them. The shakedown cruise was great; they reached northward along the Kona coast of the Big Island and then reached back on the opposite heading to *Kealakekua*. A reach was *Fair American's* best point of sail. She heeled fifteen degrees and more in gusts. She charged up and down the coast, as the sailors would say "With a bone in her teeth."

In addition to their muskets, Zachary made sure that his troops brought short spears and daggers onboard in case they were boarded during the battle. He also instructed his men on the judicious use of a belaying pin as a formidable weapon for hand-to-hand fighting.

By the time that Kahekili's fleet was amassed on the southern end of Maui; Kamehameha had assembled his own large fleet. When word came that Kahekili appeared ready to depart Maui, Kamehameha began to amass his fleet. Runners were sent to the various coastal villages to spread the call to arms. They were spread along the western coast of the island north from *Kealakekua* to *Kailua-Kona*, and *Kiholo* among other bays.

Fair American weighed anchor and headed to sea escorted by a large fleet of war canoes. Spirits were high in hopes of a decisive engagement. The catamaran canoes had no problem keeping up with the schooner and if they had any problem, it was slowing down enough to keep the big displacement ship in a formation. As the fleet passed bays and villages on their way north, additional war canoes and outriggers joined their ranks. By the time the fleet rounded Upolu, the northernmost point of the Big Island, the ranks had increased to over two hundred canoes.

Spies had alerted Kamehameha that Kahekili was going to land his fleet at Waipio Bay, so he planned to arrive there before his enemy and wait for their arrival. In case Kahekili was able to break through his fleet and land his forces, Kamehameha had troops assembled on the beach at Waipio. Since Kahekili was attempting to join Keoua, Kamehameha also had to send enough troops to the south to ensure that Keoua was kept in check while he faced Kahekili.

The spies had been correct; Kahekili's fleet left Hana and headed for Waipio. The Hawaiian strategies, similar to the early Greek and Roman sea battles were much the same as land battles. The vessels were placed in formations similar to the army units on a field. The fleets would close and attempt to board each other's vessels so that they could engage in hand-to-hand combat to decide the outcome.

Kahekili's fleet arrayed itself in the familiar crescent formation with the cannon-bearing war canoes in the center of the formation, flanked on either side with canoes carrying musketeers.

Kamehameha's fleet was similarly arrayed with *Fair American* in the center of the line.

In the fresh trade winds, the two fleets converged at full-speed. Coming out of Waipio Bay, the *Fair American* was close hauled into the Tradewinds on a starboard tack. Her square-rigged foresail and fore topsails were furled. Davis would rely only on her fore and aft sails, which increased her maneuverability.

Kahekili's *Haole* commander, Mare Amara planned to attack the strength of Kamehameha's line, the big schooner in the middle. If he could disable or capture the only sizable vessel in the fray, he could decide the battle. He expected that *Fair American* would have all but her square rigged foresails furled as was normal, making the ship a floating gun platform and preventing the lower sails catching fire during the engagement. He was surprised that the schooner was not furling its sails, but her capture remained a main objective in the battle. He believed that even if *Fair American* was under sail, his speedy canoes would have no problem overtaking the schooner.

As the fleets closed, a roar of shouts and hollers arose as the sides taunted each other. Kahekili's lead canoes had their cannon loaded with round shot and fired at the oncoming *Fair American*. The first ball splashed in the water at the starboard side of the schooner. The second ball struck the hull on the portside well above the waterline, cracking some boards below the taffrail, and then bounced into the sea.

Davis knew that it was in his best interest to remain a mobile gun platform and not get into a boarding situation. As the fleets converged, Davis ordered the helmsman to bear off to avoid collisions with the oncoming canoes. The enemy canoes on the other hand were attempting to get close enough to board.

Young knew that he had to clear the decks of the enemy's war canoes and had loaded his cannons with grapeshot. He held his fire until the fleets were engaged; and then he gave the order to fire. The grapeshot cleared part of the gun crew from one of the lead war canoes. The small pivot guns wounded and knocked men out of two other canoes.

Zachary had his muskets at the ready with one squad on either side of the deck. He commanded the port squad and Kaleo commanded the starboard squad. As a hail of hurled stones and spears began landing on *Fair American's* hull and deck, he hollered to Kaleo, "Hold your fire until they stand up to throw their weapons!"

Kaleo nodded his acknowledgement, and then ordered, "Ready men! Ready! Fire!"

A moment later Zachary also gave the order to fire. Enemy troops took the brunt of the volley, some falling overboard and some merely slumping into their canoes.

Before they could reload, several opposing muskets appeared on nearby canoes and fired at *Fair American*. One of Zachary's men groaned and fell to the deck mortally wounded. As Zachary gave the order to take him below, two musket balls whizzed past his head.

Zachary hollered up to the two sharpshooters he had stationed in the foremast's platform, "Get those bastards!"

His sharpshooters fired and wounded one of the opposing musketeers. Another warrior in the canoe retrieved his weapon and then proceeded to load it for another shot.

Zachary did not wish to take additional casualties from opposing muskets if he could help it. He ordered, "Men, kneel behind the bulkheads and fire over the gunwales!"

Except for the middle of the lines where *Fair American* had managed to keep its distance from enemy canoes, the two outside lines converged and engaged in close combat. *Fair American* had broken entirely through the opposing line and was now more than a hundred yards to the backside of the action.

Davis gave the command, "Ready About!"

He paused as the crew manned their stations. "Helms a Lee!" The helmsman responded, "Helms a Lee, Aye!"

The bow swung through the eye of the wind slowing until the sails filled on the opposite tack.

As *Fair American* picked up speed on port tack, Davis saw that four enemy canoes had also come about to pursue the schooner. They were now on a converging course.

Davis called to Zachary and Young, "Clear those bastards!"

The two forward most swivel guns fired. As the cloud of black powder smoke cleared Davis could see that both sails and men had been shredded on the two closest canoes. Zachary's men fired at the ones that were still moving. The two trailing canoes now closed on *Fair American* and both the cannons and muskets were empty. Zachary's men hustled to reload their weapons.

The oncoming canoes crashed against either side of *Fair American's* bow with great force since *Fair American* was up to nine knots and the canoes coming in the opposite direction were moving at twelve. The collision caused *Fair American* to lose way and luff up into the wind. The canoes' occupants threw grapple hooks onto *Fair American* and attempted to climb aboard. The entangled vessels now dead in the water began to float away from the main battle line, pushed by the current and the wind.

Davis ordered, "Prepare to fend off boarders!"

Three of Zachary's troops had reloaded and fired down into the canoes. One had been so excited that he had not removed his ramrod before firing. The ramrod went through an enemy followed by the ball both exiting the victims back and into the water.

Though the war canoes were large, they were much lower than *Fair American* causing their warriors to climb up the sides of *Fair American's* hull. Zachary and the crew on *Fair American* took advantage of their higher position, using spears to stab downward at their foes. One of Kahekili's warriors grabbed the main shrouds and was pulling himself up onto the gunwale when Zachary pierced his neck with a short spear sending his body back into his comrades.

On the other side of the deck, Kaleo and his squad were also engaged in keeping the enemy from boarding. However, several of Kahekili's warriors made it over the pinrail and established a foothold upon which other troops might follow them. Additional canoes were breaking from the battle line and sailing toward the *Fair American*. Young and his gun crew came to Kaleo's aid, using their rams and swabs to push the enemy back against the gunwale. Davis joined the fray wielding a short spear in one hand and a belaying pin in the other. After ten minutes of ferocious hand-to-hand fighting, the decks were cleared of the enemy. All of the troops from the two canoes were either dead or severely wounded. The additional enemy canoes were almost upon them.

Davis began shouting orders. "Cut those frickin' boats loose and let's get underway." As he turned to return to the afterdeck he commanded, "And load all weapons."

As *Fair American* made way and gained speed, Davis gave the helmsman a heading and continued downwind from the battle line. Two enemy war canoes were gaining on them, now within fifty yards.

Davis hollered forward, "Are you loaded gentlemen?"

Young waved his affirmation and both he and Zachary responded, "Aye sir!" Davis, "Very well." To the helmsman, "Bring her up on to a starboard tack." Davis shouted forward, "Don't dress the sails yet, men!"

Fair American quickly lost speed, her sails luffing off to her leeway side, providing a clear view of the oncoming canoes and a relatively flat gun platform.

Young had a clear shot at point blank range and gave the order to fire the brass cannon. The grapeshot did its wicked deed. As the smoke cleared, Young could see that the shot had killed or maimed everyone on the closest canoe and shredded the canoe's single sail. The second canoe was now obstructed from directly approaching *Fair American* by the first canoe, which was floating adrift between them. Also having just seen the annihilation of their comrades, they were reluctant to attempt to attack the schooner by themselves. Zachary and Kaleo brought all the muskets to bear on the canoe, picking off its occupants until it turned and retreated back to its battle line and the relative safety of fighting ships its own size.

Fair American was still downwind of the battle. Davis commanded the sails to be close hauled and they began a long tack away from the battle so that they could get upwind of the action. The bodies of the dead were thrown overboard without ceremony and the wounded were taken below.

Back on the battle-line the knots of opposing canoes had fought to a stalemate with many casualties on both sides. Kahekili's forces still had a few muskets and small cannons mounted on canoes and were inflicting great damage with them. Kamehameha's major weapon, the heavily armed schooner, was presently out of the fray and his forces were being pushed back.

Finally, after a half hour of tacking away from the battle, *Fair American* was upwind of the action. Davis gave the command to come about. They remained close-hauled, sailing for the upwind end of the battle. As they drew close, Davis ordered the *Fair American* off the wind so that they were now in a broad reach behind the enemy fleet. Using the small pivot guns loaded with grapeshot, the muskets, and thrown spears, they caused havoc aboard the enemy's canoes. Kahekili's fleet was caught in a pincer between Kamehameha's fleet of canoes and *Fair American* at their rear.

Several of Kahekili's canoes attempted to turn and engage *Fair American*. However, having been boarded once, Davis made sure he kept some distance from the enemy canoes. *Fair American's* cannon and muskets kept any enemy canoes which ventured too close at bay.

One medium sized outrigger canoe broke from the fray and headed straight into the path of the charging *Fair American*. The helmsman could not avoid the much smaller canoe.

Davis bellowed, "What's that bastard think he's doing! Brace yourselves, lads!"

Fair American barely shuttered as her stem ran over the outrigger tipping the canoe towards her oncoming bow. As the canoe tipped it ejected its occupants before being split by the schooner's bow and driven under. One of the canoe's crew had grabbed on to the bowsprit and attempted to climb onto the deck; however, one of Zachary's troops fired a musket ball into his forehead, hurling him backward into the sea.

The battle had raged for over two hours and the sea was littered with broken canoes and bodies of the casualties. Numerous sharks wove and darted around the melee, taking no sides. They feasted on the remains of many unfortunate souls from both armies.

Fair American made it to the downwind end of the battle and Davis prepared to haul upwind again to repeat the previous maneuver. However, Kahekili's fleet was now, not only being pushed back, but many canoes were breaking off their engagement and turning back toward Maui.

Everyone had as much fighting that day as anyone could stomach. The surviving canoes of both fleets separated. Except for a couple of parting musket shots, the battle was over. This battle became known as *Kepu-wala-ula* or "The Battle of the Red Mouthed Gun." It brought an end to Kahekili's attempts to invade the Big Island, though he still controlled the other islands in the archipelago.

Keoua of the Red Cloak heard of Kahekili's defeat while attempting to come to his aid. He realized that his situation remained desperate. He was standing alone facing the ever-stronger armies of Kamehameha. He remained haunted by the fact that even the Gods had turned on him.

Kamehameha sent emissaries to Keoua to talk about peace. They bid that he accompany them to the dedication of the great *Heaiu* at Puu-kohola that he might discuss the terms of peace with Kamehameha.

Neither of these old adversaries was about to trust the other. Keoua feared that his end might be near, but if so, he would face it as a true warrior. Keoua chose his favorite feathered cape for the meeting. He picked those trusted warriors with whom he would wish to die to accompany him on his most impressive war canoe for the trip around the island. As a sign of his total defeat, Keoua stopped enroute near Kailua-Kona and performed a rite called the Death of *Uli*, which is basically a self-inflicted circumcision.

Kaleo came running down the beach toward Zachary and his musketeers, who were resting under the shade of some coconut palms. "Zachary bring the troops; we have been ordered to go out to await the arrival of Keoua." Waking excitedly, "Olohana will take one squad on a canoe and we will take the other to be in formation on the beach."

As Keoua in the lead canoe approached the beach at *Kauai-hae* his foreboding was confirmed. Kamehameha's army was arrayed on the beach with Kamehameha and his chiefs in the middle of the group awaiting his arrival. As Keoua's canoes approached the beach, several of Kamehameha's canoes converged on them escorting them toward the beach. Keoua was surrounded and some of the canoes carried men with muskets and others carried small cannons. Keoua had no choice but to play out his role until the end.

Zachary and Kaleo were just beyond hearing what was said, but Keoua called out to Kamehameha and Kamehameha responded by waving him ashore. Keoua jumped into the knee-deep water but after only a couple of steps, Ke-e-au-moku, one of Kamehameha's trusted chiefs, leaped forward and stabbed Keoua and pushed him down into the water.

Next the relative silence was broken by a volley of muskets from a canoe which fired into the group of Keoua's chiefs on his canoe. Kaleo called, "Koa Kai we must fire!"

Zachary had seen plenty of violence in his time in the islands, but this was beyond his comprehension. He stood fixed, his mouth agape.

Kaleo, "Koa Kai, Fire!"

Kaleo then pushed Zachary from his position at the right of his squad, and ordered them to fire. As the smoke cleared after the volley only two of the *Alii* on Keoua's canoe were alive. The violence was over as quickly as it had started.

Until that point Zachary and Kaleo had never had cross words, but the scene Zachary had just witnessed ran counter to his whole sense of morality. After the brief conflict was over Kaleo turned to Zachary, "I am sorry I had to push you my friend, but the muskets were needed."

Zachary exploded, "What was that?"

Kaleo replied in a calm voice, "That was the end of hostilities on this island." He continued, "You had a job to do to bring this to an end and you did not, so I did what had to be done."

Zachary was still incensed. He spoke thoughts that he never uttered before, "You people might own me and I may have to fight in battles for reasons I don't understand, but that was not a battle between honorable warriors, it was a massacre for no good reason at all!"

Kaleo responded, this time more forcefully. "You have fought bravely at my side and I value you as my own brother. However, like any soldier you cannot pick your battles, you must do as you are told."

Zachary reiterated, "But this was not a battle, it was murder. Every time that I believe that you people are more than savages, you prove me wrong!"

Kaleo, "It was necessary. Keoua has sometimes been an ally of Kahekili and then at the first chance made war against us. This has been going on for years. If he had been allowed to live, he would have rebuilt his army and waited for the first chance to attack us again. This was the time to end the wars on this island and what better sacrifice to Ku than the body of the enemy chief?"

The discussion was ended; Zachary had nothing more to say on the issue, but was left disconcerted by the propensity for violence among his adopted people.

The remaining warriors on Keoua's other canoes were allowed to come ashore without harm.

Keoua's body was then carried to the *Heaiu* and placed on the altar as a tribute to the war god Ku. Kaleo was right, this act of assassination ended hostilities forever on the Big Island of Hawaii.

CHAPTER 16

THE FINAL BATTLES

WITH THE DEATH of Keoua in 1791, the war on the Big Island was over. Kamehameha was in firm control of this island, but his archenemy, Kahekili still had allies and controlled the other islands. The adversaries continued to raid and harass each other on a regular basis, but after the major sea battle of *Kepu-wala-ula* there were no more major engagements for the next few years. Both sides were intent on consolidating their positions and accumulating as many *Haole* weapons as possible.

The major event of 1792 at *Kealakekua* Bay was a brief visit in March by Captain George Vancouver with his ships *Discovery* and *Chatham*. Vancouver had visited this bay in 1779 as a midshipman aboard Captain Cook's old *Discovery*. Now Vancouver was on his own voyage of discovery with a new ship of the same name. Kamehameha was away from *Kealakekua* when Vancouver arrived. Kaiana was there and took Kaleo and Zachary along with other chiefs and warriors to visit the *Haole* warships.

Zachary was impressed, the only war ship he had ever seen was the Spanish ship at San Diego and that was at a distance. The row of cannons on either side of the gun deck showed the potential destructive power of this British man-of-war. Zachary could picture the effect that such a vessel would have had in the sea battle at Waipio. One ship like this and it would have been a very short engagement.

Kamehameha and his chiefs had similar thoughts when they had seen Captain Cook's ships in 1779. One ship such as these would tip the balance and decide the outcome of the inter-island wars. Ke-e-au-moku made his pitch to Vancouver to gain his assistance against Kahekili, but to no avail.

Vancouver was not in the Pacific to take sides in a war, but to explore more of this vast Pacific Ocean.

After a few days at *Kealakekua*, Vancouver weighed anchor and headed northwest toward Oahu and then to the coast of North America.

Vancouver had hoped to rendezvous with his supply ship *Daedalus* at *Kealakekua*, but the ship did not appear. *Daedalus* made it to the islands in May 1792 arriving at Waimea Bay on the north shore of Oahu. The chief in that district, eager to acquire *Haole* weapons by any means, attacked a shore party from the *Daedalus* killing three of the ship's company including an officer. After not finding Vancouver's two ships, Daedalus proceeded to North America where it did find Vancouver and reported the incident on Oahu.

Zachary settled in as a respected warrior and member of his new society. Within three months of Zachary's return from the battle of *Kepu-wala-ula*, Pua became pregnant. Prior to this announcement, sex to him had been as a young man and especially a sailor viewed it, a way to temporarily quell the fire that burned in the breeches, if not the hearts of young men. But Pua was with child and he had come to love her dearly. Now there would be his offspring to also love.

The night came when the wahine midwives came running with torches and the *Kahuna*s gave prayers for the child of their *Alii* woman and the *Haole* warrior. Ipo Lani Bower was born just before sunrise in August 1792. The word was passed, more prayers were given, and the joy passed throughout the village. Zachary was now a true family man. His perceived ties to the white man's world were now completely severed.

Ipo Lani was a healthy child, the strong product of a mixed gene pool. Pua Lani recovered from the anguish of childbirth and regained her tall slim attractive figure.

One morning after exercising with the other warriors, Kaleo announced to Zachary his plan for the rest of the day. "Brother, I woke up early this morning and was thinking; that what I really need is one of the short swords the *Haole*'s carry." Waving his right arm back and forth in front of his body he went on with his plan. "There has been a *Haole* ship in the bay for the past three days and they have been trading arms for food. If I had a fine pig, I could trade it for such a sword."

Zachary replied, "Cutlass, the *Haole*s call their short swords a cutlass."

Kaleo was not interested in details. He went on with his plan. "I have heard tell of a big boar hog that lives in the forest up on the mountain." Always animated Kaleo gestured with his arm outstretched. "If we were to hunt and kill this great pig, I could trade it for a sword."

Zachary had learned that in the Hawaiian society if someone asked for your help, it is expected that you give it freely. It would be disrespectful to do otherwise. Anyway, Zachary had not had an adventure for quite some time and was ready for one. He replied, "OK, my friend when do we go?"

Kaleo, "Now, get your short spear and dagger and we will go."

Within twenty minutes the pair were marching toward the slope of the mountains, dressed only in their *malos*. Each had a dagger tucked into their *malo* and a spear over their shoulder. Being barefoot most of the time had toughened the feet of the lads so walking up the rocky path did not affect them.

Being on the "*Kona*" or leeward side of the island meant that there was little rain to moisten the landscape except for the rainforest at the top of the mountain. Kaleo and Zachary followed a dusty path toward the thick vegetation above them. After two hours they were into the thick vegetation. It was hard to be stealthy crunching through the growth. They used their spears to push away bushes and vines ahead of them. It was slow going as there was now enough moisture under the vegetation to make the footing slippery.

Kaleo whispered, "If I had my sword, I would hack right through this *opala*."

There was a deep snorting sound from somewhere in the dense bushes ahead of them. Zachary motioned Kaleo to be silent. They squatted down and listened. After a few moments there was another snort clearly from their left. They remained still, for they had to determine exactly where the hog was if they were to surprise it. The next snort came from directly in front of their position. The hog was moving, but to where?

After what felt like a painfully long time of silent listening the bushes in front of the hunters began to rustle and then exploded apart as the boar, bigger than either of them had ever seen, charged out of the thicket. The great animal was on them almost before they could see it. The boar charged between the hunters swinging its head from side to side. A tusk slashed Zachary's right calf and knocked him off his feet. Kaleo was also knocked to the ground, but as he fell, he was able to push his spear between the ribs of the boar. The boar let out a loud squeal as it ran past them down the slope into the next blind thicket.

Jumping to his feet Kaleo shouted, "Come I got it!"

Kaleo ran after the hog and Zachary unmindful of his wound followed the sounds and broken vegetation. After about twenty yards Kaleo found the handle of his broken spear. He surmised that the head was still embedded in the hog, but now armed with only his dagger and a broken spear he was definitely no match for the great animal. Kaleo did not want to lose track of his quarry so he proceeded more slowly, hollering over his shoulder for Zachary to hurry.

Kaleo's spear head had punctured one of the boar's lungs so it could not run far and was forced to rest under a *lauhala* tree. Kaleo followed the hog's tracks and the trail came into an opening in the brush next to the *lauhala* tree. The boar hog, seeing his pursuer, summoned his remaining energy and charged out from under the tree knocking Kaleo to the ground. The boar raked Kaleo's ribcage with his tusks and then bit Kaleo's legs. Kaleo's only defense from this mauling was his dagger which he stabbed at the beast indiscriminately. He hollered for Zachary to come to his aid.

Zachary was close behind Kaleo and ran toward the snorts and shouts and flailing bushes. He came upon Kaleo pinned to the ground by the beast. Zachary holding his spear in both hands lunged downward stabbing the boar repeatedly in the back of its massive neck. One of the stabs slipped between two of the hog's vertebra and pierced its spinal cord. The animal fell on its side still twitching and kicking, some of the kicks struck Kaleo. Zachary stabbed the quivering carcass repeatedly until it stopped moving.

The boar lay still but it remained on Kaleo's legs. Zachary pushed the carcass until Kaleo was freed and hurriedly tried to pull Kaleo to his feet.

Kaleo moaned, "No so fast my friend. I don't feel so good."

Zachary leaned Kaleo against the caged roots of the *lauhala* tree and said, "I need to get you out of here and to some help."

Kaleo replied, "We can't leave my pig behind. I will be alright. Just let me rest a few minutes."

After several minutes of argument over the need to tend to Kaleo rather than the pig, Zachary gave in and prepared a rude skid upon which he rolled the large boar. Kaleo rose to his feet and leaned on Zachary as they slowly moved down the path towards their village at *Kealakekua* Bay. It was slow going. Zachary had the weight of the skid on his shoulders plus Kaleo with cuts, bruises and several cracked ribs, he moved at a shuffling pace.

After an hour they broke out of the thick vegetation into a clear view of the bay below them.

The late afternoon sun told them that they would be lucky to make it to the village before dark.

The silence of the moment was broken by Kaleo's sputtering. Below them the merchant ship had already unfurled its fore and main topsails and was heading for sea. Kaleo was at first speechless, he then sputtered a few unintelligible oaths and then a few seaman's curses he had learned from Zachary. Kaleo then fell silent again for a few minutes and then said, "Hey brother, I guess with this big sucker, we eat good for a couple days."

With the urgency of getting the hog to the ship no longer an issue and Zachary not relishing the prospect of dragging Kaleo and the boar down the slope in the dark, Zachary made Kaleo and his pig as comfortable as possible and then jogged down the slope to get help.

Soon after dark Zachary returned with two dozen men to carry Kaleo and the boar to the village.

The next day the boar hog was baked in the *imu* oven and there was indeed good eating at the men's dining hut for the next two days.

After ten months surveying the coast of North America, Captain Vancouver returned to the Sandwich Islands going directly to the Big Island and the domain of Kamehameha. After the attack on the men of the *Daedalus* by warriors of Kalanikupule and Kahekili on Oahu, Vancouver felt more secure in the domain of their enemy. Kamehameha was becoming more political and would attempt to win the weapons he desired through diplomacy rather than violence. Kamehameha treated Vancouver to the same pomp and ceremony that had been afforded Captain Cook on his arrival to *Kealakekua* Bay.

The two leaders entered into lengthy negotiations in which Kamehameha ceded the Big Island to Great Britain in return, he thought, for a major *Haole* warship. Vancouver brought gifts of cattle and sheep from the west coast of North America and his crew assisted Kamehameha in the construction of a small *Haole* style ship. However, Vancouver did not provide cannons to arm the new vessel, *Britannia*.

Vancouver had hoped to broker a peace between Kamehameha and Kahekili. Vancouver discussed peace with Kamehameha, and then in an act of early shuttle diplomacy, went to Maui and met with Kahekili. Both leaders were eager to declare what a scoundrel the other one was, but not about to agree to end hostilities. However, before Vancouver could make any true progress, in mid-1794, Kahekili died of old age. Vancouver left the islands later that year with the Big Island as a new member of the British Empire. However, Parliament never ratified the action, so Hawaii remained an independent nation. By the same token the British never supplied the man-of-war Kamehameha thought he had gained from the deal.

The menagerie of warlords continued. Kahekili's son Kalanikupule and his half-brother Kaeokulani began to fight for control of Kahekili's empire. After several engagements, both sides having *Haole* weapons and advisors, Kaeokulani was killed in battle along with his major chiefs. Kalanikupule had been aided by an English Captain William Brown who commanded two ships *Prince Lee Boo* and *Jackall.*

Kalanikupule decided to capture the two ships and have them directly under his command. The attack was successful, Captain Brown, his second-in-command Captain Gordon along with some of his crew were killed and the ships captured. For the first time Kalanikupule had an advantage in cannon and muskets; and ships that were superior to Kamehameha's vessels, *Fair American* and *Britannia.*

Kalanikupule forced the remaining crewmembers to sail the ships for a formidable attack on the Big Island. *Jackal* and *Prince Lee Boo* sailed out of Honolulu harbor commanded by the mates of the two ships: George Lamport and William Bonallack respectively. The ships were followed by an armada of war canoes.

Rather than heading for the Big Island Lamport tacked *Jackal* out to sea. *Prince Lee Boo* followed closing ranks with *Jackal.* When the time was right Lamport signaled his men, who produced muskets and forced Kalanikupule, his wife and accompanying chiefs over the side. Bonallack saw what was happening and did likewise. War canoes picked up the wet and humiliated Kalanikupule and his entourage.

Lamport and Bonallack sailed their ships to the Big Island, reported the plot and its outcome to Davis and Young. The two ships then departed the Sandwich Islands for Canton.

During the three years of relative peace, Kamehameha continued to build his forces with *Haole* weapons and advisors. The musket platoon commanded by Zachary had grown to a battalion. Isaac Davis took command of the battalion with Zachary and Kaleo as his company commanders. John Young was joined by another English seaman, Peter Anderson to command the battery of cannon.

While Kalanikupule and Kaeokulani struggled for control of the other islands, Kamehameha bided his time, building his forces. Information from spies kept Kamehameha informed of events on the other islands. When Kamehameha heard of the two large ships at Oahu, he felt it best to continue to wait rather than launching an attack that might be countered at sea by superior forces. The news of Kalanikupule's foiled attack and subsequent loss of his superior naval advantage was the break for which Kamehameha had been awaiting. Kalanikupule's would be preemptive strike gave Kamehameha the provocation for another war and it was time to act before Kalanikupule could again gain the advantage. With *Britannia* as his flagship, in February 1795, Kamehameha's fleet sailed unopposed from the Big Island to Lahaina and Kaanapali on Maui.

With the now larger army the young brothers would not stand side by side in battle. Kaleo with his company of musketeers would travel on *Britannia* while Zachary and his men would travel on *Fair American*. As they hugged each other on the beach before departing for their respective ships, Zachary proclaimed, "For the last time, let us be victorious and be done with this war."

As the hundreds of war canoes landed on the west coast of Maui, the local commander Koa-lau- kane confronted by overwhelming forces, departed for Oahu taking his commanders with him. Unlike the savage battles that took place during previous campaigns, the conquest of Maui was almost unopposed.

After re-provisioning, Kamehameha's army crossed the Pailolo Channel to Molokai and except for a few minor skirmishes took this island unopposed. Zachary and Kaleo joined forces again at Papohaku Beach on the West side of Molokai. Their companies were camped there to rest before the expected invasion of Oahu. Standing on the beach the two warriors inhaled the fresh salt air of the brisk trade-wind. The sand beneath their feet was still warm from the intense daytime sun. A third quarter moon was rising above the tree line to their east.

"Look my friend." Kaleo pointed to the west. "You can see the fires on Oahu through the darkness."

Zachary replied, "It is beautiful, and it seems so close."

Kaleo's expression turned more serious, "Soon we will take our canoes to Oahu and confront Kalanikupule's remaining army. The last two islands have been easy, but Kalanikupule will fight like a cornered boar hog to defend his home on Oahu."

Zachary, "But once we take Oahu the war should be over."

Kaleo, "There is still Kauai, but it is quite a distance from here, over the northern horizon." He thought then added, "But that is in the future my friend, let's take one island at a time."

In the mixing bowl of Hawaiian politics, sex and war, it seems that Kaiana one of Kamehameha's trusted advisors for years, had a recent affair with Kaahumanu, Kamehameha's favorite wife. This caused strained relations between the three involved in this love triangle as well as strained relations between Kaiana and Kamehameha's other advisors. Feeling that his life might be in danger, Kaiana plotted to defect and join Kalanikupule. When Kamehameha sailed across the Kaiwi Channel to Waimanalo on Oahu, Kaiana with over ten percent of the canoes and army broke off from the rest of the fleet and put into Kailua, Oahu to join Kalanikupule's forces.

Kamehameha established an encampment at Waimanalo and consolidated his forces for an advance on Kalanikupule's capital at Waikiki. He waited to see if Kalanikupule would make the first move and challenge him on the Windward side of the island, but Kalanikupule remained in a defensive position. The defection of Kaiana also made Kamehameha cautious; he needed to determine if he had other would be defectors in his midst before going on the offensive.

Having amassed his forces at Waimanalo, Kamehameha was ready to move on Waikiki. Most of the cannon had remained on *Britannia* and some canoes, to be carried around the island to the point where they could be landed to support the troops who were also moved by sea for an amphibious assault. The fleet rounded Makapuu Point and Koko Head. Troops landed at Maunalua Bay and Wailupe to march on Waikiki from the east. When the landing parties received no resistance, it was decided to land forces directly on Waikiki Beach.

Zachary and Kaleo's musket companies landed at Waikiki in the second wave of canoes. They immediately formed their battle line and followed the previously landed warriors into the capital. Everyone was alert for a potential ambush. They worked their way through the abandoned huts to the swamps on the other side of the village. There was no resistance. Kalanikupule had abandoned his capital without a fight.

Kamehameha ordered his forces to advance to the north and west until they made contact with the enemy. The leading elements were engaged by Kalanikupule's retreating rear guard, but this only served to slow the advance.

Kalanikupule had picked his defensive position up the slopes of the *Nuuanu* Valley. The steep mountains on either side would protect his flanks forcing his adversaries to be jammed together in the narrowing valley where his spears and muskets could do their damage. Kalanikupule stationed his troops and waited for Kaiana's forces to march from Kailua to join him. Some low stone walls were erected as protection from Kamehameha's muskets. This position would force a decisive outcome, since there was no escape routine that could accommodate a large number of retreating troops; either Kalanikupule would break the center of Kamehameha's army or be vanquished on these slopes.

Contact was made with Kalanikupule's skirmish lines at the base of *Nuuanu* Valley. Having apparently found the enemy, Kamehameha waited for his forces and weapons to be brought up, as they were spread between *Waikiki* and *Nuuanu*.

Kamehameha's cannons were mounted on much better carriages than the earlier campaigns when a hundred men were needed to haul *Lopaka* into position. Large crews were still needed to haul the weapons, but the new carriages allowed them to be moved faster and to be more maneuverable.

When Kamehameha's troops were arrayed in a wide formation with the musket companies in the middle, he gave the order and the advance began up the valley. Zachary looked across to Kaleo's company and gave his friend a salute. Kaleo responded with the big grin shouting, "Koa Kai this is it!"

Halting beyond the spear range of Kalanikupule's first defensive line, the order was given and the muskets caused casualties in Kalanikupule's line. The musket companies fired several more rounds and Kalanikupule's line began to waver. Seeing this, the order was given, and Kamehameha's troops advanced on the enemy's flank, turning it and forcing the defensive line to retreat. The musket troops had become much better marksmen over time and now sharpshooters picked off retreating enemy soldiers at will.

The remnants of the retreating defenders made it to the stands of bananas that somewhat protected the second line of defense. Possessing muskets of their own, Kalanikupule's gunners fell a few of Kamehameha's men as they proceeded up the valley, but it was not enough to slow the advance. However, the order was given to halt, again beyond the spear and stone range of Kalanikupule's formidable second defensive line. They waited until cannons were brought up to aid the troops. The musket companies took their shots and kept the enemy off-balance and unable to mount a counterattack.

Kalanikupule's men could see a mass of *malo* clad warriors moving up the valley to reinforce Kamehameha's position. It was not until the mass reached the Hawaiian line that the cannons, they were pushing came into view. Kalanikupule's troops began to waiver in their lines at the sight of the guns. Heretofore they had been shouting and taunting their enemy, but as the cannons were aimed in their direction, they fell silent.

Young and Anderson had the four cannons loaded with grapeshot. After a volley from the muskets, the cannon fired a salvo cutting down men and banana stalks indiscriminately. As the cannon began to reload, Kalanikupule's forces began to retreat. When the smoke cleared enough to expose the retreating men, the muskets began to pick off random troops. The cannons again ripped into the defenders until the retreat became a rout. Many fleeing troops ran past the next line of defense and kept on running up the narrowing pass toward *Nuuanu Pali*.

The signal was given, and Zachary moved his company forward. To his right Kaleo moved forward with his company. The advance slowed as they climbed upward through mud mixed with trampled vegetation and the blood of the fallen. Bodies were strewn randomly before them forming their own silent barriers to the advancing army. An occasional enemy musket cut down one of Kamehameha's men, but with no effect on the advance.

The more mobile and conventionally armed warriors had now moved well ahead of the muskets and engaged the third line of defense which was fortified behind walls of piled stones. Kamehameha's troops had advanced into spear range of the wall and had taken some casualties before withdrawing to await support from the muskets.

"Hurry, *wiki, wiki*!" Zachary spurred on his panting troops as they moved up the valley toward the position of their comrades below the next defensive line.

Upon reaching the site, Zachary formed the two platoons of his company. Kaleo was close behind and did likewise.

Zachary ordered, "First Platoon, Ready, Fire!"

A moment later Kaleo's First Platoon also fired. The thick smoke obscured the view of the enemy's position, but several of their troops that had been showing above the stone wall fell from sight. Any troops that had not been hit by the volley ducked behind the fortifications.

Zachary commanded, "Second Platoon, pick a target and fire at will!" Waving his short spear, he ordered, "First Platoon load and fire at will!"

As the enemy ventured above or beyond the wall, they were immediately fired upon. One of Kaleo's troops took great glee in knocking the red feathered helmet from the head of an enemy chief that protruded above the stone wall.

Except for the occasional musket shot the battle had come to a standstill at this wall. However, the Hawaiian advance guard was catching its breath and patiently waiting for reinforcements and the cannons.

The reinforcing units began arriving and after an hour the cannons arrived. The main body of Kalanikupule's forces were trapped behind the series of stone walls. If they had mounted a counterattack before the reinforcements had arrived, they may have been able to turn the tide, but the muskets had kept them behind the walls and in disarray. If they moved now into the open to retreat, the muskets and cannon would most assuredly chew them up.

The cannons were moved into position. Seeing the fortified position of the enemy, Anderson ordered that the cannons be loaded with round shot. On his command the four cannons fired a salvo and blew holes in the crude stone walls. As the smoke and dust cleared enough to see the enemy, the muskets began to inflict casualties on the exposed enemy. Kalanikupule's forces began to abandon the walls and retreat up the narrowing pass.

Kaleo, always less disciplined, hollered to Zachary, "Come on, let's finish it!"

The older and slower Davis had arrived on the scene. Zachary looked to him for direction.

Knowing that he could not restrain his young warriors; he waved them on shouting, "I'll take care of the muskets. You lads take care of yourselves!"

Zachary turned uphill to see Kaleo already charging forward waving his war club. Zachary followed but lost sight of Kaleo as he was engulfed in a knot of hand-to-hand combat. Zachary had reached his advancing comrades as a dozen enemies had turned to fight rather than be struck down from the rear by their adversaries. Zachary stabbed one of the foes in the side with his short spear. Grabbing the handle of his war club, which was slung over his shoulder, he struck the same adversary across the head with the club, knocking him to the ground and off the blade of his spear. A second foe stabbed at Zachary with a spear. Zachary parried the thrust upward with his spear, but the blade slit his left cheek. Zachary retaliated with his club against the attacker's left ear, driving him to the ground.

Having vanquished the small covey of enemy, they moved on up the narrowing pass to the *Pali*, the cliff that overlooks the windward side of Oahu from *Kailua* to *Kualoa*. The melee became more frantic with small knots of hand-to-hand fighting and the backsides of fleeing enemies clubbed and stabbed from behind by their pursuers.

Back at the wall fortifications, Davis had advanced with the musket companies to find that one of the cannon shots had struck the wall at the point where Kalanikupule's staff had been huddled.

Though Kalanikupule was not among the dead, bodies of the turncoat Kaiana and many of Kalanikupule's leading chiefs were strewn among the broken lava rocks.

Zachary had lost contact with Kaleo for some time and tried to avoid some of the small skirmishes along the path so that he could overtake his friend. Finally, he saw Kaleo at the forefront of the assaulting troops; he had managed to advance well beyond the protection of his own forces and was in the midst of the enemy swinging his war club to fend them off. Zachary hailed a half dozen Hawaiians to assist him and laid into the rear of the group of Oahuans surrounding Kaleo. Swinging their clubs, they made it to Kaleo in short order.

The winded Kaleo greeted them, "Good to see you lads!"

Kaleo then turned back into the thick of the fray which had now pushed into the clearing before the cliff at the Pali lookout. Zachary soon lost contact with Kaleo again.

With their backs against the cliff, the remainder of Kalanikupule's troops had no choice but to fight or die. The hand-to-hand combat was furious for about half an hour. The overwhelming force of Kamehameha's army pushed the warring mass closer to the edge of the cliff. Many brave warriors were clubbed or stabbed in the melee. Some were pushed over the cliff by the mass of pressing bodies, and some of Kalanikupule's troops jumped rather than surrender. The base of the cliff was strewn with broken bodies.

Then, it was over. The battle was won. Kalanikupule and a few of his troops had escaped down mountain paths and headed to Kailua, but his army was vanquished. Kamehameha had conquered Oahu in one decisive battle.

Zachary sat on a rock and rested a few minutes in the midst of the bleeding and broken bodies. He then thought of Kaleo and got the same sick feeling in his stomach that he had on Maui when his friend disappeared in the battle. Zachary forced his fatigued body into movement. He returned to the edge of the clearing where he last saw Kaleo and then began checking bodies strewn in the clearing. Not finding his friend he felt added apprehension as he neared the edge of the cliff. Finally, he looked over the side of the cliff. A chill went through his spine as he looked over the side.

"Hey brother, I was hoping you'd come by," announced Kaleo who was wedged between a rock outcropping and a bush about six feet over the side of the cliff.

Pointing to his leg Kaleo added, "I think I broke something."

Zachary's apprehension turned to joy on seeing his friend. He replied, "Don't move, I'll get help."

Kaleo responded, "I'm not goin' too far."

Zachary called on some troops that were assisting the wounded, to come to his aid. Tying a rope around his waist Zachary lowered himself over the side of the cliff with three *kanakas* on top giving him slack as he descended. When he reached Kaleo and rested his feet on the rock outcrop he checked Kaleo's right leg which was definitely broken.

"Kaleo I wish you would wait for me in these things." He added, "I am getting tired of huntin' for your ass at the end of every fight."

"Oh Koa Kai, I know. Next time I wait for you."

Zachary thought for a moment and replied, "After today, hopefully there will be no next time." Zachary hailed the troops to bring a litter and more ropes. After they were delivered, he moved Kaleo onto the litter and tied him and especially his broken leg to the poles of the litter. Given a signal, the troops above pulled the litter up the side of the cliff. Zachary held it off the rocks as best he could from below.

Once Zachary was back at the top of the cliff he followed along with the litter as they carried Kaleo down the path and into the valley for treatment.

Kaleo attempted to be jovial in spite on his aching leg. "A 'we, I lost my best club in today's fight. Kalanikupule's men probably left some good ones. I'll find another one I like."

Zachary retorted, "You almost lost your favorite butt today. If we have to do battle again, I won't let you out of my sight."

Kaleo, "Hey, what a friend!"

CHAPTER 17

PEACE IN THE ISLANDS

KAMEHAMEHA'S TROOPS PURSUED Kalanikupule and his small remaining force through the Koolau mountain trails for three months before capturing him. To ensure that the business on Oahu was finished, Kalanikupule was dutifully sacrificed to the War God *Ku*. With the conquest of Oahu, Kamehameha controlled all of the inhabited islands in the archipelago except Kauai, which was over one hundred miles of open ocean from his new capital at Waikiki. If an invasion of Kauai was needed; it would take much planning and preparation.

Kamehameha had become more politically astute over the years. Now, he hoped that he might gain the loyalty of Kauai's king Kaumu-alii through diplomatic means as opposed to force. Kaumu was the son of Kaeokulani, Kahekili's half-brother and nephew of Kalanikupule; therefore, a long-term enemy of Kamehameha. Kamehameha sent emissaries inviting Kaumu to come to Oahu and discuss peace. However, Kaumu had heard of the assassination of Keoua of the Red Cloak on the Big Island and the more recent sacrifice of his uncle Kalanikupule. Fearing for his life, Kaumu declined to meet with Kamehameha.

Lizzie and her aunt returned to Boston from England in the late fall of 1795. It was a rough passage, but at least it was after hurricane season. Immediately upon reaching port, Lizzie posted a letter informing her mother of their safe arrival. Within days, Lizzie received a return note from her mother bidding her to come home. It had been over five years since she had been whisked away from her home. She felt pangs of homesickness for the first time in years. She decided that it was time, and if she took the coach within the next few days, she would be home to help her mother prepare for the holidays.

Arriving in New London in a cold December rain, Elisabeth Hopkins, now quite the cultured young lady, returned home. Mabel and Edmund were elated when their only child arrived on their doorstep. Edmund had long ago regretted his rash actions in banishing Lizzie from New London. Then, when it turned out to be an extended separation of several years, he felt that it was he who was being punished for being overly zealous. It had been so long that he felt she might marry in Boston or somewhere abroad, and never return to her home. Though Edmund had worried about Lizzie being under the long-term influence of his flighty sister-in-law; he was truly impressed with the educated, well-mannered and worldly woman that she had become.

Lizzie reestablished her friendship with Emily and thereby learned of Zachary's journey at sea and subsequent disappearance. Now at home, she had many more thoughts of the young man of her first affections and prayed for his safe return.

Mabel had never forgiven Edmund for his actions. Since Lizzie had left there had been a cold silent animosity between Mabel and Edmund. Because of Edmund's ministry, their personal situation was not to be revealed to the public, but those who knew Mabel could see the silent bitterness in her expression. Those who paid attention could tell that Edmund's sermons had lost any feel of warmth and love. However, Lizzie's return brought about an end to the hostilities in the house. Mabel's motherly love once again showed in her expression. Though Edmund always had a hard time showing his emotions, he too was much more pleasant in his demeanor and his sermons again carried messages of joy and love.

Emily was married and had a small townhouse a few blocks from the docks, the two young ladies could share their confidences over lunch.

Lizzie's adventurous life in Boston, London and Europe had reached New London via her many letters to her mother and several to Emily. Emily was eager to hear of Lizzie's exploits.

The subject finally turned to Zachary. Lizzie asked after him and Emily told the lengthy story of his putting to sea with her father, his being lost, and that they now knew that he was alive on an island somewhere in the Pacific. She related the letter to Mr. Worthington in hopes that her father might retrieve Zachary.

Lizzie: "Emily that is an amazing story. I shall pray for his safe return." Emily: "You two sure caused an uproar around here."

Lizzie: "Isn't that the truth? An innocent picnic outing and it ended changing my life. If it hadn't happened, I would have never ventured out of New London. And poor Zachary, it sounds as if it changed his life too, but much to the worse. I do feel sorry for him."

Emily: "Father said that he had become a fine seaman."

Lizzie: "I think of him every once in a while." Blushing she added, "He was the first boy I ever kissed."

Emily: "I'll venture not the last." They both laughed. "I'm amazed that you are not married, with children at your apron strings."

Lizzie: "I have been courted, both in London and Boston. Fine young men, with first rate pedigrees, which my aunt finds so important. I still receive letters from a gentleman in Boston, who professes his love and pushes for my hand. But I don't know. I just have not found the one with whom I wish to spend my life."

Zachary and Kaleo were enjoying the role of conquering heroes. For the first time in years, it seemed that war was not imminent, and the young warriors could let their guard down and relax.

Being at Kamehameha's new capital at Waikiki was good duty. It did not take long for Kaleo to find some willing consorts among the wahines of Oahu, though having one leg in a splint was somewhat cramping his style. He worried about Zachary's unwillingness to participate in such amorous escapades. Zachary tried to explain the *Haole*'s concept of fidelity to one's spouse, but it was so foreign to

Polynesian concepts of vigorous interplay between the sexes, that Kaleo could not comprehend why a man would do that to himself.

Long before Zachary had taken Pua Lani to his hut, he understood that sexual interplay was fairly open in Polynesian society. It was obvious that the chiefs had several wives and even more courtesans. Women did not appear to have multiple husbands, but that did not seem to stop them from having amorous encounters with other men. Though there were tense situations generated by some individual affairs, the general concept appeared to be accepted in the society.

The freewheeling sexual mores of the Polynesians ran counter to Zachary's staunch Christian up- bringing. After it was determined that Pua Lani was going to remain in his hut as a de facto common-law wife, Zachary tried to explain to her the restrictions placed on married couples in his society.

Though the concept of monogamy was foreign to Pua Lani she agreed to Zachary's request and was somewhat complimented that he would only have relations with her.

The final campaign of the war had kept Zachary from his home at *Kealakekua* for most of the first half of 1795. In that time, they had swept across Maui, Molokai and Oahu. Now that he was stationed at the new capital at Waikiki, he had no idea when he might return to his home and Pua Lani. But things were about to look up.

Even though Kaahumanu remained Kamehameha's favorite wife, she had not given him any children from their relationship. Kamehameha greatly wished to have a male heir that was born of the highest caste. To achieve his desire, he decided to marry the sixteen-year-old, Keopuolani. He had the girl and her mother brought to Waikiki and plans were made for a lavish wedding.

High caste *Alii* came from the other islands to Oahu to witness the royal event. This included Pua Lani and her child Ipo Lani. Zachary was overjoyed at the prospect of her arrival and had a larger hut constructed for their residence.

The royal wedding took place in July 1795, after which, Pua Lani decided to stay in Oahu with Zachary. They were happy in their new surroundings. Zachary had continued military duties, but there was plenty of time for fishing, games, and love making. Zachary even tried his hand at surfing, though he never came near matching the grace and agility of the locals.

Not only had Kamehameha conquered the other islands, but he put faithful allies in charge of the conquered territories and set about developing a political and administrative system that would knit the islands together as one kingdom and forever end the feudal wars.

In October 1795 the *Impatience* rendezvoused with *Setauket* at San Diego. Her skipper, Captain McDonald reported to Israel on *Setauket. He* brought with him the mail which had been sent to the ship, including the packet of letters from Jessica. Israel invited McDonald to return for a dinner of fresh beef that evening. They could discuss the status of the expedition over some of the wine McDonald had brought with him.

After McDonald departed, returning to *Impatience*, Israel sat at the small desk in his cabin and began reading his mail. Always a company man, Israel first read the letters from the owners. As he had hoped they wished him to complete his load with the assistance of the *Impatience* and then proceed home with all dispatch.

Israel began reading the letters from Jessica and Emily. He read the letters in date order so that he would have the events discussed in the proper order. He finally got to the last letter and could not believe his eyes. Jessica wrote, "I have just received a letter from Zachary. He is alive and sounds to be well. He did not say so, but I fear that he may be some sort of captive of the Hawaiian king. He said that he was on the island of Hawaii in the Sandwich Islands. Israel, please find a way to bring Zachary back to us."

Israel read the passage again and then let out a hoop, "Praise the Lord, Zachary is alive!"

Israel heard eight bells, the change of the watch. Running out on deck Israel called to the mate. "Mr. Bolton assemble the crew!"

After a few minutes the ship's company was assembled before the poop deck. Israel could not help but spread his joy. "Lads, I have just been informed that Zachary is alive and well."

A cheer went up from the crew, for they had either known Zachary from the previous voyage or had heard the story of his disappearance.

Israel continued, "I know that you all are eager to get home, but Zachary is in the Sandwich Islands. After we have accumulated a full load, we will call in the Sandwich Islands on our way home."

The crew cheered their support. Israel motioned to Bolton. "Carry on Mr. Bolton and have the cook issue an extra ration of rum with the dinner."

Bolton, "Aye, aye Sir."

Israel returned to his cabin to contemplate the journey to Hawaii. He did not have charts of the islands and would have to trade with other ships to gain the needed charts.

At dinner that night Israel was in the best of spirits. Even though his guest Captain McDonald was usually rather stuffy, the second bottle of wine went quite a way towards loosening his stiff collar. The conversation was quite jovial; especially with the news from America, including McDonald's description of the Whiskey Rebellion that had taken place just before he departed Boston. After months of sea rations the taste of fresh beef was a joy to McDonald's palate.

Israel told McDonald the story of Zachary's disappearance and the news of his location. Israel asked McDonald to take *Impatience* north to Monterey and then work his way south accumulating hides. At the same time, the crew of Setauket would continue to prepare the hides it had for shipment to the east coast.

Several *Haole* ships visited Oahu during the second half of 1795. Kamehameha was still trading for weapons in preparation for an invasion of Kauai. The new harbor was the village of Honolulu, discovered and established by the English Captain William Brown during his time at Oahu. Honolulu harbor was one of the few anchorages in the archipelago protected by a barrier island.

Kaleo was moving slowly with his leg in a splint, but Zachary and Pua did what they could to take care of him and keep him amused while his leg healed. Being young he healed fast and after two months Kaleo could put some weight on his leg.

The number of foreign ships transiting Honolulu brought diseases to the islands. No sooner had Kaleo's leg begun to improve than a visiting ship brought measles to the islands. Hundreds of people on Oahu including Kaleo got sick within the first week.

Zachary had his bout with measles when living with Jessica and was therefore immune. He expected that people on Oahu would be sick a few days and then get well, just as in America. It didn't happen that way; the Hawaiians had no inherited immunity to this white-man's disease. Within a few days people began dying with high fevers which ended with convulsions and death.

Kaleo had the itchy spots and a high fever. Zachary decided it would be best to keep Pua and his daughter away from the sick people as much as he could, while he ministered to Kaleo. There was no way to measure Kaleo's fever, but it was obviously high when he became delirious. Zachary was panicked, unsure what to do. All he could think of was to cool Kaleo's burning body.

Throwing Kaleo's limp body over his shoulder, he carried his friend to the surf and held him up in the gentle Waikiki surf. "Come my friend, you can make it." He continued to extol his friend. "Come on, we didn't fight for four years for you to give up to a kids' sickness."

After an hour in the surf, the fever broke, and Kaleo became more lucid. "Koa Kai can we get something to eat?" Pulling himself up onto Zachary's squatting body he said, "The surf always makes me hungry."

Zachary responded, "Stay here you ox, while I get your crutch."

Zachary ran back to the hut and returned with the crutch and helped his friend hobble back to the hut to rest and eat. The strong young Kaleo survived the measles epidemic, but many on Oahu were not as fortunate, hundreds of people, particularly the very young and the very old died from the disease.

While ministering to Kaleo, Zachary had not seen Pua and Ipo Lani for two days. After Kaleo's fever had broken and he was obviously on the mend, Zachary went to his hut to be reunited with his family. Upon arriving he found that his attempt to keep Pua and Ipo from being infected by the measles had not worked, Ipo had the telltale spots on much of her body and a high fever. Pua was just beginning to break out.

Zachary began to minister to his family in the only ways that he knew. He made Pua lay down and covered her in an attempt to sweat out her fever which was just beginning. He scolded Pua and Ipo to stop scratching their itchy blemishes.

As Jessica had done when he was sick, Zachary called for a chicken and made a chicken soup using what he had to work with, basically chicken, water, sea salt and some luau leaf for vegetables. He served it to his two patients and then bade them to sleep and sweat out their fevers. After two nights of little sleep while looking after Kaleo, Zachary had a third night of cat naps as he watched over his patients.

A little after sunup the next morning, a much improved Kaleo dropped by to roust out his friend. Kaleo found Zachary slumbering in the corner of the hut; and both Pua and Ipo pale with fever. Seeing the state of affairs, he immediately sensed the dire situation.

Koa Kai wake up!" He poked his friend, "We must do something."

Zachary sat up in a start and immediately felt the burning foreheads of Pua and Ipo.

Seeing Zachary's concerned expression, Kaleo urged him to action. "Come my friend, if the ocean's waters took away the fire from my body, it can do so for Pua and Ipo."

Kaleo scooped up Ipo and exited the hut. Still hobbling, he headed to the beach. Zachary picked up the limp and unconscious Pua and followed him. As he had done with Kaleo, Zachary laid Pua in the water and held her head up to breathe. Kaleo sat in the water next to him and did the same thing with Ipo's small body. However, the cure did not work After an hour, Ipo's breathing became fainter. Kaleo vainly tried to breathe life back into her, but to no veil. Ipo quietly died in the water.

Zachary looked to the sky, "Oh my God! No!"

Still holding Pua he pulled the little body to him, rubbing his nose to Ipo's. "*A 'we, A 'we*" he moaned in the Hawaiian manner, "Oh no, my little one."

His thoughts returned to the still unconscious Pua. He hugged her limp body, "Come my love you must be strong and break this fever."

The white man's disease was too strong. Pua soon began convulsing. Zachary held her as tightly as he could, but to no avail. Pua breathed her last without regaining consciousness. Zachary sat in the waves, holding his two women, the salt water of his tears mingling with the salt water of the ocean. Kaleo's big arms wrapped over them, as he joined his friend in sorrow.

In the days and weeks after the death of Zachary's family, he became reclusive. Kaleo's attempts to draw him out were in vain. Zachary, his spirit broken, was lost in his own self-incriminating thoughts. He drank when he could obtain rum from a visiting ship; he chewed awa, the native narcotic and became a derelict consumed by his own remorse.

Zachary remembered passages from the jealous, vengeful God of the Old Testament. The God that destroyed Sodom and Gomorrah, The God that flooded the world to remove the wicked. Zachary was sure that he was the wicked, and he could not help but feel that God was punishing him for his great transgressions. He thought, "What worse sin could he have committed than to have fought and killed on behalf of pagan gods." He had loved and lived in sin with a pagan woman, but now a vengeful God had taken her from him. His transgressions had cost the lives of the two people most dear to him.

He questioned: What had he done to deserve these trials? Why had he not died in the waters off Maui with the rest of *Fair American's* crew? Why had he not been killed in one of the many battles of the past four years? Early death would have saved him from the loss and misery that he must now endure.

As part of the Hawaiian mourning rituals, they many times broke out teeth or otherwise disfigured themselves as part of the lamentation. Zachary felt a hurt in his heart that caused him to understand and contemplate such an act. He sat alone on a rock outcropping, with the remnant of a bottle of rum. He stared at the endless ocean below his perch. He looked at the rock and considered bashing his mouth into its jagged edge to break his teeth. However, even in his drunken stupor, he could not bring himself to perform such an act; not because of the pain, but because of his deep feeling that the Christian God was punishing him for his previous pagan acts.

On several occasions during his drinking bouts, Zachary would attempt to pray to his Christian God, but it would not last, as he would soon curse the kind of God that would take his beautiful Pua and Ipo from him.

On other occasions Zachary would look into his empty bottle and see his past life. He looked down from his perch at the thatched huts of the village and thought that these were not his people. His people wore clothes and went to church on Sunday and had only one wife and paid homage to one God. He pictured his Aunt Jessica setting a proper table for dinner, and Emily who always worried that her dress might be rumpled and that every hair was in place.

He thought of Elizabeth for the first time in two years. Her sparking blue eyes and the way her nose wrinkled when she laughed. Where was she? He had been gone so long that she could be married to some God-fearing New England lad of proper upbringing.

The more Zachary thought of his former life the more he felt the urge to return home. He had mentally broken the binds with his adopted people. As a result of his revelations Zachary came out of his shell and attempted to participate with Kaleo and in the community, but without the relish that once accompanied his actions. Kaleo was pleased to have his friend back, but could feel the distancing.

Even when sober, Zachary contemplated his return to America. There were an increasing number of *Haole* ships visiting the islands. He could ship out on one of them. However, he understood that even though he was treated royally by the Hawaiians, he was their captive and they might not let him depart, as they had stopped Davis, Young and him almost five years ago. From what Davis and Young had told him they had no desire to return to the civilized world, so he had better not tell them of his plans to escape. Also, he had never been sure whether Kaleo was only his friend and mentor, or might be there to keep watch on him. Zachary decided that he would keep his own counsel and tell no one of his plans.

After leaving Monterey, *Impatience* worked her way down the coast of California stopping at San Pedro before proceeding to San Diego. They arrived in mid-November. The crews of both ships worked together for the next two weeks preparing hides for shipment, until *Setauket* had a full load in its hold.

Though Israel still did not have nautical charts of the Sandwich Islands, Captain McDonald had met a seaman in Monterey who claimed he was in the islands with Captain Vancouver. The seaman provided a rough latitude and longitude for the islands and an equally rough sketch of the islands they had visited. Armed with the rough sketch, on the first of December 1795, *Setauket* weighed anchor and headed southwest toward the Sandwich Islands.

After months of cruising the coast and working to prepare hides on the shore, the crew of *Setauket* was enthused to have the clear salt air at their backs. *Setauket* charged through the swells, with the fair TradeWinds pushing her downwind. Spirits remained high; one quick stop at the Island of Hawaii and then it would be homeward bound.

On the seventeenth day out of San Diego the lookout cried "Land Ho!" as the tops of the clouded mountains rose above the western horizon. Using the sketch from the seaman in Monterey, Israel plotted a course toward the large mountains to the south. The sketch was good enough to allow *Setauket* to drop anchor at *Kealakekua* Bay the next afternoon.

Israel and Bolton rowed ashore to make contact with the locals and with luck find the whereabouts of Zachary. Upon reaching the beach they were escorted to the hut of the chief who was now in charge of this district.

Passing the *Heaiu* and seeing a number of skulls on stakes, Bolton commented to Israel, "What kind of heathen place have we come to?"

Israel replied, "Easy Mr. Bolton, hopefully all will be well."

To Israel's amazement more than one of the chief's subordinates spoke some English. After some pleasantries Israel got to the point of the visit. "We are looking for a boy." Holding his hand about five and a half feet from the ground, "Blonde hair, and blue eyes."

The chief and his advisors looked at Israel blankly. It was clear that he was not communicating.

Bolton leaned over to Israel. "Sir, we haven't seen him in over four years, he could be a whole lot bigger."

Israel thought for a moment and looked at his assembled crewmen. He stepped over to a tall blonde headed lad and said, "Myers take off your hat."

Israel pointed to the mop of hair, "Blonde hair." He then pointed at Myers' eyes, "Blue eyes." The Hawaiians conferred and then the chief responded proudly, "Koa Kai, a fine warrior." Israel asked, "Is he here?"

The chief responded, waving his arm in a roughly northern direction, "No, Koa Kai is on Oahu with the army of the great king."

The chief motioned to a young warrior, "Kalani will take you there, but first we must eat."

The chief then rose up and proceeded to the eating hut. Israel, Bolton and the crewmen followed. Looking out across the bay, Israel could see a number of canoes around his ship. He was afraid that *Setauket* was being pirated.

The chief seeing the panicked look on Israel's face said, "It is good. It is only some wahines.

Come let us eat."

Israel did not understand most of what was said, but was a bit comforted by the chief's calm voice. However, Israel did not know what to do under the circumstances; he did not wish to offend his host and lose the offer to take him to Zachary, but at the same time he did not want to lose his ship.

Israel sat uneasily through the dinner and dancing that followed.

Finally, well after dark, Israel, Bolton and Kalani were rowed out to *Setauket*. In the moonlight Israel could see movement on the decks. As they got closer, he could hear hoots and hollers, though of a jovial not menacing tone.

As they came alongside, Nimmo rushed to greet them, his shirt unbuttoned and a lei around his neck. "Sir, I tried to keep them off, but they were just too persistent."

A giggling unclad girl ran behind Nimmo chased by a similarly unclad sailor.

Climbing upon *Setauket's* deck, Israel was intent on bringing order on his ship. "Kalani, get these people off my ship!"

Kalani barked some commands in Hawaiian and the women and a few Hawaiian men scurried over the side into the waiting canoes. The process took a few minutes, as other women appeared from below decks and also slid over the side.

Israel looked at his disheveled deck and crew. "Thank you Kalani." He turned to Bolton, "Mr.

Bolton please bring some order to this place."

Bolton replied, "Aye, sir." Turning to the half-clad crewmen, "Ok, you sons of whores, your mischief is over. I want this deck squared away before anyone turns in!"

The next morning the crew, still giddy from their first experience with the local hospitality, weighed anchor and made way in a reach to the northwest. Arriving just before sunset, Kalani suggested that they remain offshore for the night and make the entrance to Honolulu harbor at daybreak. *Setauket* tacked offshore towards Molokai for several hours and then three hours before dawn, tacked back toward Koko Head, east of Waikiki. At sunrise *Setauket* bore off to the south past Waikiki beach heading to the entrance of Honolulu harbor.

Though Zachary had been left to himself to mourn his losses, the moment he rejoined the community he was thrust back into his military role. The plans to invade Kauai were proceeding and he was again drilling his musket troops for yet one more campaign. Being kept busy was a good thing, for he had little time to grieve. Time and activity were easing the pain.

Staying busy reduced Zachary's time to plan his departure from the islands. He told himself he would act when the opportunity arose. With this thought firmly in his mind, he could go back to his duties.

But when alone Zachary would see his beloved Pua and Ipo and the depression would return. It was hopeless. There was no escape from the paradise which had become his hell. He purchased another bottle of rum and found himself again on the heights above the crashing waves.

"Maybe that is the answer," he thought, "the way out of this misery. Just step off the edge of the cliff, as so many of the enemy warriors had done in the final battle."

Before he could execute his own demise, he passed out from the strong rum on a hot day.

Zachary awoke; his head was pounding. His face hurt from the burn caused while sleeping with his face in the Sun.

Zachary again considered ending it all at the bottom of the cliff. He stood for a few minutes on the edge. He waited for the courage to take that one step off into the end. The trade wind blowing in his face helped to sober him. He then thought, "Suicide is not an answer, it would only add to his sins." Zachary dropped to his knees and prayed to the white man's God, the God of New England, and the God of home. He confessed his perceived sins and begged forgiveness. The tears streamed down his cheeks. He prayed with an emotion that he had not felt in prayer since he stood over the grave of his mother, so many years ago.

Zachary looked out from his perch and saw a distant ship reaching past Molokai toward Oahu. Zachary looked, not believing what he saw; he rubbed his eyes. It was either *Setauket* or the closest sister ship he could imagine.

Zachary leaped to his feet in joy, and ran down the path toward the beach. He stumbled several times in his haste.

Winded but still running, Zachary saw Kaleo ambling along the beach with his net over his shoulder. Zachary shouted to his friend with uncontrolled excitement. "Come Kaleo we must go to that ship."

Kaleo was taken by surprise, he had not seen his friend that exuberant in months and it was usually his role to be eager to visit *Haole*'s ships. "What is it my friend?"

Zachary grabbed Kaleo's arm pulling him toward the beached canoes. "Come, *wiki, wiki*, I think that I know that ship."

Zachary's plan to disappear from the islands without Kaleo or anyone else involved was now out of the question. Kaleo was there and if this was truly *Setauket*, he would know what was about to happen.

Pulling Kaleo to one of the canoes, Zachary prodded his friend, "Come Kaleo, let's paddle out to the ship."

Taking a small outrigger canoe, the two paddled swiftly after the ship. As Zachary had hoped, it was reducing sail and turned toward the harbor entrance. After two hours of hard paddling Zachary could see the stern and that the ship was in fact *Setauket*. The canoe came along the side of the now anchored ship along with other canoes which were coming to greet the visiting ship.

Having had his ship overrun by the locals at *Kealakekua* Bay and a number of metal objects stolen, Israel was in no hurry to have his ship boarded by the locals again. He ordered, "Mr. Bolton ask Kalani to keep these people at a distance."

Seeing a mop of blonde hair in the canoe alongside, Bolton replied, "I think that you will want these lads aboard, Sir."

Kaleo and Zachary scurried onto the deck. Zachary shook Bolton's hand, "Mr. Bolton."

Zachary then proceeded to the after deck. Addressing Israel, he said, "Permission to come aboard, Sir."

Israel rushed forward, overwhelmed with emotion, tears welled up in his eyes and he hugged Zachary. "No standing on ceremony lad. It is wonderful to see you."

Seeing this, the crew on deck led by Danny cheered, "Hurrah, Zachary Hurrah!"

After Israel finally released Zachary, he shook hands and hugged Bolton, Nimmo and the other members of the crew.

Joy was rampant on *Setauket* and through the outpouring of emotions Kaleo stood silently. It was obvious that this was Zachary's ship and his people and the only reason they could be here was to retrieve him.

Zachary, seeing that Kaleo was left out of the proceedings, went to him and pulled him toward the group. "This is Kaleo, my friend, my teacher, and my brother." Pulling him in front of Israel Zachary added, "Please welcome him."

Israel shook Kaleo's hand as did the mates and many of the crew. Kaleo was a little disconcerted by all the attention and still in a quandary over the morning's events.

Israel invited Zachary and Kaleo to his cabin to hear a brief account of Zachary's adventures. At the end of the dissertation, Israel said, "So now that we have found you, it is time to head for home."

Zachary responded, "Well sir, it may not be that easy. I am in the service of the king and have a duty to him. He must release me."

Israel objected, "Nonsense we can up anchor and be out of this harbor within an hour or so."

Zachary replied, "These people have been my family and have been good to me. I cannot sneak away and just leave them. I want no one to be punished for my departure." Grasping Kaleo's shoulder he added, "I must talk to Kaleo and then if possible, I will leave with you."

Israel acknowledged the sense of duty and honor in Zachary's demeanor and agreed to stay until Zachary could seek his leave to depart.

Though he was reluctant to leave the *Setauket*, now that he had found her, gesturing to Kaleo, Zachary said, "Let us go, my friend."

While paddling back to *Waikiki*, Zachary explained to Kaleo, "As you can see, my uncle has come for me. I know that your job has been to keep track of me, and I would not wish that you be punished because of my leaving. You have been my friend and brother and you and your people are dear to me. But these are my real people and I wish to go with them." He paused, "However I will not sneak away. I have fought on behalf of the king, Kamehameha and wish his permission to depart. If he does not give this permission I will continue to serve."

Kaleo silently paddled the canoe, listening to Zachary's dissertation. Speaking to Kaleo's back, Zachary could not see the tears rolling down Kaleo's cheeks.

Zachary continued, "I must have an audience with the king and request his permission."

Kaleo finally spoke, "As much as it grieves me, my friend, it will be better that I speak to the king on your behalf."

Zachary replied, "*Mahalo*, brother."

They were then silent during the remainder of the trip back to Waikiki, each engrossed in their own thoughts.

It took two days for Kaleo to gain an audience with Kamehameha. During that time Zachary visited *Setauket*, but spent his nights on shore as a sign that he was not going to leave without permission, and he packed his few accumulated possessions for departure.

During the audience Zachary milled around outside of the royal compound in case Kaleo called upon him. Inside Kaleo extolled Zachary's deeds in combat, told of the death of his Hawaiian family and ended with an eloquent request for his freedom.

After the verdict, Kaleo bowed respectfully to his king and backed out of the large room where Kamehameha held court. Once out of the hut, Kaleo ran from the compound and grasped Zachary's hand. "Zachary you are free to go."

Zachary hugged his friend, as it occurred to him that Kaleo had never called him "Zachary" before. Was this a sign of their parting?

Zachary said, "Come my friend. Let's go to the ship and tell my uncle."

It was two more days before *Setauket* was fully provisioned and her water casks filled for the long voyage. It was an emotional parting. Davis and Young along with many of Zachary's wartime colleagues came aboard to wish him well. Zachary had talked with his uncle and arranged for a special gift for Kaleo, since he would be the hardest friend to leave behind.

As expected, Kaleo was visibly upset at this parting. Just before the bon voyage party was leaving the deck of *Setauket*, Zachary turned to the after deck and called to Israel. "Captain Redden, do we have something for my friend?"

With that Israel reached behind the binnacle producing a cutlass. "That we do, Mr. Bower."

Zachary took the sword and handed it to Kaleo, "*Mahalo* my friend for keeping me well all these years."

Kaleo hugged Zachary, almost speechless, "*Mahalo nui.*"

Kaleo and the others then climbed over the side to the awaiting canoes. Israel, "Mr. Bolton, weigh anchor if you please."

Bolton, "Aye, Aye Sir." Turning to the crew, "Ok, you sons of whores to the windless."

Zachary turned to take his station, but Israel kept him at the after deck. When a crewman shouted that the anchor was free; the order was given to make sail. All sails were unfurled, and the fore and aft sail set to sail, the ship close-hauled out of the harbor. As *Setauket* made way, Israel ordered the helmsman to bring her up on the wind to beat, out of the harbor.

As *Setauket* built up speed heeling in the fresh trade wind, Zachary waved to the canoes. Kaleo stood up in his canoe, tears running down his cheeks, waving the cutlass wildly over his head shouting "*A Hui Ho!*" ("Until we meet again," because Hawaiians don't say goodbye).

CHAPTER 18

HOMEWARD BOUND

Setauket took a heading of south-southeast and traveled down the archipelago toward the southern Pacific Ocean. Though Zachary had long hoped and prayed for this day, he was nostalgic as he watched the islands pass by. His years in the Sandwich Islands had taken him from a boy to a man. He had learned to kill, and he had learned to love in the most profound of ways. While there, he had experienced the maximum swings of his emotional pendulum, fear and hate followed by love and elation, the greatest of joy and the greatest of sorrows. He knew that the islands would always be in his heart and mind.

First Molokai slipped by to port, followed by Lanai on the starboard, and Maui to port. As the low sun in the west made the cone of *Haleakala* glisten, Kahoolawe appeared off the port bow. Zachary thought of his beloved people, Pua Lani, Ipo and Kaleo. He said a prayer for them before going to his old familiar hammock.

During his watch in the middle of the night Zachary could see the light of fires at villages along the coast of the Big Island. The sun came up between Mauna Kea and Mauna Loa, the major summits of the Big Island. *Setauket* continued on until the southernmost island was astern and only the empty Pacific lay before her.

The ship's company fell into its routine, as they reached south in the fresh trade wind breeze.

Zachary found the drudgery of scraping and cleaning to be an old and familiar friend. He even decided that he had missed hearing Mr. Bolton's bellowing, "Ok, you sons of whores!"

It was not long before Danny began asking Zachary about his past years since they had lost him in California. Of course, Danny's first questions were about love life in the islands, though there were parts of the story that Danny was not prepared to accept. Zachary explained the availability of sex to Davis, Young and him.

After the explanation, Danny was incredulous. "You mean to tell me that those people were offering you women anytime you wanted, and you weren't sure that you wanted any?" He scratched his head. "I always worried about you lad." He paused to add emphasis. "If they had offered that to me; by the end of a week I'd have been shriveled up like a prune. They would have had to throw me in the ocean to put some water back. Maybe I should have stayed behind and told them people what a good friend of yours I was."

Zachary was also asked about his adventures during dinners at the Captain's table. At first Zachary was reluctant and uncomfortable telling the stories, but as time went on it became easier. He explained the training as a warrior and then the many battles in which he had fought. In the evenings when the sailors would normally play music or tell stories, they came to gather around and press Zachary to spin a yarn about the islands.

After six weeks at sea, on a quiet night watch, Zachary got up the gumption to tell Danny of Pua Lani, Ipo, his love for them and their untimely demise. Danny leaned against the rail listening to the story, for once in his life, without comment. When Zachary had finished Danny shook his head, "Damn, man, that is tough. I feel your pain."

As *Setauket* worked her way south, Zachary reacquainted himself with navigation and the other skills that he had been studying before the incident in San Diego. He eagerly read everything he could find on board. After the trials of the past years, the prospect of being a student had a new and painless attraction for him.

The voyage south was relatively uneventful. *Setauket* called at Island Juan Fernandez to fill its water casks and added some provisions before once again rounding Cape Horn. Upon departing Juan Fernandez the light sails were stowed, and the heavy sails replaced them as they prepared for the rounding.

By thirty-eight degrees south, *Setauket* was feeling the full effect of the Southern Ocean with frequent squalls, high seas, and one gale. The west to east rounding is usually the easy direction because ships can run before the storms and make a fast passage as opposed to the weeks of beating into the weather when passing the other direction. However, there are still substantial dangers during the west to east passage. Charging down large waves in a gale can cause a loss of rudder control and a "broach" (Being broadside to the wind and waves) which can then cause the ship to be rolled or swamped by the next series of waves. There have been stories of small ships running down huge waves and being "pitch-poled", (Rolling stern over bow), but this may just be sailors' tales.

Having made this passage before, Israel was prepared for the wild ride before raging storms. He had two anchor rodes ready at the stern. As the seas built, he ordered the watch to "stream warps" dragging the anchor rodes astern. This produced enough drag to aid the ship on her heading and reduce the chances of a broach or pitch-pole.

Having talked to other captains since his previous rounding, Israel had decided to take the shorter route through the Straits of Magellan, cutting hundreds of miles from the journey. Having first established a good celestial fix at fifty-two degrees south he ordered a more easterly heading to enter north of Cabo Deseado.

Within hours of entering the restricted waters between Isla Santa Ines and Brunswick Peninsula the barometer began to fall as a major storm approached from the west. The disadvantages of the short cut became immediately obvious as the seas began to build. In this constricted passage the seas were steeper and more confused than in the open ocean. Having entered the channel, the ship was committed; there was no turning back in the rising storm. She would have to run before it to survive.

Under only reefed topsails, a reefed main royal and her smallest fore staysail, *Setauket* charged into the blackest of nights. The pea green seas were streaked with froth. The gusts blew froth and foam off the wave tops. Even after streaming warps, the men at the helm fought the wheel to maintain control of the ship. Running down the face of the swells she would approach twenty knots only to slow in the troughs and climb the back of the next swell at six knots.

Zachary and his watch huddled under the sparse protection provided by the break of the after deck attempting to stay out of the horizontal rain and sleet. Zachary and a colleague had just finished their turn at the helm and were rubbing and blowing on their hands attempting to warm them. Danny and a crewman known as the Scott were at the helm. Zachary shivered under his wet clothes. After years in a tropical climate, Zachary's thinned blood, ill prepared him for the biting cold of the Southern Ocean.

Bolton had just roosted out the off watch when a particularly harsh gust caused a reef line on the main royal to part. The port side of the shortened sail arched out in a round billow, two more reef lines broke in a row; but, no more and the sail did not split. The unreefed half of the sail arched high lifting above the yard. The uneven distribution of sail caused the helm to become even more unwieldy. Israel and Bolton aided at the helm as Israel called for the errant sail to be secured.

Nimmo who had just come on deck jumped to the windward shrouds with Zachary close behind him. Two other crewmen made for the starboard shrouds. Below, men loosed the sheets, clews, and bunts leaving the sail flailing but spilling wind. Nimmo climbed over the center of the spar and worked himself out onto the portside yard. Zachary still followed him. The two other crewmen moved out on the starboard yard.

Nimmo hollered into the wind, "Let's furl the whole sail lads!"

They struggled to grab the flailing canvas with cold and gnarled hands. The wind at their backs blew their oilskins over their heads. The driving sleet pelted their backs.

They had almost secured the sail when the shout came from below, "Rogue Wave!"

A huge wave was rolling across the prevailing set of waves hurling itself at *Setauket's* starboard beam.

The men in the rigging heard the shout through the whistling wind, but could not make out the words. They instinctively grabbed a tight hold on the jackstay when the motion of the ship began to change. First the ship lurched to starboard as the beam fell into the trough ahead of the wave. Then the wave hit the beam with full force, rolling her over on her port beam. Zachary's feet slipped from the lines, but his left hand held a firm grasp on the reef line that he had just tied. A foot of the man to his right swung toward him, but the lad hung on. *Setauket* stayed at a thirty-five-degree heel to port for a few moments, which seemed like an eternity, then she slowly came up, righting herself.

Zachary regained his footing and looked to his left. Nimmo was gone. Without a sound he had slipped away into the boiling sea. Zachary turned his head down shouting, "Man overboard!"

The crew on deck could not make out the words of the shout, but surmised what it was. All looked at their captain, but they knew that nothing could be done. To attempt to come about in this storm would most assuredly broach her.

The initial shock of hitting the frigid water stunned Nimmo, but he forced his way to the surface long enough to see the stern of his ship pass by. The warped anchor rode hit him in the side of the head, and he grabbed the rope and was dragged for a moment before the waves peeled away his grasp and drove him under. It was over for Nimmo. The Horn had gained another sacrifice to the gods of the sea.

After two hundred miles of running before successive gales *Setauket* got a respite, when it turned to a northerly heading around the south end of Brunswick Peninsula and gained the benefits of a windward shore to break the fetch of the seas and wind. The winds abated enough to set the reefed fore and main Upper Topsails and a small jib.

The respite from severe weather also gives Israel the chance to muster the crew and say a prayer for the departed Mate, Mr. Nimmo. As was the custom, the personal effects of the deceased were auctioned to the crew, who then had a few added items in their sea chests.

The day after rounding the Brunswick Peninsula, Israel called the Boson to his cabin. Seated behind his small desk, he greeted Bolton. "Mr. Bolton, please sit down."

Bolton: Thank you, Sir."

Israel: "With the tragic loss of Mr. Nimmo we must select a new Second Mate." Bolton: "Aye, Sir."

Israel: "I want your suggestion before I make the decision." Bolton replied without hesitation, "The lad Zachary, sir."

Israel: "That was my thinking too, but I wanted to be sure that I was not letting my fondness for my nephew affect my judgment."

Bolton: "Not at all sir. You gave the lad the opportunity to learn the skills to be an officer and he has applied himself to those studies. He gets on well with the crew and as a seaman he can do anything that any of the other lads can do."

Israel: "He is over twenty years, and his stint with the Hawaiians certainly matured him." Bolton: "Aye sir, he is not the swab that stepped aboard six years ago."

Israel: "Then it is done. Assemble the crew at the change of the watch and I will make the announcement."

The elevation to Second Mate came as a complete surprise to Zachary. In less trying times he may have considered himself for the position; but, in the storms of rounding the Horn, he like all of the crew stood his watches and tried to gain some sleep and warmth in their pitching bunks the rest of the time. The major adjustment was to take a managerial role over the people who had been his peers for so long. Due to the continued rigors of the Southern Ocean, Zachary had no choice but to command his watch to perform its duties. By the time *Setauket* emerged from the east end of the Straits of Magellan, he was comfortable in his new position.

Setauket proceeded east to the Falkland Islands for provisions, before continuing north and home. The voyage north was for the most part uneventful. However much of it was close hauled on a starboard tack into the trade winds providing for a swift passage to windward. Once *Setauket* entered the Florida Straits, she rode the Gulf Stream north. She continued a northerly heading staying offshore about 75 nautical miles to take advantage of the current and heading to stay outside of Cape Cod. After Israel had a celestial fix which confirmed his position as being north of the cape; he ordered a westerly heading toward Boston.

Zachary became more and more eager to get home. He pictured Jessica, Emily and especially Lizzie. He had asked Israel about Lizzie, but his uncle only knew the story of her trip to Boston and he had heard that she had also gone on to England. Zachary worried that after five years she might very well be otherwise attached. He thought, "She may be engaged or even married, to some gentleman of Boston or maybe England. She may have very well found a gentleman, not a country lout such as me."

To his eye, she remained the most beautiful girl he had ever seen, and would be a prize in any of the places she had visited. Zachary asked Israel if she were married or engaged, but Israel knew nothing of her marital status.

Before actually heading for its home port *Setauket* put into Boston to unload its cargo of hides. There was excitement at reaching port after the long voyage which rippled through the ship's company.

The sailors anticipated a meal other than sea biscuits and salt pork and the opportunity to drink their fill and have the company of women of loose virtue.

Between the local stevedores and *Setauket's* crew it would take three days to unload the cargo and load on some goods that were destined for New London. Danny was ready for a frolic ashore. He showed due respect to Zachary's new position, but they were still shipmates and friends. He approached Zachary, "Mr. Bower, it is a fine day to be putting ashore. I find that it will soon be my duty to frolic with some young beauties in yet another port. Oh yes, and of course visit my dear mother. Would you be pleased to join me in the pursuit of pleasure?"

The thought had passed through Zachary's mind. He knew that in this, as in all seaports, there would be female companionship available for a small fee. But at the same time, he had been contemplating Lizzie and their meeting. He could not arrive at that point bearing one of the diseases that plagued so many sailors. Yet he did not wish to offend his friend and appear as an overly officious ship's officer. He responded, "Danny my friend, I would be more than happy to raise a pint with you, and let the day follow its course and see where it takes us."

After *Setauket* was secure in its berth, Israel reluctantly allowed the crew to go ashore by watch. He knew again that there would be no more harmony on board if after the many months at sea, the crew got this close to American soil and did not get to kick up their heels a bit. He was reluctant because he knew the crewmen were sure to overindulge, get lost in some brothel and/or get thrown in jail. He needed all able bodies to unload cargo, so they could head for their home port in a timely manner.

Zachary did join Danny and the rest of his watch in a nearby pub. As the officer of their watch he was pleased to buy the first round, which was greeted with cheers from the crew. It did not take long for the group to be joined by a number of ladies. Though Zachary was again tempted for a quick sexual encounter, he told himself that he would be celibate for the time being. He reasoned that he should stay virtuous for his true love, at least for the present. If he found that she was engaged, married, or not at all interested in him, he promised himself that he would whore his way from one end of New London to the other. Soon Danny and several other crewmen disappeared with their new found loves. Zachary quietly returned to the ship and his own cold bunk.

Zachary lay in his bunk, unable to sleep due to the anticipation of this voyage finally ending.

When he had first been retrieved by his uncle, he had been overjoyed to be heading home. He knew that the voyage would be long, and he settled into the ship's routine, satisfied in the fact that he was heading home. Months had now passed since his leaving Hawaii and now, the thought of being as the crow flies, less than two hundred miles from his destination, made his anticipation almost unbearable. He finally consoled himself that he made it this far, and he could contain himself for the next few days. Helped by several drinks, Zachary finally fell asleep, to dream of his return to New London and Lizzie.

Upon arrival in Boston, Israel met and dined with Mr. Worthington and the other ship's owners. Having hustled Jessica's letter out to *Impatience* that nasty February day, Worthington was interested in the retrieval of Zachary. All were quite pleased that he had been successfully retrieved. Over dinner Israel related some of the stories Zachary had told of the wars in the Sandwich Islands. The owners were impressed with the stories and toasted Zachary (in absentia), the profitable voyage, and the future voyages of *Setauket*.

Worthington: "Captain Redden that was a splendid story. Zachary was an impressive lad when I met him at your home, some years ago. I am happy to have had a small part in retrieving him."

Israel: "Well the lad saw a lot of war while he was in the Sandwich Islands and has matured beyond his years. After the loss of Mr. Nimmo, Zachary was the obvious choice to become my Second Mate."

Worthington: "I am sure that he was a good choice, but does he have a proper uniform?"

Israel: "Not really, I gave him Mr. Nimmo's old uniform, but it was pretty threadbare."

Worthington: "Well if I may borrow him tomorrow morning, I would be happy to take him to my tailor and have him fitted for a proper dress uniform."

Israel: "You are too kind; you do not have to do so."

Worthington: "Nonsense it would be my pleasure to properly outfit an officer of our finest Captain."

Israel: "Then thank you sir, on both accounts."

Worthington: "Good it is done then. I shall call for the lad at 09:00 and have the uniform before you are ready to depart Boston."

The next morning Mr. Worthington was on time and took Zachary by carriage to his tailor for measurements. Worthington gave orders that the uniform should be finished within four days.

Three days later Worthington arrived at the dock and took Zachary along with Israel back to the tailor to try on the finished product. Zachary in the fine dark blue uniform cut a dashing figure before the tailor's full-length mirror. Far from the boy who had left America six years before, he was now a young man of twenty-one years. He stood slightly over six feet tall with the broad chest and shoulders of his father and brothers. He had lamb chop sideburns similar to those of his uncle and a bit of a scar on his left cheek from the combat in his past.

Zachary was overjoyed by the gift and heartily thanked Mr. Worthington and praised the tailor for his work. He returned to his work clothes before departing the tailor's shop. The uniform would only be for the most important of occasions.

Upon returning to *Setauket*, Israel met in his cabin with Worthington to discuss future voyages. Zachary and the crew finished loading the cargo and preparing the ship for sea. Late in the afternoon *Setauket* was pulled out of her slip and anchored in the harbor to await the night's high water which she would ride out of the harbor and then out to sea, heading south to the mouth of Long Island Sound.

High tide was at ten o'clock at which time all hands were called to weigh anchor and make sail.

The breeze was from the northwest and would aid in a swift departure from the harbor. Zachary was pleased his crew pulled the first watch, as he was too excited to sleep. He watched as the twinkling lights of Boston fell astern and then disappeared. In a day and a half, he would be home. He looked forward to this moment for years; but now that it was close, he felt some trepidation about the homecoming. For months Zachary had eagerly longed for home and the pursuit of the lovely young girl who had caught his fancy so long ago. He pictured Lizzie in his mind as the beautiful sparkly eyed teen of his memories. Now that he was close to home, he was apprehensive. She could have married long ago. After all, Emily had married a local merchant when Israel was last at home.

Zachary remained on deck after the change of watch. As the night waned, *Setauket* was offshore from Cape Cod, close enough to shore to see an occasional light. He gazed at the bioluminescence sparkling in the bow wave and thought about how Lizzie could have become so sophisticated that she would have no interest in a questionably educated sailor. It had long ago occurred to Zachary that Reverend Hopkins' objection to him was fueled by a disdain for a person below his class. Possibly this was a class difference which could not be overcome. Also, she could have changed and not be the beauty he remembered. She could be sickly or fat or any manner of thing that would make her much less desirable than the girl in his mind's eye.

As the last of the shore lights disappeared astern and the glow of the coming dawn painted the eastern sky first with pale pinks and then a rich pallet of oranges and reds, Zachary buckled up his self-esteem and told himself that whatever was awaiting him, he had no choice but to face it like a man. If Elizabeth Hopkins was not to be his love, there should be other young beauties available for a dapper young ship's officer.

The northwest breeze continued to speed *Setauket's* progress south, passing between Martha's Vineyard and Nantucket. Upon passing Orient Point on Long Island, she entered her home waters of the Long Island Sound.

Once they came into the Sound the breeze died and the water was like glass. The dog days of Summer were kicking in early this year. After a painful day with little progress up the Sound, the sky clouded over, the wind shifted to the west for a short period and then to the southeast which brought a series of squall lines and the strong winds associated with them. With a favorable breeze, *Setauket* now headed for home.

The same old fisherman alerted Jessica that *Setauket* was seen on the Sound. She hurried up the street to inform Emily and her husband Clarence. They all bathed and dressed to meet the ship. On board *Setauket* a similar ritual was underway. Zachary shaved, bathed as best he could and donned his new uniform for the occasion.

By mid-day *Setauket* was anchored. Israel and Zachary were rowed ashore in a longboat. As they approached the dock, they could see the waves of Jessica and Emily. The excitement continued to build.

On the dock Jessica first hugged and kissed Israel and then reached up and grasped Zachary by both shoulders. "Look at you, as fine a young gentleman as I have ever seen."

Jessica hugged and kissed Zachary and then passed him on to Emily for more hugs and kisses.

They strolled back to the house with a continued banter of questions and comments and gay but meaningless chatter. The joy of the homecoming was as he had hoped. He was back in the security and comfort of his adopted family.

After a leisurely lunch Zachary took Emily aside to ask the questions that burned in his mind. "Emily, what has become of Elizabeth Hopkins?"

Emily: "I knew that you would ask after her. She and I are still good friends. As far as I know she is presently at her parent's home."

Zachary: "Is she married, engaged or otherwise spoken for?"

Emily: "Not that I know. She is considered by some to be an old maid."

Zachary: "Is there something wrong with her, that she has not been swept away by now."

Emily: "Not at all, she has had several advances from local boys and receives letters from a young gentleman she met in Boston who I believe was studying at Harvard College. As yet she has not been betrothed to any of them."

Zachary: "Do you think that I should go see her?"

Emily: "Most definitely. You are quite handsome in your uniform and would most likely sweep her off her feet."

Zachary: "But what of Reverend Hopkins?"

Emily: "Her father is still a stodgy and uppity old cuss, but if you don't let him intimidate you, you can overcome him."

Zachary: "Then I shall go there."

Emily: "Yes, do it now. Call on the Reverend and then his daughter."

Zachary took Emily's advice and walked over to the rectory. On the front porch he wiped the dust from his boots on the back of each trouser leg and knocked on the door. After a long minute's delay Mabel answered the door.

Zachary straightened almost to attention. "Good afternoon Mrs. Hopkins. Zachary Bower, here to see Reverend Hopkins."

Mabel's face showed her astonishment as it sunk in who was standing before her. "Yes, please come in, I will get Reverend Hopkins."

Zachary removed his cap placing it under his left arm and entered. Mabel left Zachary standing in the entry hall and departed to the study. She opened the door and slipped into study. "Edmund, there is a young ship's officer here to see you. Though I hardly recognized him, I believe that it is Zachary Bower."

Edmund looked up from his desk. "What does he want?" Mabel: "He didn't say."

Edmund with some reluctance in his voice, "I guess that I should see him. Send him in."

Mabel returned and ushered Zachary into the study. Edmund stood and shook Zachary's hand and then sat down again leaving Zachary standing before him.

Edmund: "What can I do for you?"

Zachary: "Well sir, I know that you have had some issues with me in the past and for that I can only ask for forgiveness for any embarrassment that I may have caused you and your family."

Edmund: "Yes, yes that was long ago."

Zachary stared Edmund in the eye. "I feel that I must speak plainly. In the past you considered me to be some kind of country bumpkin, not of sufficient social standing to be seen with your daughter. Possibly this was the case."

Edmund shifted in his chair. He hated plain talk when it was aimed at him. Zachary went on. "I have now traveled much of the world, have been in wars and I am a ship's officer. I will not be treated as a lout. Therefore, I have come to properly ask your permission to see your daughter."

Mabel standing behind Zachary did not know how her husband would respond. She stammered, "Oh dear."

Edmund also squirmed in his chair and stammered, "Well a, we shall see."

Zachary responded, "Both Elizabeth and I have passed our twentieth year. Possibly she should decide if she wishes to see me."

Edmund: "Yes, of course, I was just about to suggest that. Mabel, please get Elizabeth." Motioning toward a chair, "Mr. Bower please be seated."

Upstairs Mabel announced Zachary's presence and that he had asked to see her. In true girlish fashion Lizzie responded, "But I'm a mess."

Zachary sat with the knowledge that his bold action was about to be rewarded. The tension of the previous confrontation was over, and he made small talk with Reverend Hopkins. Zachary feared that if too much time passed, the Reverend might change his mind. Edmund did not feel at all at ease, for he had been confronted and had lost the engagement. They were alone together for twenty minutes while Lizzie primped, with Mabel prodding her to hurry before the two men found something to disagree about.

When Lizzie entered the study, Zachary rose and turned to greet her. Lizzie was still tall and thin, but had filled out and was much curvier than he remembered. Her dress was blue complimenting her golden curls and matching the blue of her eyes. She had grown to be a fine woman, even more beautiful than he had remembered. He could feel the flush of red in his cheeks, as he stepped forward to greet her.

Lizzie extended her right-hand palm down and Zachary took it in his left hand, kissed it and gave a squeeze as he released. Lizzie withdrew her hand. "Mr. Bower you look well."

Zachary responded with some stammer in his voice. "Miss Hopkins you look quite well yourself."

Edmund broke in, "Mr. Bower has come and requested my permission to call on you. Though I am reluctant, I felt that you should have a say in the matter."

Lizzie nodded to Edmund. "Thank you, father." She turned her attention to Zachary, smiling with that little wrinkle in her nose, which he long remembered, he was again infatuated. She said, "I would be most pleased to be visited by Mr. Bower."

Edmund had hoped that his daughter had finally inherited some of his class consciousness, but that was not to be. Edmund with some reluctance in his voice, "So it is settled, Mr. Bower you have my permission."

Lizzie taking Zachary by the hand, "Come Mr. Bower, let us take a stroll through town on this lovely afternoon."

They walked through town making small talk. Zachary made sure that they stopped by his home so that Israel and Jessica could see his conquest. As they passed through town on the way back to the rectory, coming the other way was Toby McPhee and his two roughneck companions. Toby had gone from an overweight slovenly boy to a two-hundred-and-eighty-pound dimwitted slovenly adult. They recognized each other as they approached. Toby, who still endeavored to impress his cohorts whenever possible, motioned at Zachary. "Nice sailor suit."

Zachary felt a rage well up that was first kindled when Toby accosted Emily many years ago, but now he had no patience for louts. With a fire in his eyes none of them had ever seen, Zachary reached out and grabbed Toby by the throat and slammed him up against the wall of a store. Gritting his teeth, he growled, "I have killed men who were much better than you!"

Toby sputtered a response. "Aye sir, I didn't mean anything by it. Only havin' a bit of fun." Zachary regained his composure and released Toby. "Then be off with you."

Lizzie was somewhat taken aback by the look of rage exhibited by Zachary. Zachary and Lizzie continued their walk for some distance in silence, Lizzie holding on to his arm. Lizzie broke the silence by reaching over and touching the scar on his cheek. "You must have some stories to tell."

Zachary responded softly, "I will have some great stories to tell our children."

Lizzie stopped in her tracks and turned to him, "Don't you think that you are a bit premature, Mr Bower?"

Zachary turned to face Lizzie, holding her by the shoulders, "Elizabeth, there have been times during the past six years when the only thing that made me want to live was the vision of your face. I did not come back here to have less than you as my bride."

Afraid that he may have been overly aggressive, he took her hand, and led her over to a bench and beckoned her to sit. He began, "I know that I have been quite bold, but before I ask for your hand, there are things that you deserve to know about."

He began, "I was a warrior in the service of a heathen king. These people worshipped many gods, similar to the Greeks and Romans." His voice trembled a bit, "I do not know if I am damned for my transgressions."

Lizzie responded, "Oh, dear."

Zachary continued, "I also had a wife and a daughter."

Lizzie, whispered, "Oh, dear." Then regaining her voice, she asked, "So, you are a married man?"

Zachary replied, "No, they both died of a fever. I became a lost person for a time after that, until Uncle Israel rescued me."

Lizzie responded, "Was she pretty?"

Zachary now wished that he had not gotten into this discussion. "Hawaiians tend to be quite a bit larger than the average American. Therefore, they like large women with a lot of meat on their bones. Pua was tall and thin and not what Hawaiians would appreciate, but in my eyes, she was very pretty."

Lizzie, "Do these Hawaiian women have nice clothes?"

Zachary, "Both men and women wore a sort of loin cloth. Sometimes especially when dancing, they wore skirts made of leaves. They do not unusually wear tops, but do wear long necklaces of fragrant flowers and leaves.

Lizzie, "I don't think that we will be having any styles like that in Connecticut, any time soon."

Lizzie sat quietly for a few minutes and then responded, "Since I have listened to my father's sermons for years; I believe, as he does in a merciful loving God. Therefore, I do not believe that you are damned, though you might ask for the Lord's forgiveness and when the time comes, you might have some explaining to do."

Lizzie, holding both his arms, reached up and gently kissed him, then drew away before he could make the kiss more passionate. She said softly, "With regard to the rest of this story, I need to let it sink in and then we shall see about your intentions, Mr. Bower."

Zachary Bower, a man of his word married the lovely Elizabeth Hopkins six months after returning home from the long voyage. The wedding was planned so that Zachary's father, brothers and their cohorts could attend, having returned from an expedition to the Mississippi River and back.

Between the sailors and the woodsmen, the wedding reception was long noted as the rowdiest affair the town had ever seen. There was much singing and dancing and way too much drinking, but only a couple of friendly fights. All of this ruckus seemed appropriate for the settling down of our hero.

EPILOGUE

This story adds a fictional character, Zachary Bower into the midst of the wars to consolidate the Hawaiian Islands. Zachary and all the characters in America, on both the East and West coasts, are fictional. The happenings while in Hawaii are as close to the actual history, as possible. The names of the participants are historical persons with the exception of Kaleo, Kimo and Pua Lani who were needed to support Zachary in his immersion into Hawaiian society.

The history of Hawaii is intriguing; there is the prophesied one in which Kamehameha, who believed he was destined to unite the islands, continued to make war until he had achieved his objective. He proves that thinking can make it so. There are spies and conspiracy that go along with any war, but I know of nowhere else in history where the main combatants changed sides on such a regular basis.

Hawaiian history has love affairs that influence who allies with whom during different phases of the wars. The Polynesian mores are quite different than the Judeo-Christian restrictions regarding sex and marriage. I remember reading in a sociology book, it was most likely Margaret Mead about her studies in Samoa, a statement something like, "and adultery was their favorite pastime."

The entire story of the massacre on Maui is historical fact. The *Eleanora* and *Fair American* were the ships involved and the Metcalfe's, Father and Son, were the captains. *Fair American* was as told, the source of Kamehameha's first cannons and muskets. Isaac Davis and John Young were the two captives who were kept alive to teach the Hawaiian warriors how to use their newly acquired weapons. This incident allowed Zachary to be added as the third survivor, so that he could be involved in the rest of the story.

Kamehameha the Great, not only conquered the Hawaiian Islands bringing them for the first time under one rule, but he set up an interrelated administration that ensured that the islands would remain as one country. The nation of Hawaii survived until it was overthrown by *Haole* plantation owners in 1893. Hawaii became a territory of the United States on July 4, 1898.

GLOSSARY

Abaft	Aft of the ship's beam (mid-point).
Alii	The highest caste in the Hawaiian social hierarchy
Anchor Rode	The line and chain attached to an anchor.
Avast	The commands stating no further action until the next command.
Barque	A sailing ship with three or more masts. The fore and main masts are square rigged and aft most mizzen mast is rigged fore and aft.
Beat	To sail with the wind as close to the bow as possible. A model sloop can sail within 45 degrees of the wind. A square rigger like *Setauket* could only sail within 70 degrees of the wind.
Bow	The front of a boat or ship.
Belay	To tie off a line.
Belaying Pin	A removable pin 10" to 12" long, on to which lines are tied.
Box Haul	A combination of tacking and wearing maneuvers; used to come about in a limited space.
Broach	To roll onto the leeward beam due to excess wind or wave on the windward beam.
Captain Cook	British Captain James Cook discovered the Hawaiian Islands in 1778. He named them the Sandwich Islands after his patron.
Catboat	A sailboat with one sail.

Crosstrees	The platform at the doubling of the topmast and topgallant.
Dayman	Crewmen who are not assigned to a watch, such as the ship's carpenter, cook and sailmaker.
Doubling	Doubling the Horn refers to crossing a latitude in the Atlantic Ocean, rounding Cape Horn and then crossing the same latitude in the Pacific Ocean.
Fo'c's'le	Contraction of "forecastle," pronounced foaksel. Crew quarters in the bow of the ship.
Hampers	The uppermost sails, i.e. the Royal and T'gallant
Haole	Hawaiian word for white people. When Captain Cook discovery Hawaii, the Hawaiians did not believe that people as pale as the British sailors could be breathing. *Haole* translates to breathless.
Hardtack	A hard saltless biscuit used on ships and army rations.
Heiau	Hawaiian temple.
Holystone	A block of pumice stone that was pushed down the decks to remove any splinters.
Kanaka	The common level individual in the Hawaiian social hierarchy
Kane	Hawaiian God of living things, sunlight, and freshwater.
Kaneloa	Hawaiian God of the land of the departed.
Kapu	Taboo
Ketch	A boat or ship with two or more masts, all fore and aft rigged, with the largest sail on the main mast and a smaller sail on the aft (mizzen) mast. The mizzen mast being forward of the rudder post.
Koa Kai	Sea Warrior
Ku	Hawaiian God of war.
Larboard	Another term for the port side of the ship.
Leeward	The downwind side of the ship.

Line	A rope is a rope on land, when used on a boat it becomes a line.
Lono	Hawaiian God of the harvest, rain, sports and peace.
Luffing	Causing the sails to spill wind.
Maholo	Thank you
Mai kai	Excellent
Okole	One's posturer
Pele	Hawaiian Goddess of volcanoes.
Poop deck	The aft most deck on the ship.
Port	The left side of the ship.
Possible Bag	A homemade shoulder bag used by frontier people to carry miscellaneous items.
PuaKenikeni	Scientific name: Fagraea berteriana. A flower from a small tree that is white, but turns yellow and becomes more fragrant when warmed by body heat.
Reach	To sail with the wind off the mid-ships or beam. If the wind is aft of the mid-ships it is a "broad Reach".
	If the wind is forward of the mid-ships it is a "Close Reach". If the wind is mid-ships it is a "Beam Reach".
Reefing	Reducing the size of the sails. Normally, there are reef lines sewn into the sail so that the crewmen may partially roll up the sail, wrap the reef lines around the sail and tie them off.
Royal	The topmost sail on a barque.
Run	To sail with the wind off the stern.
Sandwich Islands	The name given to the Hawaiian Islands by Captain Cook

Schooner	A boat or ship with two or more masts, all fore and aft rigged, with the largest sails on the aft masts.
Starboard	The right side of the ship
Streaming Warps	Running anchor rode off the stern to slow the ship when sailing down large waves
T'gallant	A contraction for Top Gallant which is the second from the top sail on a barque.
Tack	Turning the ship's bow through the wind.
Wear Windlass	Turning the ship's stern through the wind. A mechanical system for hauling up the anchors.
Windward	The upwind side of the ship.
Yard	The horizontal spars that are attached to the masts. The Yard is named after the sail that it holds.
Yardarm	The end of the Yard.
Yawl	A boat or ship with two or more masts, all fore and aft rigged, with the largest sail on the main mast and a smaller sail on the aft (mizzen) mast. The mizzen mast being aft of the rudder post.

BIBLIOGRAPHY

Dana, Richard Henry, Jr., Two Years Before the Mast, New York: American Library, a division of Penguin Putnam, Inc., New York: 1964

Daws, Gavan, Shoal of Time, A History of the Hawaiian Islands, Macmillan, New York: 1968

Fornander, Abraham, Ancient History of the Hawaiian People, Honolulu: Mutual Publishing LLC, 1996

Johnston, Allen, Buckskins, Blades and Biscuits, Blaine, Washington: Hancock House Publishers, 1995

Morrison, Susan, Kamehameha The Warrior King of Hawaii, University of Hawaii Press, Honolulu: 2003

Tregaskis, Richard, The Warrior King, Hawaii's Kamehameha the Great, New York: The Macmillian Publishing Co., Inc., 1973

Wilcox, Del, Voyagers to California, Elk, California: Sea Rock Press, 1991

www.ingramcontent.com/pod-product-compliance
Lightning Source LLC
Chambersburg PA
CBHW030318100526
44592CB00010B/485